A VERY PUNCHABLE FACE

A VERY PUNCHABLE FACE

A Memoir

Colin Jost

CROWN
NEW YORK

Published in the United States by Crown, an imprint of Random House, a division of Penguin Random House LLC, New York.

CROWN and the Crown colophon are registered trademarks of Penguin Random House LLC.

Photo credits and permissions appear on page 313.

LIBRARY OF CONGRESS CATALOGING-IN-PUBLICATION DATA
Names: Jost, Colin, author.
Title: A very punchable face / Colin Jost.
Description: New York : Crown, 2020.
Identifiers: LCCN 2019059124 (print) | LCCN 2019059125 (ebook) | ISBN 9781101906323 (hardcover) | ISBN 9781101906330 (ebook)
Subjects: LCSH: Jost, Colin, 1982– | Comedians—United States—Biography. | Television comedy writers—United States—Biography. | Actors—United States— Biography.
Classification: LCC PN2287.J685 A3 2020 (print) | LCC PN2287.J685 (ebook) | DDC 791.4502/8092 [B]—dc23
LC record available at https://lccn.loc.gov/2019059124
LC ebook record available at https://lccn.loc.gov/2019059125

Printed in the United States of America on acid-free paper

randomhousebooks.com

9 8 7 6 5 4 3 2 1

First Edition

Book design by Caroline Cunningham

To my mom and dad, and my brother, Casey.

You're like family to me.

Contents

Introduction

"There comes a time when you look into the mirror and you realize that what you see is all you will ever be."

—Tennessee Williams

"I don't know what I think until I write it down."

—Joan Didion

've wanted to write a book my entire life. Partially because (as you will soon learn) I have difficulty taking what's inside my head and saying it out loud. For someone whose job is essentially *speaking*, this creates a deep anxiety and sometimes a paralysis that keeps me from expressing what I'm really thinking. Whereas the act of writing allows my brain to function in a different way. I can write and not be afraid of what I'm going to say.

I also just love books. They were my first escape and the only way I traveled and learned about the world without leaving the island I grew up on. Books were my ticket to a good high school and a good college. And books were how I learned about the people I admired, from Teddy Roosevelt to Tina Fey (the modern Teddy Roosevelt).

Some of you know me from *Saturday Night Live,* where I've

been a head writer and co-anchor of Weekend Update (the real fake news) for the past six years.

Some of you know me from *OK!* magazine, where I'm standing on a red carpet next to my much more famous fiancée.

Some of you *think* you know me, but you're actually just thinking of the villain from an '80s movie who tries to steal the hero's girlfriend by challenging him to a ski race.

And some of you, I'll admit, were duped. Because half the copies of this book were titled *Becoming 2: Michelle's Got More to Say.* And for that I apologize, even as I continue to fight Mrs. Obama aggressively in court.

Regardless, thank you for reading my book. I'm not a person who opens up easily. I'm half German and half Irish Catholic. So it's never a good sign when your German side is the *less* repressed one.

That's why I rarely post anything on social media or do any serious interviews. I feel ashamed when talking about myself, even though everyone else is doing it.

But doing it in book form puts me at ease somehow. Because, again, books were my friends. Math was my girlfriend. And I lost my virginity to spelling.

I called this book *A Very Punchable Face* because multiple friends have told me: "Colin, you have a very punchable face."

These are *friends,* mind you. So I can only imagine what my enemies are saying.*

I'm so punchable that I've been punched in at least four different sketches on SNL, including one where my boss, seventy-

---

* Actually I don't have to imagine. That's what Twitter's for.

five-year-old Lorne Michaels, punches me in the face fifteen times. (He demanded multiple takes. Said there were "lighting issues.")

Leslie Jones has punched me. Tiffany Haddish has punched me. Cecily Strong has spit vodka in my face and vomited red wine all over me.

I've learned that anytime I get physically abused on camera, people laugh.

That is why many chapters in this book involve me getting hit in the face, verbally assaulted, sliced open, pummeled by fruits and vegetables, thrown out of a wrestling ring, or metaphorically punched by trolls and critics. And yes, there's also a chapter about me shitting my pants as a grown adult. Sorry, Grandma!

And listen, I understand why some people want to punch me. I'm self-aware enough to realize what I look like.

I look like a guy who's always on the verge of asking, *Do you know who my father is?* Even though my father was a public school teacher on Staten Island. If you had Mr. Jost for mechanical drawing freshman year, then you know who my father is!*

I also realize that I look like the president of the Young Republicans Club, even though I've voted Democrat in every election for every single office, even the weird ones like "State Supreme Court Bailiff" where half the names could be fake and no one would ever know.†

---

* So far, name-dropping my father has only ever gotten me a free pretzel from one of his former students working at Auntie Anne's.

† I once voted for a judge because his last name was "Ice" and I just thought that was awesome.

And it doesn't help, punch-wise, that I'm one of the whitest white people outside of *Frozen*.

Here are some names I've been called on social media as well as regular media: "Bland," "Pasty," "Transparent," "Milquetoast" (gross), "the Whitest Man in History," "Powder," "If Milk Became a Person," "Milk-Face," "Milk the Movie," "You Tall Glass of Egg Whites" (™ Leslie Jones), "Casper," "Gay Casper," "Chicken Salad," "If Jizz Became a Person," and of course, "The Actual White Devil."

Sometimes these names are hurtful. Sometimes they're just confusing. (What is a "Mayonnaise Yeti"?) But mostly they make me laugh. And I learned very early on that laughing at yourself is a terrific survival mechanism.

As someone who was bullied growing up, I realized that it's way easier to play into the bullying rather than fight it. If you're better at making fun of yourself than a bully is, then the bully has no room to operate. (Except punches. They still have punches. Oh god, do they have punches.)

I've applied this childhood approach to my adult whiteness. If people are going to make fun of how white I am, then I better do it before they do.

After all, I'm so white, golf plays me!

For this reason, I almost called my book *White Guy* until I realized that it miiiiiiight feel a liiiiiiitttle politically charged in the wrong way.

So instead I went with *A Very Punchable Face*.

Except in Russia, where it's called *Mayonnaise Yeti*.

A VERY
PUNCHABLE
FACE

Finding My Voice

"Let thy speech be better than silence. Or be silent."
                                    —DIONYSIUS OF HALICARNASSUS

"If you just don't interfere with yourself, you're quite interesting."
                                    —ROBIN WILLIAMS

wasn't able to speak until I was almost four years old. I didn't know this at the time, but apparently that's insane. Most kids start to speak by the age of one and a half or two. So speaking for the first time at the age of four is like having sex for the first time at the age of seventy-five: You can do it, but no doctor recommends it.

My parents claim they weren't too worried, but a four-year-old who doesn't speak isn't normal. It's the opening of a horror movie. They said I could understand what people were telling me, but I couldn't respond verbally. I would point or grunt but couldn't form any actual words. I was a shorter, less charming Mr. Bean.

My mom finally admitted, "We were a *little* worried, since every other child we knew was talking in full sentences. Whereas the only three sounds you ever made were 'Ma,' 'Ba,' and 'Da.' But you made good eye contact with people and you were exceptionally good at miming!"

Okay, now *that* is a horror movie. A four-year-old staring you dead in the eyes and "miming" while repeating "Ma, Ba, Da" until blood pours out of his eyes.

I have a vague memory from that age of feeling really frustrated, like I was trying to will the words to come out but couldn't do it. It felt like trying to talk underwater. Or rap in outer space. My mom said I would get angry a lot and lash out.

"You very much identified with *He-Man* at the time," she said. "So if other kids were communicating with words, you tended to respond with violence."

Not sure if that was the message behind *He-Man* . . . "Use the Power of Grayskull to defeat the power of words! Silence your friends with your fists! And punch your way to justice!"

Other times I would get scared and not know how to express it. My mom said that when a fire alarm went off, I grabbed her hand and mimicked the sound of the alarm. Then I pointed to my heart, like, "It's making my heart beat faster because I'm scared." I might have been a chimpanzee?

I've told friends that I couldn't speak until I was four and their usual response is: "Oh yeah, that makes sense." And I'm like, "What the hell does that mean?" And they say, "I don't know, you just seem like someone who didn't speak until they were four." And I say, "Oh yeah? Well, you look like someone who has sex with their cousin." And that ends the discussion pretty quick.

But I kind of understand what they mean. To this day, I'm in my head a lot of the time. I create entire monologues and have full, detailed conversations with friends—entirely in my head.

And then I get frustrated because that whole carefully constructed dialogue will never see the light of day. It just exists fully built in my brain like a ship in a bottle, and then it floats away before anyone can see it. It's like rapping, but in outer space.

I still have a deep fear about speaking. Not public speaking, but regular speaking. Once I get going I'm okay, but it's *starting* to speak that's the problem.

I've noticed that I say "Uhhhh" a lot in conversation before I speak, and it's because I'm stalling to let my words catch up with my brain. It's like a pinwheel spinning on a computer, waiting for me to locate the information somewhere in my mind. "Uhhhh . . . want to go out for lunch? And uhhhh . . . don't go in the kitchen, it's on fire."

I even get scared when the phone rings because I think, *I'm not ready to speak yet. I haven't figured out what to say.* But when I push through that fear and start saying words, I'm instantly relieved. That's why answering the phone and talking to another human still feels like a huge psychological accomplishment. (And that's why I currently have 254 un-listened-to voicemails. The oldest is a call from Omaha Steaks in 2007!*)

That's also why I loved performing, even as a kid. It forced me to speak with conviction and to express emotion in what I was saying. If I didn't have an outlet as a writer and as a performer, I don't know what I would have done. It would have been like trying to rap, but in outer space. (Sorry, I'll stop.)

---

* My credit card was declined for the "Surf and Turf Sampler" I bought my grandparents for Christmas.

I'm always happiest when I don't have time to think or plan ahead. If I'm onstage and someone yells something from the audience and I just have to react, that's when I'm most comfortable. Or when I wake up in the morning next to my future wife and we can talk and joke around while I'm still half asleep and not paralyzed by my own thoughts yet.

An ex-girlfriend gave me some great advice: "You need to say what you're thinking a lot more and not be afraid of being judged or being inarticulate or offensive or even boring."

Being boring is what I fear most, so I tend to keep a story or a joke in my head until it's ready to tell other people. Sometimes this is good, because the story might be better by the time I relay it. But a lot of times it's bad, because I could have just blurted it out and found the funny part of the story in real time. The more I get it outside my head and onto a stage or page (huge rhyme alert), the better off I am.

When I was four, however, my parents weren't worried about my future career as a performer. They were worried about their child not saying a single word. And that's when they sent me to Staten Island University Hospital to work with a woman who saved my life.

I remember my speech therapist as this glowing blond angel who started pulling words out of my brain. Like when Ursula steals Ariel's voice in *The Little Mermaid,* only she was putting the voice *into* me, while doctors removed my vestigial fish tail. And even though she was from Staten Island and probably had a thick *Green Book* accent, in my memory she sounds like the

fairy godmother in *Cinderella*.* "Come on now, Colin! Enunci-
ate! Let the magic of words transport you!" Instead of what
she really said: "Repeat after me: *My ex-husband is trash. If I
catch him with another Perkins waitress, I'm getting Uncle Lou to
break his thumbs.*"

I asked my mom recently if my speech therapist was actually blond and she said, "Oh yes, she was striking! What a
beautiful woman! I'll never forget her!"

"Oh great," I said. "What was her name?"

"I have no idea!"

In fairness, my mother suffers from Giant Irish Family Syn-
drome, where she can't even remember her own children's
names without cycling through multiple cousins first.

"Hey . . . Sean, I mean Patrick, I mean Colin!"

It could be worse. She often gets to the dog's name before
my brother, Casey.

I've tried many ways to track down my speech therapist because I wanted to thank her. But clearly my mother is no help
("Was it 'Brenda'? I know it started with a letter . . ."), and according to my dad, my medical records before the age of fifteen have "disappeared." (Either my parents misplaced them
or they're covering up a much darker secret.)

So if you're reading this and you were a speech therapist at
Staten Island University Hospital around 1986, please know: I
am eternally grateful to you for giving me the power of speech.
It was so much more effective than the Power of Grayskull. I
don't remember any of the exercises we did together. I just

---

* I only know Disney movies.

remember feeling that anger and frustration slowly fade away. I remember not being scared anymore. And I remember how happy I felt when I could finally express myself. I didn't have to punch my way to justice anymore.

I'm still learning how to speak and not be afraid of what comes out. But you taught me that once I get going, it will be okay.

Now, whenever my mom meets a new mother whose child is having difficulty speaking, she says, "Don't worry, my son was a very slow talker and now he makes a living from it!"

"Oh, which son?"

"Dylan. I mean Billy. Wait, no, Colin. Whichever one does the news."

Wait, You're from Staten Island?

"Where you grew up becomes a big part of who you are
for the rest of your life. You can't run away from that.
Well, sometimes the running away from it is what makes
you who you are."

—Helen Mirren

"There's no place like Staten Island!"

—Donald J. Trump

When I tell people I'm from Staten Island, they're usually
confused. Most people have an impression of what
someone from Staten Island is like based on characters from
Jersey Shore, Mob Wives, or this cartoon Italian man on pizza
boxes:

In reality, *Jersey Shore* types make up only a very small percentage (40 percent) of Staten Island's population. The rest are grounded, hardworking, normal-speaking humans, who almost never stand outside their house shaking a rolling pin and yelling, "I'm a-gonna a-kill you!"

Yes, Staten Island is the most Italian county in all of the United States, beating out even Meatball, Indiana. But the beauty of Staten Island is that anyone who lives there long enough, regardless of ethnicity, just *becomes* Italian. Now we have Russian Italians, Korean Italians, Egyptian Italians, and Sri Lankan Italians.* You'll see a red-haired, freckled Irishman named Danny O'Doyle, then he opens his mouth and it sounds like Marisa Tomei in *My Cousin Vinny*. If you go by accent alone, even members of the Wu-Tang Clan sound like they could be in *Goodfellas*.

I did too, believe it or not.

When I finally learned to speak, I swear to god I sounded like Carmela Soprano. There are videos of me at age eight where I'm trying to sell my bike to whoever's filming me and it's like an ad for a Mazda dealership on Route 9 in Jersey. "Yeah, you know, you gotta check dis thing out cuz it's got more wheels than it knows what to do wit! The chrome on dis thing is insane, bro! And talk about a seat! Dis is gen-u-wine snakeskin. Straight off the snake's back. So come on, let's get dis deal done, I got a sauce on!"

Eventually, I trained myself not to speak that way because I didn't want people to single me out. I wanted to fit in other

---

* Oddly, Staten Island has the largest population of Sri Lankans outside of Sri Lanka.

places, not just where I grew up. That's why I now sound like an Ohio weatherman—neutral, friendly, and almost fully recovered after escaping that cult.

People don't know much about my hometown. When you google "Staten Island," the first questions that pop up are: "Is Staten Island a real island?" "Is Staten Island dangerous?" And weirdly, "Was Kareem Abdul-Jabbar ever married?" (Answer: Yes, to Habiba Abdul-Jabbar, from 1971 to 1978 . . . Why is this related to Staten Island?)

Although Staten Island is technically part of New York City, it's physically (and spiritually) closer to New Jersey. It was a Dutch island before the British took it over, and the Dutch word for river is *kill*, which makes a lot of places on Staten Island sound even more violent than they already are. Arthur Kill. Fresh Kills. The Kill Van Kull. When you're dumping a body in a river, calling the river a "kill" seems like . . . well . . . overkill.

And sure, Staten Island has a bad reputation and is often looked down upon by other boroughs in the city. But I did some historical research on my beloved hometown and discovered . . . that its reputation used to be even worse!

The Lenape tribe that lived there hundreds of years ago called it *Eghquhous,* or "The Bad Woods." That's right. Staten Island was the butt of even Native American jokes. (By the way, never a good sign when Native Americans *willingly* leave a place.)

But it gets worse. During the American Revolution, Staten Island was solidly supportive of the British crown, and George

Washington called Staten Islanders "our most inveterate ene-mies." Wow. When George Washington calls you a piece of trash, that hurts.

The island was even used by the British as a staging area for attacks on the rest of New York. And this tradition is alive today, as Staten Island voted almost 70 percent for Donald Trump—a clear fuck-you to the rest of the city. (And no won-der Trump loves Staten Island. When our local baseball team won the Little League World Series, they defeated Mexico.)

Even our patron saint and beloved explorer, Giovanni da Verrazzano (after whom the Verrazano Bridge was misspelled), only anchored in Staten Island for *one night*. Then his friends were like, "Is this seriously where you hang out?" And he yelled, "Anchors up! Let's get this puppy to Manhattan!"

My family was not like that punk Verrazzano. We have been living continuously on Staten Island since at least 1890. Half of my mother's Irish ancestors* immigrated to New York during the potato famine of the 1840s (historical proof that it's hard to give up carbs). They moved from the West Village in Man-hattan to Brooklyn, and then to Staten Island—apparently in search of worse and worse real estate. The other half came directly from County Cork to Staten Island in the 1890s, set-tling on the north shore for the next hundred years. Once we got to Staten Island, we never wanted to leave.

That's why my parents moved directly next door to my grandparents, like a real-life *Everybody Loves Raymond*. Also on the same block: my uncle, my cousin, my other cousin, and

---

* Last name "Kelly," so that should really narrow it down.

my other uncle. When a house comes up for sale on our street, I get a call telling me to buy it or details for a relative's funeral.

My mom always said that she loved Staten Island because it still felt like a small town. You would go to the supermarket and see a friend. You would go to church and see your enemies. And thanks to the Mafia, you would go to the park and see the dead body of your friend's dad. You know, small-town stuff.

And I really did know everybody's name. Not only because it was a close-knit community, but also because the people I grew up with had fantastic names. Salvatore Salmieri. Lenny Leone. Krystal Volpe. Michael Abbatantuono. And my second-grade girlfriend, Christina Martini.*

I loved growing up on Staten Island because it felt like kids doing regular kid stuff. We played a lot of sports and wandered around unsupervised, and with the exception of that Cropsey serial killer and several neighborhoods with the worst crime rates in all of New York City, it felt safe! Plus, you would see things that could only happen on Staten Island. Like my neighbor who had a Virgin Mary statue on his lawn, but the statue started to lean forward, so, to secure it, he tied a rope around her neck. Anyone driving by would think: *Oh, this man is hanging the Virgin Mary. I guess he hates religion?* When in fact, he loved religion *so much* that he refused to let the mother of God touch his Astroturf lawn.

Of course, Staten Island has changed a lot since my relatives settled there. It used to be almost entirely farmland, and when

---

* Her father, Spiros Martini, ran a haunted catering hall.

I was growing up in the '90s, there were still horses in a stable down the street. (Weirdly, that stable is now a graveyard . . . maybe for those horses?)

More than anything, it's just a lot more crowded than it used to be. In the past couple decades, the population of Staten Island has more than doubled, but the number of roads stayed basically the same. As a result, "traffic" is the number one topic of conversation at any Staten Island gathering.

I visit my family and the first fifteen minutes will be: "How did you get here? How was the traffic? Did you take the expressway or Clove Road? Are you going home the same way? Why not? Is there gonna be traffic? *What do you know that I don't know, you son of a bitch?*" Then, twenty minutes after the party starts, someone gets up and says, "I have to leave now to avoid the traffic."

I actually want to make a horror movie called *The Traffic* and set it on Staten Island. It can star my grandpa, who flees every event two hours early in fear of spending one extra minute in traffic. And he's ninety-five! What is he even racing home to? (Also, should he be driving?)

Maybe that's why most people never move off Staten Island—they're terrified of hitting traffic on the way out.* But I was desperate to see other places and have experiences that were decidedly *not* Staten Island.

I remember when I was seventeen, my swim coach Jimbo Cooney (another great name) was giving me a trophy at the end-of-the-year awards ceremony, and he said to the crowd, "Let's face it, folks, this kid's future is not in swimming. And

* Plus, the bridge to Brooklyn costs nineteen dollars.

it's not on Staten Island. He's going places." (It was a lot nicer than what he said about the next kid: "This guy is a terrible swimmer and I'm actually surprised he showed up tonight.")

But he was right:* I was at least physically "going places." And only many years later could I look back and appreciate how Staten Island informed the rest of my life.

The truth is, I've always had a chip on my shoulder about my hometown. But it stems from a deep insecurity that I don't really belong anywhere.

One of my favorite moments on Weekend Update was when fellow Staten Islander Pete Davidson came on and talked about how I'm beloved in our hometown and he's despised.† But even Pete would admit that's not entirely true. Pete seems way more "authentically" Staten Island than I do, which is probably fair, even though it's a little alienating for me. If I'm not "really" from my hometown, then where am I from?

At the same time, I feel defensive about Staten Island because the people I knew growing up were great people. A lot of them were first- and second-generation immigrants from all over the world‡ who worked really hard to become doctors, lawyers, teachers, shop owners, businessmen, and, yes, sometimes suspiciously wealthy "garbagemen."

And that thing about Staten Island being super Italian? Well,

---

* About both of us.
† Example: One reporter complimented my golf swing while another threatened to murder Pete.
‡ For every Lou Tobacco and Tommy "Tommy Naps" Napolitano, there was a Harini Rao and a Sameer Murukutla.

a study on Italian communities in Pennsylvania found that people in those areas lived longer, had a much greater sense of family and belonging, and were generally happier and healthier. There is a deep psychological comfort in feeling like you're part of a larger community. (Which is probably why I'm still at SNL after fifteen years. The Staten Islander in me doesn't want to give up a good family.) I still go back home at least once a month, because it's part of me and I feel weirdly revitalized every time I visit. It's like Superman's Fortress of Solitude— only replace the space crystals with a plate of linguine fra diavolo.

I've come to resent the negative depictions of Staten Island on TV because they've given my hometown a terrible reputation, which it only sort of deserves. Yes, until recently, Staten Island was home to the largest landfill in the *entire world*. And yes, as a result, miles of the island smelled like rotting garbage. And yes, my main cultural touchstone as a child was the Staten Island Mall. And yes, only a year ago, a mob boss was whacked outside his house for snitching to the cops.* And yes, the local St. Patrick's Day parade is the only parade in New York that still bans gays from marching.

But there are also like 170 parks! That's so many parks, guys!

And George R. R. Martin said he based King's Landing on his view of Staten Island from his home in New Jersey. That's pretty cool, right? (He also based Cersei on a woman he met in the parking lot of our Costco.)

The reality is: Staten Island is like 90 percent of the country— it's slow to change, but most of the people are fundamentally

---

* I would write more about this incident, but I wasn't raised to be a rat.

good people. They're just set in their ways. After all, it's an island. It has its own evolution. Even if the Galapagos Islands had three bridges to New Jersey, they would still have some freaky iguanas.

So if you're like me and you're not always sure how to feel about your hometown, remember what Method Man once said: "I'm in between homes right now, but my last house was dope."

You're Gonna Need Stitches

"Scars have the strange power to remind us that our past is real. The events that cause them can never be forgotten."

—CORMAC MCCARTHY

"Again?!"

—STATEN ISLAND HOSPITAL

I have had six sets of stitches on my face.

These are their stories.

"Dun-dun." (™ *Law & Order*)

I.

There was a game I played in kindergarten that I have not encountered anywhere outside of Staten Island. It was called "The Firefighter and the Fire." One child would play the firefighter and the other would play the fire. And it was up to the firefighter to chase down the fire and tackle it. As a potential fourth-generation member of the New York City Fire Department, I was eager to play the firefighter. This had the additional advantage of not being the one who got tackled.

My friend Michael Bodnar was the fire. I yelled "Go!" and he started running and waving his arms in the air, to simulate what a fire might look like while it was running. I chased him with my "hose" (penis) (kidding) for about ten seconds, before Michael Bodnar made the brilliant strategic decision to duck under a nearby metal table.

I followed him at full speed, but forgot the part about ducking. The corner of the table hit about half an inch from my eyeball and ripped open my eyelid.

The fire, unchecked, proceeded to burn down thousands of homes on the island.

II.

Any time a story starts with one child chasing another child with large metal scissors, it never ends well.

The situation was: I was extremely angry at my younger brother, because he was younger and before him there was only me. Now he was here too, and that meant less attention for me. (This was a major ongoing problem.)

So, when I was eight and he was five, I decided to grab the scissors from my dad's desk and stab my brother in the back.

"Boys will be boys!" I imagined telling a therapist, years after the funeral.

The main flaw in my stabbing plan was: My brother Casey was fast. He had gotten even faster through years of escaping attacks by snow shovels, golf clubs, kitchen knives, and baseball bats. When he saw me holding large metal scissors, he thought, *This could end poorly for me.* So he started running down the hallway.

Our hallway was only eight or ten feet long, but halfway down the hallway, the basement door opened outward. Casey, sensing that his fast running might not be fast enough, threw open the door as he passed. I proceeded to slam into the door at full speed, face-first, like Wile E. Coyote, and my chin exploded with blood.

The hero escaped to live another day. The villain was scarred once again.

I shook my fist and yelled, "You haven't seen the last of me, Dr. Jones!"

And Dr. Jones said, "Please hold still, Colin. I'm trying to sew four stitches into your chin."

III.

Every public golf course on Staten Island has a secret alter ego. At night, the second hole of South Shore Golf Course turns into a keg party for teenagers. (I know this from when I was a teenager. It's not like I go to teenage keg parties now. Unless some cool teens *invited me* . . .)

The tenth hole of La Tourette Golf Course also becomes a teenage keg party, and if you disable the regulator on the golf carts, you can race them straight downhill at fifty miles an hour until your friend flips a cart and smashes his leg into twenty-five pieces. Or you can be like my other friend and get so drunk that you drop a lit cigarette and burn down the 150-year-old clubhouse. He's a lawyer now!

Silver Lake Golf Course has two alter egos. The eighteenth hole was a mass grave for Irish immigrants in the 1800s. So that's always fun to think about when you're strolling up the fairway on a sunny afternoon. And in much less morbid news, the seventh hole has probably the best hill for sledding in all of Staten Island. So whenever it snowed, my brother and I went straight to Silver Lake, fleeing the ghosts of Irishmen with every step.

Now, my family had a rule: We were only allowed to use Radio Flyer sleds, the heavy wood and metal ones from, I want to say, the 1860s. (I believe Lincoln rode one to Gettysburg.) But one day when I was eight years old, my mother—in what she recently described as "a moment of weakness"—let me try one of those newfangled round plastic sleds that I borrowed from my second-grade friend Mark Gravante, whose name I've changed because shortly afterward he disappeared into the witness protection program. (But for real.)

Say what you will about Radio Flyers, at least they have a steering mechanism. It's a piece of string attached to a piece of wood, but it's *something*. A round piece of plastic is less of a conveyance and more of a battle between momentum and obstacles.

In my case, the obstacles won. I flew straight down the hill into a grove of elm trees that I believe was planted to maim slow-witted children. For the second time in what would become a series of "almost lost an eye" moments in my life, I smashed into a tree, eye-socket-first. (I've discovered firsthand how well-designed the human eye socket is. Apparently, natural selection really favors "keeping eyes.")

But the real damage was done to my forehead, which required fifteen stitches. To this day, my mother has never forgiven herself. And if you check our garage, there are still only Radio Flyers hanging on the wall.

IV.

When I was ten and my brother was seven, we would play a game called "Wolverine and the Wolf." (For some reason all our games sounded like Aesop fables.) It wasn't really a "game" so much as it was "a full physical fight." We called it "Wolverine and the Wolf," but a better name would have been "Child UFC."*

There were no rules except for one: The Wolverine (me) was "allowed to stand up." Which meant the Wolf was *not* allowed to stand up, and thus had to crawl around on all fours. This meant that the older brother (me), who was already taller and hella fat, had the additional advantage of "standing." So the Wolf would have to crawl around while I stood over him and took my time punching him in the back.

It was even more insidious because every time we played, I would ask my brother beforehand: "Do you want to be the Wolverine or the Wolf?"

He would choose "Wolverine," because he saw how poorly it had gone last time as the Wolf. Then I would really talk up the benefits of being the Wolf instead. "The Wolf has sharper teeth, it's bigger and stronger, it can eat more cinnamon rolls," etc. My brother would hear all these amazing benefits, and switch to being the Wolf.

Once my brother had locked in "Wolf," I would describe the benefits of being the Wolverine. "You can stand up on two legs instead of having to crawl. You can punch in addition to

---

* Now I really want to create Child UFC.

scratching. You can hold the Wolf down and punch it. And you can hold objects in your claws and use them to hit the Wolf."

I know. I was a legitimate monster. To quote my grandfather after I punched my brother in the back, "What a rotten kid."

But my brother finally got a modicum of revenge when—*against the established limitations on the Wolf*—he reached up and raked his nails across my face, leaving a scar that's still fairly prominent on my right cheek.

The Wolf had finally slayed the fearsome Wolverine. And the Wolverine was taken to see a plastic surgeon to put his face back together. And then the Wolverine was taken to the doctor a second time after he saw the wound scabbing over, thought, *Oooo, a scab!,* and tore it off his cheek, reopening the wound.

Shortly after this, the Wolverine and the Wolf would see a child psychologist.

V.

I owned a snake-themed bicycle called a Rattler.

My friends had real bikes, like a Huffy or a Mongoose. They bragged about having "chrome caps" and "shocks" and "gears." I had a Kmart bike made of Chinese steel with no gears and ten stencil drawings of snakes.

I went a lot of places on that bike. In fact, I rode it through all five boroughs of New York during the annual forty-two-mile bike race. (I guarantee you I was the only one who did it on a Rattler.) I also ate about twenty PowerBars along the way because they kept giving them out for free at every rest stop, so I probably gained five pounds biking forty-two miles.

When I first got the Rattler, I decided to charm it, as one does with a snake. I did this by pedaling as fast as I could down my street, then suddenly slamming the pedals backward to activate the brakes. (Again, this was not a good bike.)

At the time, I had not yet been exposed to the basic principles of physics. Therefore I did not understand that when an object (like a bike) is in motion and a person (like me) is attached to the object, that person assumes the velocity of the object he or she is attached to. However, when the object's velocity suddenly changes to, say, zero, the velocity of the *person* remains at the original velocity until it is reduced to zero by a second object, such as the pavement.

"Mah? I gah go to hostital again."

VI.

Now, call me crazy, but when you already have five sets of stitches on your face, and you're thirty-three years old, you sort of assume you're done getting stitches on your face. And when your face is on TV, you would assume you'd be extra careful not to damage that face, so people don't flip to your channel and think it's Shark Week.

Well, both of these assumptions were foolish. As are many decisions I make in my life.

Some quick background: I am not a great surfer, but I'm an okay surfer. I can do "most surfing stuff," as no surfer would ever say. If you saw me on a wave, you'd never think, *That dude's ripping it! He must be a pro!* But you also wouldn't yell, "That guy's a kook! Let's murder him!"

That's where I'm at, surfing-wise. I'm fairly cautious and, more than anything, I try to stay out of other people's way.

Okay, background over.

On the Fourth of July in 2016, I was down the Jersey Shore visiting my then 101-year-old grandmother in the town of Lavallette. I had just bought a new surfboard and I was excited because there were supposed to be waves that weekend and I had never surfed in Jersey before.

I walked to the beach at 11 A.M. (a.k.a. "Dawn Patrol") and there was only one other guy in the water. He seemed to be actively bad at surfing, so I thought, *Sweet, I can get all the waves!* (All the mushy two-foot waves.)

I paddled out, which on the Jersey Shore takes about three seconds, and caught my first wave. For history's sake, let's just say it was a hundred feet high and a perfect barrel. I jumped off my board, turned around to paddle back out, and was immediately hit in the face by the other guy's board. Apparently, he had just "let it go" so the board could ride a wave on its own, directly into my nose.

If you haven't gotten hit in the face by a ten-foot surfboard, it really, really, really hurts. I give it "one star."

I touched my nose and it was bleeding. I thought, *Goddammit, did my nose just break?* Then the dumb part of me thought, *Goddammit, does this mean I have to stop surfing?*

I actually debated staying out and surfing more because I was so pissed off at this guy for ruining my day after one wave. Then I touched my nose again and there was *more* blood and I thought, *Maybe bleeding a bunch in the ocean* isn't *a great idea?*

I walked back to my grandma's house, in no mood to celebrate the birth of our nation. My mom took one look at me and said, "You're gonna need stitches."

Then she said, "You know how many plastic surgeons are working on the Fourth of July? Zero."

So two days later, I got stitches. I really hope for the last time.

I Become a Commuter at Age Fourteen

> "A journey of a thousand miles begins with one step."
>
> —Lao Tzu

> "I know what you did, motherfucker! First day on the job, you was *rapin' crackheads*!"
>
> —An insane woman on the subway, to me,
> a fourteen-year-old

My grandfather worked four jobs. He was a fireman, a handyman, a substitute teacher, and a housepainter. With those jobs, he was able to put four children through college. That's where he spent all his money, because he knew that education was the best way to get ahead in life. (This was before Instagram and sex tapes.)

"Protect your brain!" he always told me. "Because it's all you got! Your brain is your ticket to wherever you want to go."*

---

* His other lesson was: "People are crazy!" Which is so simple, yet shockingly helpful. I have often wanted to verbally or physically fight someone before remembering that people are crazy and anyone could have a gun. This was proven last year when I honked at a swerving car and the driver got out and yelled, "You want to fight?!" And then showed me a gun.

My brain was definitely my ticket out of Staten Island, because it got me into a Catholic high school called Regis* that would change the course of the rest of my life.

I was extremely lucky to get accepted to Regis because (a) it's one of the best high schools in the country, and (b) it's *free.* For Catholics in New York, Regis is almost like the Watchtower for Jehovah's Witnesses. Tens of thousands of kids apply for 120 spots in each class. To this day, if a Catholic mother hears I went to Regis, she will grab my face and say, "God bless! What a wonderful place!"

The only catch: Regis is in Manhattan. So on a good day it took me an hour and a half each way to get there.† I took a bus, then a ferry, then a subway—which, when you type it into Google Maps, looks like you're emigrating from China to San Francisco in the 1840s:

🚶 → 🚌 → 🚶 → ⛴ → 🚶 → 🚇 → 🚶

But no one complained about the commute because, again, it was a free high school and we all felt insanely grateful to be there. As my grandfather reminded me, "If you don't want to make the trip, there are plenty of kids who would take your place!" Then he'd say, "By the way, did you hear about the boy who stuck his head out the bus window and hit a tele-

---

* Regis Philbin was named after my high school but then didn't get in, so he went to Xavier High School, which was full of kids who beat the shit out of kids who went to Regis.

† And mine wasn't even the longest commute. Some of my friends traveled almost two and a half hours from upstate New York and rural Pennsylvania.

phone pole and his head ripped clean off his body? People are crazy!"

Initially, my parents were very worried about their fourteen-year-old boy commuting alone into the city and taking the subway home late at night. Especially when their fourteen-year-old boy looked like this:

If that doesn't say, "Come and get it!" to a subway pedophile, I don't know what does.

And like many of the kids at Regis, I was book-smart and street-illiterate. But I would learn and experience so much over the next four years that by the time I graduated, I looked like this:

There was a nickname for New York in the 1930s that I always loved: the Wonder City. And for most of us, coming from the suburbs and suddenly being in the middle of Manhattan with no adult supervision after school ended, New York was a Wonder City on every level.

Some of my friends used this freedom to do actual fun things, like taking Ecstasy and sneaking into clubs like Limelight (an abandoned church where you could dance on the altar) or Tunnel (which got shut down once a month because someone OD'd or got stabbed in the bathroom). Police referred to Tunnel as "an open-air drug supermarket." (Which today is just a Walmart.)

I was way too afraid to try drugs because, again, my brain was all I had! So I enjoyed the nerdier perks of Manhattan, like seeing a David Lynch movie that never would have played on Staten Island. Or sneaking in to watch the funeral of Robert Giroux, one of the partners of the publishing house Farrar, Straus and Giroux. You know, crazy teenage hijinks!

I wasn't always so squeaky clean, though. Occasionally I signed out from school under the guise of visiting a nearby museum but instead snuck off to play billiards at a local pool hall, like one of the troubled teens in *The Music Man*. Or my friend Milosz and I would go to the Knitting Factory or a performance art space called ABC No Rio. We'd share a 40 of malt liquor and watch a twelve-person band called the World Inferno Friendship Society perform punk/klezmer songs about Weimar Germany, Paul Robeson, and Austro-Hungarian actor Peter Lorre. The closest thing we had to that on Staten Island was a waiter who sang "That's Amore!" And sometimes, my friend Pete and I would go to an Italian restaurant downtown and order "One glass of red wine, please!" and they would serve us! One glass of red wine for two out-of-control teens!

Then we stumbled home, flying from the wine but also terrified because we thought *The Blair Witch Project* was real and the witch was coming for us next. (Did I mention we were booksmart?)

I also got to meet the most intimidating and sophisticated girls in the world. Girls who attended fancy neighboring schools with names like Marymount, Chapin, Spence, and Nightingale—names that just *sounded* rich. We somehow convinced them to attend our high school dances, and I felt like a way chubbier Jay Gatsby, faking a cultured air to mask my Staten Island bootlegger upbringing. (To this day, that's how I feel 95 percent of the time.)

All my friends and I would hang out after school for hours because no one wanted to go home. The adventure of the city was so much more exciting than anything waiting for us in the outer boroughs. It was like a slightly more grown-up version of *The Goonies,* only our treasure? Was knowledge. And our Sloth? Was a guy on the subway who looked like Sloth. And look at that . . . he's masturbating! "Heyyy, you guyyyys!!!"

The upside of having an hour-and-a-half commute is that you can get a lot of homework done on the way home. (And on the way to school in the morning, you can cram for all the tests you didn't study for the night before.) There were also many days where homework and studying were disregarded in favor of extremely juvenile and dangerous behavior. Like doing "dips" on the chain-link ropes between two moving subway cars. Or seeing who could run across all four subway tracks to the other side of the platform without "touching the third rail" and "dying." Or tying your friend's hands to the subway pole and then "pantsing" him so he was naked in the middle of the train and couldn't pull up his pants. And then if a stranger on the train tried to help him, you'd yell, "He's touching that kid!" Really smart, cool stuff like that.

One of my most vivid memories in high school was when our cartoonishly uptight dean of discipline sat down next to my friends and me at lunch and said, "Is there something you fellas would like to tell me about what happened on the subway today?" So many terrible things happened on the subway all the time that we truly had no idea what he was referring to. So we just stayed quiet. He said, "Really? Nothing happened? You boys weren't overheard . . . saying something like . . . *SUCK MY COCK!?*" And he said it with such an *Aha, gotcha!* tone that we all immediately burst out laughing. We still had no idea what he was talking about, but we were so excited that a random stranger on the New York City subway had called our high school to complain about a group of teenagers using the phrase "suck my cock." I can only imagine the complaints they receive at 311. "This morning a teenager told me to eat his butthole! And I *refused!*"

There were also scarier moments, like when a group of older, much stronger teenagers followed us off the train late at night, jumped us, and broke my friend Pete's nose. Or the time when I was standing on the corner of Houston and Bowery and I watched a man step into the street and get hit at full speed by a city bus and his body basically exploded in front of me. That was very, very disturbing, and I can still close my eyes and picture pieces of him lying on Houston Street. But it's also New York, so fifteen minutes later you just move on with your day! Like you didn't just see a human being turned into meat-loaf. (That's the verse they cut out of "New York, New York.")

I take it for granted now, but New York is intense and over-whelming, especially when your brain is still developing. The shit you see—including many piles of actual human shit—definitely affects you and hardens you. (I know, when you see me you think, *How'd he get so* hard?) When you walk into a subway station at 9 A.M. and there's a man standing halfway through the turnstile with his pants down and his entire fist inside his butt, that definitely alters your sense of what's "nor-mal."

I was always on edge when I traveled home alone late at night. Because again, I was this boy:

Except I was very conscious of never smiling because I was afraid that if I smiled, someone would punch me. I actively tried to look sad, and, in keeping with my slow-to-talk, living-in-my-head approach to life, I would invent awful things that had happened to me to tell a robber so he would feel guilty and then not rob me. Like I expected a robber to say, "Wow. I'm so sorry, Colin. I was going to steal your ten dollars, but after hearing that your cat killed your sister, I simply cannot in good conscience take your money. In fact, here's five dollars from me. In memory of your sister, Noxzema."

When the subways weren't empty and scary, they were loud and crowded. So I got used to reading and focusing while standing in the hottest, sweatiest corner of the train as a panhandler screamed about Jesus coming back to Earth to send us all to hell, and would we like to hear a song about that?

It was actually great preparation for SNL, where on any given Saturday someone in the crew is yelling about a technical problem, the musical guest's forty backup dancers are arguing with an actual llama that just took a dump on their craft-service table, while a cast member is crying and throwing glass bottles in their dressing room because their sketch got cut after dress rehearsal. And I'm standing in the middle of all of this with a script for a sketch that airs in fifteen minutes, thinking, *What's a funnier way to say "front butt"?*

And then there was the *boat* portion of my trip, which is always a funny element to sprinkle into a morning commute. No one has ever transferred from a city bus to a subway and thought, *There should be a boat ride in between!*

If it sounds glamorous to arrive in Manhattan every morning via ship, let me assure you it was not. Even my immigrant ancestors arriving at Ellis Island would have seen me on the ferry and thought, *There has to be a better way.*

The Staten Island Ferry is the busiest passenger ferry in the world, with almost 25 million riders a year. By my own unofficial calculations, it also holds the record for "Most Exposed

Public Restrooms" (somehow designed so that any casual pass-ersby can see the entire bathroom, all of the stalls, and every single drag queen fixing her makeup in the mirror), as well as the record for "Most Dead-Eyed Businessmen Staring at the Sea Contemplating Whether to End It."

Riding the ferry was not a "yacht lifestyle." The bins under the seats were marked LIFE JACKETS but should have been marked A HUNDRED RATS LIVE HERE. The ferry is known for its amazing views of the Statue of Liberty, but it's also a great place to watch a raccoon eat a passenger's leftover meth. And look, the raccoon is reading the New York Post! Cuuuuuuute!

There are many questions that come to mind while riding the Staten Island Ferry. Questions like, "Why does the donut store on the ferry sell 25-ounce cans of Foster's Australian beer?" Or, "Why is a janitor telling me, 'Let's go! Get off the boat!' when the boat is still moving at full speed nowhere near the dock?" Or, "That Russian woman just threw a stroller off the back of the ferry—is that something I should report?"

All I'm saying is, you've never experienced a New York sun-set until you've seen it from the deck of the Staten Island Ferry—as a seagull pukes up mouse bones onto your geome-try textbook. You'll think, Are we in the Mediterranean? And a drunk ferry hand will burp, "Naw, sweetie, that's the Hudson Bay! Where all of New York's sewers meet for breakfast!" You can almost hear "Come Sail Away" playing in the background as you pass an open trash can full of Bud Light Lime cans and actual printed pornography. Hey, something's gotta pass the time! And time flies when you're having this much fun/teta-nus.

.   .   .

After the subway and the ferry, getting on the bus on Staten Island to finish off my evening commute actually felt like a relief. I knew I was almost home, plus everyone on the bus was resigned to a defeated silence. It's like we all thought, *We live in a place full of cars, yet we're riding a bus. Let us never speak of this to anyone.*

The bus snaked its way up Victory Boulevard, which was dedicated to the American victory in World War I but also showcased the modern victory of having a Golden Krust Jamaican Beef Patty restaurant share an office space with H&R Block. It was the heyday of the Wu-Tang Clan, and every day my bus passed an official Wu Wear clothing store.* Then one day the store closed and someone replaced it with a pet store. But the new owner was either too cheap or too big a fan to take down the giant *W* from the Wu Wear sign, so they kept it and named the store "Walking Dogs."

Then we passed my Catholic church, with its enormous banner reading: "ABORTION IS MURDER! ALSO, WE'VE ADDED A SPANISH MASS AT 1 P.M.!" And as the bus crested the hill by Clove Lakes Park, I could look back and see all of Manhattan in the distance. I felt the sense of accomplishment that comes with completing any journey, even a daily commute by land, by sea, and by underground rocket toilet.

---

* One of my great joys in life was making a movie with Method Man, who told me he would never leave Staten Island because it was the only place in America where he could get pulled over and the cops were actually excited to see him.

To this day I'm always more productive while traveling because I know the journey itself is getting me somewhere, and that frees my mind to be more creative. There's a reason it took an American to invent the rocking chair—because even when we're sitting still, we like to feel like we're in motion.

I exited the bus every night at the base of a cemetery run by stray dogs, which then chased me up the street to my house. Eight hours later, I woke up and did it all over again.

Sports for Nerds

"Swimming is a confusing sport, because sometimes you do it for fun, and other times you do it to not die."

—Demetri Martin

"Speech and Debate is not a sport."

—Urban Dictionary

rowing up, I played basketball, baseball, golf, and soccer. I was decent at all of them, but not nearly good enough to play at a higher level. I mean, *physically* I was NBA-ready—a classic lottery pick—but emotionally I was too immature to handle the sudden fame and fortune. So I told a young LeBron James, "Sorry, man, you're gonna have to do this without me."

The one sport I was actually good at was swimming. I swam and dove competitively from ages four to eighteen. But I peaked at the age of eight. That's when I won a gold medal in diving for all of Staten Island (by one point over Steve Deppe. Suck it, Steve!) and qualified for the Junior Olympics in the 50- and 100-meter breaststroke (I placed 16th and 32nd. Suck it, Me!).

But even though I loved being in water, I never enjoyed swim meets. It always seemed like they were imposing structure and stress on something that should have been freeing and fun. For example, going down a slide is awesome. But if you had to show up every day for slide practice at 7 A.M. and then compete against your best friend in slide competitions, while grown-ups screamed at you to slide better, until your friend won and you cried, slides would seem a lot less awesome. And yes, I cried after the 1994 breaststroke finals when the official said I lost even though *technically* I had a faster time. And yes, I was beaten by Steve Deppe. And yes, I just googled Steve Deppe and discovered he now runs a successful wealth management business in San Diego. And yes, his online corporate profile says, "As a former athlete, Steve continues to exercise daily, whether it's lifting weights, running, *swimming,* or playing sports." And yes, the fourth example he gave of "exercise" was "sports." And yes, I just went out and bought goggles and a Speedo and went down to my local pool and didn't leave until I swam a hundred laps, hoping that would be more laps than Steve Deppe swam today. BUT REALLY, WHO EVEN CARES ANYMORE, RIGHT??? NOT ME!!! IT'S NOT A COMPETITION, EVEN THOUGH I'M NOT EVEN MARRIED YET AND STEVE IS ALREADY "THE PROUD FATHER OF HIS DAUGHTER, CAMRYN." PLUS, HE'S "AN AVID SPORTS FAN, WHO NEVER MISSES HIS FAVORITE TV SHOW, *SPORTSCENTER.*" WE GET IT STEVE, YOU FUCKING LOVE SPORTS!

Anyway.

By the time I got to high school, I was pretty burned out on swimming. And my new commute made it almost impossible to get home in time for afternoon practice. So I made the decision, once again, to prioritize my brain over the inefficient body that housed my brain.

I would also like to point out—and this is a real F.U. to Michelle Obama's "Let's Move!" program—the more sports I played as a kid, the fatter I got. WHY? IT DOESN'T MAKE SENSE! I was a *five-sport athlete* and I looked like Pizza the Hut was eating an additional pizza.

It's actually a testament to how incredibly caloric American food was in the '90s that a boy who exercised constantly could steadily gain weight. My mom was a *family doctor*, who should have theoretically understood nutrition, yet at least once a week my brother and I split an entire can of Pillsbury cinnamon rolls. That's four cinnamon rolls each. For *breakfast*.

It didn't help that after every practice or swim meet, we'd go to McDonald's and my dad would ask, "What do you want to order *in addition to* your Value Meal?" Because a Double Quarter Pounder with Cheese, plus an extra-large fries and an extra-large Coke, wasn't enough to satisfy the

nine-year-old garbage disposal I had become. I also needed a "regular" double cheeseburger "on the side." And some chicken nuggets "for the table." (The table consisting of me and my dad.)

Then we would go to Wendy's *after McDonald's* to polish it off with a chocolate Frosty.

I SHOULD BE DEAD. I mean, look at this photo: ⟶

This is right before I appeared in *Young and Busty, Volume 12*. Which led to a starring role in *Ten-Year-Old Titties*.

I swear to god, I spent most of my childhood convinced I had breast cancer. One of my nipples was puffier than the other one (probably a cinnamon roll had gotten lodged in there) and I thought, *That's the lump. I have breast cancer. I'm the first male tween with breast cancer.* I didn't know what to do. Should I tell a doctor? Would they have to make a special awareness ribbon for me that was half pink, half blue, with the faces of all five Backstreet Boys?

I remember thinking, *I can beat this thing. I'm not gonna become another statistic.* There were no statistics. No ten-year-old boys had breast cancer. But every time I touched my nipple (which was fifty times a day), I felt terrified. (And then, of course, hungry.)

But back to swimming! I quit the only sport I was ever good at, but not before I spent one last summer lifeguarding at Hillside Swim Club.

Hillside had by far the best swim team on Staten Island. Every kid was super competitive and trained year-round so they could win the championship. (Which they did. *Twenty-five years in a row.*)

The adults at the club were also super competitive, only their sport was drinking. They had only a few months of summer and they didn't want to remember a single day of it!

As a lifeguard, you were expected to watch their kids and make sure no one drowned. But what they *really* expected of you was to switch the keg before it ran out of beer, or they would legit fire you. (Somehow they skipped over "tapping a keg" during CPR training.)

In order of priority, it went:

1. Check the keg
2. Double-check the keg
3. Get the backup keg on ice
4. Clean the toilets decimated by adults who drink fifteen beers a day
5. Really double-check the keg
6. Don't let a kid die
7. Check for glass on the pool deck because someone dropped a bottle of beer while the keg was being switched over

There were three lifeguards on duty at all times to monitor a pool that never had more than ten kids in it. We were bored out of our minds. The closest I came to a rescue was when a kid yelled, "Hey! I've got a cramp!" And I said, "Then stand up. You're in three feet of water. Also, why are you eating a sandwich in the pool?"

Between lifeguarding shifts, I was also commuting back into Manhattan to intern at Merrill Lynch three days a week, under the tutelage of a financial adviser named Rocco. This was right before the dot-com bubble burst, so employees at Merrill Lynch were saying things like "This company can't lose!" and "Our stock price just keeps going up and up! I'm sure that will continue forever!"

My bosses would show me a printout of how much money they were making—millions of dollars a year—and say, "What a job! And I'm barely doing anything!" To this day, I distrust all money managers because I saw how little they actually managed anything. My boss would say, "Hey, Colin, here's a pie chart of where Mrs. Reynolds is keeping her money. And here's a pie chart of how she *wants* her money invested. Can you click a few buttons to make the pie charts look the same?" That was 90 percent of the job. The other 10 percent was lunch.

When I worked there, Merrill Lynch's stock price was 120 dollars per share. They were later bought by Bank of America for 29 dollars per share. Here's a pie chart for that:

Still, I was determined to learn as much about our financial system as possible. So while I sat in the lifeguard chair (ostensibly monitoring lives), I would read textbooks about finance with titles like *Investor's Guide to Treasury Bonds* and *The Mechanisms Behind the Stock Market*. Needless to say, I was single.

Next to me was a lifeguard named Anthony (pronounced "Ant'ny") who was joining the Navy in three weeks. He wouldn't *sit* in the lifeguard chair—he would hang from it and do pull-ups while every girl at the swim club watched and ovulated. Anthony was, you might say, "more popular" than me.

The last week before the summer ended, Anthony snuck us two beers from the keg and asked me, "So what are you gonna do if you don't swim no more?"

"I don't know. Maybe I'll focus on academics instead."

"Yeah. Yeah, I was gonna say, you should definitely do that.

'Cause the physical stuff, where you need to use your body and muscles to do things, that might not be for you."

"Yeah, maybe not."

"No, like a hundred percent not. I mean, this isn't an intervention or nothing, but seriously, don't do sports no more."

"Okay, got it."

"Do you, though? 'Cause I'm worried about you doin' more sports. It could affect your breast cancer."

"I promise I'll stop."

"Good. And hey, go Navy."

We clinked glasses and then he left to have a threesome with the two hottest female lifeguards.

And my days as an athlete were officially over.

Or were they . . .

Speech and Debate is a sport, okay? There are trophies. There are tournaments. You have to stand on your feet for upward of ten minutes at a time. It's a goddamn sport.

It has to be. Otherwise my high school bedroom was a joke. It was filled with trophies and plaques that looked exactly like sports trophies, except there was a beautiful angel on top with golden wings and oddly large breasts. (Just like mine!)

Oh, and the other difference is that if you looked at the inscription on the trophy, instead of saying *MVP, Baseball* or *Most Assaults, Lacrosse Team,* my trophies said—and I'm paraphrasing—*Will Not Have Sex in High School. Repeat: Colin Will Remain a Virgin Until He Stops Doing Speech and Debate.*

If you're an overprotective parent, here is my advice: Get your child involved in Speech and Debate *today*. It's like a chastity belt with a condom wrapped around it, so if someone tries to have sex with the belt, the belt won't get herpes.

I don't quite understand why it works that way. If anything, Speech and Debate should have *helped* me have sex. I was away most weekends for tournaments in hotels in random cities with girls from other high schools. Yet sex was the farthest thing from anyone's mind. It was like trying to get laid in a cemetery. Just saying the word "oratory" was like a magic spell that ensured sexlessness for another year.

But that's not to say we didn't have fun!

I mean, my friends and I would pretend to be WWE wrestlers and wrestle each other on the hotel bed . . .

Or while my friend Chris was sleeping, my friend Tim would put his nuts on Chris's face . . .

Or a whole group of guys would order a porno on the hotel TV and just sort of . . . watch it together . . .

You know, cool, "not sexually repressed" stuff like that!

But let me start with some fundamentals.

For those of you who don't know, Speech and Debate is like Track and Field for nerds. And that's saying a lot, because Track and Field is already pretty nerdy. As with Track and Field, Speech and Debate has many different categories and there was a real divide between the "Speech" team and the "Debate" team. Just like "Track" is made up of runners and "Field" is made up of a bunch of weirdos throwing things around a field.

The style of debate at my school was mostly "Lincoln-Douglas," modeled after the historic debates between Linkin Park and Michael Douglas. Each tournament had a resolution for the two sides to argue about, such as "Handguns ought to be outlawed in the U.S.," "Adolescents should make their own healthcare decisions," or "Dogs are great and cats are dumb." And you'd alternate taking the pro and the con, so it forced you to think through both sides—even though any sane person would agree that dogs are great and cats are dumb.*

I got really frustrated competing in Debate because inevitably some tool-bag I was debating would find a way to make every topic devolve into a potential nuclear holocaust. He'd say, "Well, if we don't ban abortion, then one of the unborn babies will survive and become an evil genius and steal our nuclear weapons, and at that point there's a greater-than-100-percent chance of COMPLETE NUCLEAR HOLOCAUST." And I would stand up and say, "Judge, this man has no dick." And somehow that didn't win the argument.

So I quickly moved over to the Speech side, where I could do my own thing and not worry about accidentally calling my opponent an asshat.

Speech included "intellectual" categories like Extemporaneous Speaking (for those who dreamed of being president) and Student Congress (for those who dreamed of being a state senator); but it also had artsy categories like Dramatic Interpretation ("I have AIDS!"), Humorous Interpretation ([sung] "I have AIIIIDS!"), and Duo Interpretation ("We both have AIDS! In unison!"). Those categories were for theater kids who weren't cool enough to do actual theater. (Like myself.)

---

* Disagree? Send proof that your cat is smart to:
  The Association of Idiots
  Attn: Yourself
  123 IsAllYouCanCountTo Road
  Dogs Rule, The Earth 90210

There were also in-between categories that were neither intellectual nor artistic. Those included "Original Oratory" (you wrote a speech and performed it); "Declamation" (you borrowed a speech from someone like Martin Luther King, Jr., and delivered it with twice the volume and ¹⁄₁,₀₀₀th the impact); and "The Oral Interpretation of Poetry and Prose," which I believe was a category invented by homophobic bullies. Who else would put the words "oral" and "poetry" in the same name? Everyone called it "O.I." for short—as in, "*Oh, I* should never read poetry aloud for ten minutes and expect my peers to still respect me."

I prided myself on doing as many different categories as I could, probably because I was already scared of commitment, but also because I liked the variety of performing in different ways. Like how a lot of mimes are also serial killers.

Also, if you only compete in one category, then you have to hear the same speeches from your opponents hundreds of times. If I had to listen to some kid with a thick Long Island accent recite "The Road Not Taken" by Robert Frost for an entire school year, the road *I* would have taken would have been blowing my brains out.

That's the strangest thing about Speech and Debate—how self-serious some of the kids are. There were white kids from private schools on the Upper West Side performing excerpts from John Leguizamo's *Ghetto Klown* with no sense of irony. You haven't lived until you've heard a kid named Ezra Kleinman very earnestly deliver the line "I did what any other Spanish kid raised in the ghetto would do—I acted like a retard!"

I did "Original Oratory" a lot, where you write your own speech. And I essentially treated it like stand-up, where I would have a loose theme and then try to tell as many jokes as possible. There was always a moment when you walked into the classroom and saw the titles of the speeches your competitors were going to perform, and you immediately knew when it was gonna suck.

You'd see titles like:

Come and Get Me, Cancer!
My Mom, the Ghost
What We Found in Grandpa's Attic
Oops, No Arms

and:

How My Vacation to Aruba Quickly Descended into
    Dolphin Rape

Then I would have to go up and write the title of whatever goofy speech I had come up with, like "I'm White and It's Fun!" or "It's Pronounced Colin Not Colon!" And I'd just hope for a judge who wanted to laugh and not contemplate: "Where Did Our Innocence Go?" (A real title of another student's speech. His answer? Video games stole it! That's right, a fifteen-year-old was like, "These damn newfangled video games! Always stealing our precious innocence!")

My friends and I spent half our time re-creating the cheesy performances from other schools, which was so much more fun than earnestly doing our own pieces. For example, *The Elephant Man* is a beautiful, moving play, but not one that should be performed by a blond teenager from California named Zeke. "I'm not an animal! I'm a human being, bro-ham!"

There were also genuinely amazing performers who made me realize how limited my own skills were. I remember seeing this one guy, who was a few years older, named Josh Gad. He won every national tournament my freshman year, and I said, "This kid's going places!" like I was a 1920s silent movie director. Then I completely forgot about him until I went to see *The Book of Mormon* on Broadway and thought, *Who is* this *talented fella!* I looked at the Playbill and thought, *Another Josh Gad?*

And there was Hallie Jackson, who I'd always see at national tournaments for Original Oratory, and she was one of the few people who wrote good speeches and was also cool. Then I ran into a "Hallie Jackson" who was a reporter for MSNBC at the Republican Convention in 2016 and thought, *You look just like the Hallie Jackson I knew from Original Oratory, except you're no longer a foot taller than me!*

And most important, just like getting into Regis helped me discover the world outside of Staten Island, Speech and Debate helped me discover the rest of America, including major universities where a lot of the tournaments took place. It was like doing a college tour, only with your friends instead of your parents. (Plus a Catholic priest as a chaperone, but I'll leave those jokes aside for now.) And it motivated me to work harder in school, because I really wanted to get into one of those colleges.

By my senior year, I had qualified for the national championship in Original Oratory, Declamation, Student Congress, Duo Interpretation, and the Oral Interpretation of Poetry and

Prose (😃). I also qualified for the state championship in all of those categories, plus Extemporaneous Speaking and Lincoln-Douglas Debate.

Let's just say I had a lot of busty angels on my bookshelf.

And those trophies actually meant a lot to me because, again, I started out at a zero in terms of talking, so Speech and Debate at least validated that I *could* talk and might even excel at it someday.

Plus, whenever I did fail (which happened just as frequently) or I had a strange experience with a judge (one of them wrote, *Your performance was a little too Jewish . . .**), I learned that it was okay because there was always another tournament the next week where I could redeem myself. It's a lesson I still remember every week at SNL, where even the most successful writers and cast members get their sketches cut all the time. It sucks in the moment, and it takes a few days to get over, but there's always another chance next week.

And that is how my vacation to Aruba quickly descended into dolphin rape.

---

* I guess because the tournament was in Georgia, anyone from New York was automatically Jewish? Also, if you thought *I* was too Jewish, just wait until Ezra Kleinman does *Ghetto Klown*!

What Is Harvard Like?

"If you guys were the inventors of Facebook, you would have invented Facebook."

—MARK ZUCKERBERG, *The Social Network*

"My advice to you is to start drinking heavily."

—JOHN BELUSHI, *Animal House*

Harvard is a really weird place. Not just in terms of the school itself. The *concept* of Harvard is really weird. Of all the colleges in America (and maybe the world), it has this other thing about it, which is partially just name recognition (people in rural Mongolia have heard of it) and partially some kind of mysterious aura that makes it feel like a gathering of the Illuminati.*

The reality is that Harvard is very similar to a bunch of other schools, and if you got into Harvard, you weren't special or spectacular. You just had good grades and something that

---

* In fairness, I *am* a member of the Illuminati, but I'm only a Mystic Templar, so I've barely glimpsed the Minerval Sanctum. And I assure you, being in the Illuminati isn't all it's cracked up to be, unless you like power, gold, and the ability to murder without consequence.

helped you stand out in some way that Harvard happened to be looking for that year. (Or your last name was Wigglesworth and an admissions officer gave a speech like, *"There has been a Wigglesworth at this university since 1636!"* And everyone else in the meeting was like, "Okay! Okay! Let Wigglesworth in! As long as he doesn't take a spot away from a hardworking celebrity's fake-athletic daughter.")

The secret is: Anyone who went to any of the top 25 or 50 or even 100 colleges in America could easily graduate Harvard, maybe with better grades than actual Harvard graduates.

Some people dream about attending Harvard. I did not. I dreamed about attending the University of North Carolina, because that's where Michael Jordan went. I would constantly write in a journal that I wanted to attend UNC, then go to UNC medical school to become a doctor, but then *reject medicine* and write science-fiction thrillers like Michael Crichton. My parents pointed out that maybe I shouldn't go through four years of medical school to *not* become a doctor. But guess who did just that? Michael Crichton.

There was also the simple fact that Harvard was never a place I imagined I could go. Growing up in Staten Island, no one ever said, "Are you thinking Harvard or Yale?" They said, "Are you going to college down the street or will you just stay in the house you grew up in until you die?"

To this day, no one has ever met me and thought, *He probably went to Harvard.* Most people meet me and think, *He might have gone to college?*

I certainly never volunteer that information, purely out of self-preservation. When you're starting out in comedy—

particularly stand-up comedy—being introduced as "This next guy went to *Harvard* . . ." is maybe the quickest way to get an audience to hate you.

But if people do find out, their first question is usually "Really? *You?* Huh." And their second question is: "What is Harvard like?"

Harvard is like Professor X's School for Mutants, except their mutant powers are playing cello or computer programming or being a Saudi prince. It's a quarter athletes and legacies, a quarter geniuses, and then the remaining half are fairly smart kids who suddenly realize they aren't geniuses.

I got a perfect score on my math SAT*, but when I got to Harvard I realized, *Oh, damn. I suck at math.* The first day, we all took a math placement test and were divided into five tiers of math classes. I was put in tier one (tier five being the best). I met a couple kids who made it into tier two or three, and they were like professional math-doers. "Who the hell is in tier five?" I asked.

"Sasha," they said.

And they pointed at a kid with a full beard and flip-flops who was tossing a Frisbee into a tree.

That's what Harvard was like: thinking you're pretty good at something, then meeting someone who is *really good* or maybe even one of the best in the world. And that doesn't even

---

* And a not-great score on my verbal SAT, because, again, anything verbal was my enemy.

mean they get good grades. A lot of the most famous alumni left without graduating because their work became more important than school. People like Bill Gates, Matt Damon, and Mark Zuckerberg.

And you know who *did* graduate? The Unabomber, Ted Kaczynski.

The point is: Never graduate from Harvard.

People often ask me: "Did you, like, hang out with Mark Zuckerberg?" He was a year behind me and I remember when Facebook first started, because it only operated within our school (like an actual yearbook). I was probably one of the first hundred people to join, and I immediately thought: *This is a gigantic waste of time.* I wasn't *wrong* . . . but I certainly never imagined it would become a multi-billion-dollar company. (My parents pointed this out to me several times while I was making four hundred dollars a week writing for a cartoon show.)

I was "Facebook friends" with Mark, back when that actually kind of meant something. But I don't think we ever hung out, because he was busy making a billion dollars creating Facebook and I was busy making zero dollars writing comedy pieces for a magazine that no one read. The sad part is, I probably spent more time writing those comedy pieces than Mark did creating Facebook. But is he *happy*?*

My strangest Facebook connection was that I rowed crew freshman year with the Winklevoss twins (a.k.a. "the Winklevi," which is maybe the grossest nickname in history). They

---

* (By all accounts, yes.)

probably don't remember me because they were approximately eight feet tall, 230 pounds, and excellent at rowing; whereas I was six feet tall, 160 pounds, and hadn't rowed a boat since my grandpa took me to a duck pond on Staten Island in 1993.

I "walked on" the crew team, which is what they call it when the coach humors you and lets you join the team, mostly for his own entertainment. Think of it like the first couple episodes of *American Idol,* when they're ostensibly looking for singers but actually looking for train wrecks. A lot of walk-ons flip the boat and fall into the shockingly disgusting Charles River. And if you're the crew coach, that's gotta make you laugh.

The thing about crew, though, is that there's no way to do it and *not* get incredibly fit. By spring of my freshman year, I was in by far the best shape of my life, even though I was consuming four or five thousand calories a day. Because I was rowing a goddamn boat for hours and *then* running six to eight miles.

I completed the "triathlon," which was rowing 10,000 meters, then running 10 miles, then running up and down every single section of stairs in the football stadium. That was certainly my peak athletic accomplishment. (Other than my Small Fry C Division basketball championship in sixth grade, when we were given the trophy retroactively after it was discovered that the team who beat us was using several high school players. Which is just so insane, that kids in high school would willingly put on elementary school uniforms and dunk on feeble white tweens . . . actually, now that I'm writing it down, it does sound fun.)

I was eventually moved to the lightweight crew team, which sounds like it's for pussies, but it's actually for *athletic* pussies.

Crew taught me discipline, and how to stay calm and mentally sharp even when I was physically exhausted, which is a skill I still use at SNL. It also taught me that rowing crew is really hard and maybe more demanding on a pure aerobic level than any sport except boxing. And finally, it taught me that I didn't want to do crew anymore, because it was grueling and endless, and sitting on a rowing machine twice a day for four hours was not the most satisfying way to spend half of your college life.

So by the end of freshman year, I stopped rowing crew but made the interesting decision to continue eating five thousand calories a day. Which is hard to do when you're *not* rowing a boat or running six to eight miles a day. It requires some real ingenuity—like when I would order a double-decker pizza most nights, for just myself. The joke among my friends was that I had to call the pizza place if I *didn't* want a pizza. Otherwise they'd just keep 'em coming! (And each double-decker was only four dollars, by the way, which is terrifying on a "where did they get ingredients that cheap?" level.) Also during this time period I discovered beer, which I had barely ever touched in high school and which apparently is not a "diet food."

I gained forty pounds, I would say . . . instantly? It was like a reverse fairy tale where I fell asleep on a pizza, got kissed by a pepperoni, and woke up a toad. Then I realized that my vision was suddenly fading (I guess I went pizza-blind?) and I had to get eyeglasses for the first time. Plus, I had late-onset acne, which made my *face* look like a pizza, which in turn made me even hungrier. Basically, I went through a second awkward puberty, only this time in college. And pictures of me from this time period are not pleasant to look upon.

I was also pretty disillusioned with college in general during freshman year because I really missed my high school; it was full of smart but humble kids who never took school too seriously. Whereas a lot of the kids at Harvard needed to *tell* you they were smart in a really off-putting way. I went to a reunion in New York a few years ago and the first guy I ran into sounded like a parody of a Harvard grad. I literally asked, "How's it going?" And he responded, "Well, I guess I chose the typical route: investment banking for two years, then private equity, and now I'm partnering with a VC firm in the tech space. And, not to brag, but I almost owned part of Instagram." *Almost?* That was your *brag?*

I also became disillusioned with my religion, because I was used to a certain kind of Catholic that I grew up with—the kind that's reserved and humble to the point of shaking slightly. (Unless they're drunk, in which case they're yelling, "I love you" through a veil of tears.) And I was too young (or naive) to understand the real-world implications of religion.

In high school I had gone to mass every Sunday and studied the Bible from cover to cover, but the Jesuit priests who taught us always focused on the secular, philosophical ideas behind the scripture rather than giving us a lecture on morality. Plus, my mother, who took me to mass every week, was a very progressive woman who was pro-choice, pro–birth control, and in favor of legalizing gay marriage—basically all the things the Catholic Church railed against. So I never thought of Catholicism as "strict." I thought of it as a community, and I thought of church as a place for quiet reflection once a week.

Then I got to college, and the religious kids were *really* religious. The kind who push religion on others in a way that

really freaks me out. They're like people who keep telling me, "You *have to* see *Hamilton!*" Honestly, no I don't. And the more you keep telling me, the less likely I am to actually see it.*
Super religious people are basically saying, "You *have to* see *Jesus!* Otherwise you'll never get to heaven!" And I keep thinking, *Yeah . . . but I don't want to go to heaven if* you're *gonna be there . . .*

That's essentially why I stopped going to mass once I got to college. The kids I met there were well-meaning, nice people, but who the hell wants to hang out with people like *that*? Masses involved way more singing than I'd ever experienced before. And everyone was so falsely cheerful and upbeat in a way that made it feel like a cult. It was like a completely different religion. Like a Baptist church with no cool outfits and way worse music.

Luckily, there were some truly impressive students at Harvard who were not in any way cocky, but instead went about their work and otherwise acted like cool, reasonable people. That includes current presidential candidate Pete Buttigieg (whom I now have the pleasure of impersonating on SNL—at least until they realize that Jim Parsons would do a way better job), author Leslie Jamison (who was the star of our creative writing classes from day one), NFL quarterback Ryan Fitzpatrick (who led our team to an undefeated season, no big deal), and my freshman roommate Naresh Ramarajan, who created an app in India that shows cancer patients a whole range of treat-

---

* I have subsequently seen it and it's excellent.

ment options and puts them in touch with a specialist in each field.

Naresh was incredibly brave even in freshman year. He was raised Hindu and came to Harvard to study medicine. Then, over the course of his first year, he came out as gay, dropped out of the pre-med program, and started studying *Islam* instead. That's a real trifecta for Indian parents.*

What I realized by the end of freshman year was that I didn't exactly fit in anywhere at Harvard. I felt lonely and isolated and out of place.

This is how bad and emo it got: I would wander the streets alone at 2 or 3 A.M., then return to my dorm and write *poetry*, with titles such as "A Blurred Vision," "The Artist's Flaw," "The Life of a Man," and "The Stranger You Love to Meet." So yeah, it was pretty bleak. And that was before I wrote a poem called "Shall I Flee Her Gripping Curse?" (Holy shit.) If my computer ever gets hacked, I pray they go for the photos and not the poems.

I would stay up all night feeling depressed and then oversleep because no alarm could wake me up. In fact, one time a smoke alarm went off ABOVE MY HEAD and I did not wake up until the fire department knocked down the door to my dorm room. And then, like a full-on cartoon character, I sat up

---

* Our third roommate would only listen to *either* a cappella music *or* instrumental music. Meaning he wouldn't listen to the combination of music and lyrics. And he studied intensive Japanese and played the ocarina, which is the mythical wind instrument from *The Legend of Zelda*. (Our upstairs neighbors heard it through the radiator and thought it was a ghost.) Add me and my personal double-decker pizzas into the mix, and we were a real wrecking crew!

in bed and said to the firemen, "Oh, hey, guys. What seems to be the problem?" Only I had to yell it over the sound of an alarm.

Perhaps the two pizzas a night were a sign that something was wrong. Maybe I lacked purpose or any kind of community like I had growing up. I left for summer break and went back home to Staten Island, and I knew that next year I had to find something at school that would help me feel less isolated. Something I cared about deeply. And that thing was the Harvard Lampoon.

Fools in a Castle

"Be assured there are ex-young men, here in this very city . . . who got initiated at Harvard into the Puritan mysteries: who took oaths in dead earnest to respect and to act always in the name of *Vanitas,* Emptiness, their ruler . . ."

—THOMAS PYNCHON, *Gravity's Rainbow*

The *Harvard Lampoon* is partly a humor magazine (published somewhere between zero and ten times a year); partly a secret society (but with rituals that are closer to an escape room than a fraternity); partly a funhouse filled with hidden rooms, moving panels, and very random objects (like the Skeksis' throne from *The Dark Crystal*); and partly a countercultural menace to Harvard and the city of Boston.*

More than anything though, the Lampoon is a place where aspiring comedy writers can spend all their free time with

---

* The Lampoon once had John Wayne drive a tank through campus during the Vietnam War. My era had the less historic but more entertaining version: James Brown drove a monster truck across campus yelling, "Don't be a fool, stay in school!" (We also hired a James Brown *impersonator* to hang out with the real James Brown, which made all the photos even more surreal than they were already.)

other aspiring comedy writers and try to make each other laugh. And it's one of the last places you can experiment as a comedy writer in print, because virtually no one will ever read the magazine.

Everyone who got on staff was the funny / weird / awkward / out-of-place kid at their high school, and suddenly you found a dozen other people just like you and thought, *Why would I go anywhere else?* It would be like if you were the only person in your high school who owned a ferret. And then you got to college and found a whole group *dedicated* to owning ferrets. You'd think, *Wow. I finally belong* . . . on an FBI watch list.

And for me, the Lampoon was an oasis at Harvard, where so many students were cloying faux-intellectuals who heard I was from Staten Island and said things like, "Is your dad a garbageman?"* Whereas the Lampoon was filled with all the "alternative nerds" you knew growing up who read a hundred books that weren't on the syllabus and got really into some weird hobby like philately because they truly cared about it. We were nerds who felt like outcasts even at a school full of nerds. And we liked it that way. Because within the Lampoon, a nerd could feel like a king.†

I had never heard of the Lampoon until I saw a flyer in my freshman dorm. It said, "Try out for the Lampoon, or we'll kill your parents." I thought: *This sounds like the place for me!*

The introductory meeting was in an old circular library full

---

* They didn't realize that "garbagemen" were often the wealthiest and most feared people on Staten Island.

† Or queen! The Lampoon is roughly half female and was coed before Harvard was.

of smoke. Maybe it was the cigarettes, or the day drinking, but everyone seemed extremely cool. Many of the upperclassmen I saw in that room have since become writers for *The Office, The Simpsons, 30 Rock, Modern Family, Parks and Recreation, Veep, Black-ish, Master of None, The Mindy Project,* and *The Good Place.* But back then, they were just the most intimidating nerds I had ever met. And they were really, really funny. I immediately thought, *This is the only thing I care about doing in college.**

Unfortunately, it was really hard to get in. Hundreds of people apply every semester and usually only three or four writers get accepted. Unlike most clubs at Harvard, it's entirely merit-based. It doesn't matter if you grew up rich or your mom was on the Lampoon or your dad was Saddam Hussein. The writing submissions are disguised with fake names, so members vote purely on the content, not on the person submitting it. That's probably why, for the most part, the writers are not wealthy kids and legacies, but working- and middle-class kids who are Jewish, Irish, Korean, Indian, African, Middle Eastern, and Australian—basically every ethnicity that the founders of the Lampoon would have hated. Some still have hilariously old-timey names like MacDonald C. Bartels (a real person), but others have names like Aisha Muharrar, Alice Ju, and Sakura Christmas (maybe one of the best names of all time). And getting accepted typically means writing every day for at least a year, sometimes two or three.

I wrote thirty pieces my first semester and got rejected. The next semester I wrote fifty pieces and got rejected again. And

---

* Sorry, economics!

you couldn't get published in the Lampoon unless you were a member, so I had no other outlet for my writing. I just had a folder with eighty pieces of trash in it.

It was weird to have friends and family back home ask, "What are you doing in college?" And I would say, "Trying to write for the Lampoon!"

"So . . . they won't let you write?"

"Nope!"

"And this is a college humor magazine?"

"Yup!"

"What about that kid in your class who's starting Facebook? Maybe you should work on that instead?"

"No way, Dad! Facebook's going nowhere! The real money is gonna be in *magazines!*"

Part of the lore of the Lampoon is the building that houses the magazine. If you've ever walked down Mount Auburn Street in Cambridge and thought, *What is that creepy house with eyes and a mouth?* That is the Lampoon Castle.*

It was designed by an architect named Edmund March Wheelwright, who was once the city architect for all of Boston. The Lampoon was the last building he designed before he went insane and was committed to a mental institution. So it has a few "flourishes of madness," like a spiral staircase that goes the wrong direction, plus the "face" on the front of the building and a stained-glass butthole in the back. (Nothing says

---

* "Castle" is generous. Real castles might be offended.

"I'm heading to a mental institution" like crafting an anus out of stained glass.)

It was financed mainly by William Randolph Hearst, who was a member of the Lampoon in 1884. He was expelled from Harvard for one of the Lampoon's first pranks. At the time, an organization called the Hasty Pudding Club gave out decorative "Pudding Pots" to their favorite professors. Hearst gave out "Chamber Pots," which were pots you took a dump in. And he put his *least* favorite teachers' photos at the bottom of the pots. Hey, it was the 1880s. All the "pot humor" was based on actual pots.

After he was expelled, they expunged his name from the academic records, and the only evidence of him being a Harvard student was his name on the masthead of the Lampoon. He and Isabella Stewart Gardner (an honorary Lampoon member) went on a trip around the world collecting precious artifacts. Everything she bought went to the Gardner Museum in Boston. Everything Hearst bought went to the Lampoon.* So being inside the building is like visiting a museum where nothing is roped off. There's a priceless ornate cabinet in the Gardner Museum that's protected and pristine. And the same exact cabinet sits in the Lampoon, only the door is broken and the drawers are full of rolling papers and cartoons of half-men/half-penises.

When Ray Stantz describes Dana Barrett's apartment building in *Ghostbusters* as "a huge super-conductive antenna that

---

* Hearst also brought back a pet crocodile named Champagne Charlie. Then someone fed it champagne at a party and it died. Oh, and he started the Spanish-American War. That too.

was designed and built expressly for the purpose of pulling in and concentrating spiritual turbulence," that's what I think of when I'm in the Lampoon.

Hardball host Chris Matthews once stopped by because he was moderating a debate in Boston. He looked around the building, then approached a twenty-one-year-old me and whispered, "Where is this place in your dreams?" Might be the best and creepiest first line anyone has ever said to me. Yet it was also a very intuitive question. The building does still appear in my dreams, the way Neverland probably appeared in Peter Pan's dreams. (The island, not the ranch.)

As much as I believe there is magic anywhere in the world, I believe there is magic in the Lampoon. There is something deeply supernatural about the building. It feels like the last act of a possessed man before the devil leaves his body and he is reduced to a blabbering old husk of a human, seated dead-eyed in his wheelchair until he suddenly grabs a nurse's wrist and whispers to her: *"My castle! Bring me to my castle!"*

No one lives there, but many people have effectively lived there because they were homeless, expelled from school, addicted to nitrous oxide, or had gone slowly insane in the building and were now afraid to leave. (A paranoia perhaps exacerbated by the nitrous oxide.)

The third time I applied, after eighteen months of writing constantly, I finally made it. When they told me I got in, it was the happiest moment of my life* and the first time I ever felt like I

---

* I can still say that because I haven't gotten married or had kids yet.

belonged somewhere. For a lot of us, the Lampoon was a place we didn't know existed, but once we found it, we couldn't imagine our lives without it. It was our Hogwarts, only somehow nerdier. (At least three of my friends wore capes. And they were human adults, not child wizards.)

I never wanted to leave that building, and for the most part I never did. I spent about eighty hours a week at the Lampoon, and took an approach I would later take at SNL: I wrote more than anyone else because I wanted to improve as fast as I could.

I submitted dozens of pieces for every issue, and even if only a couple made it into the magazine, I was still learning from all the rejections, too. My thought process was always: *Keep writing new stuff. Don't worry about what gets accepted or rejected. Just keep moving forward and keep improving.*

Eventually, a way higher percentage of what I wrote got accepted, and over the course of my two and a half years on staff I had more than a hundred pieces published in the magazine (maybe two of which still hold up). It was the first time I was willing to put 100 percent of my effort into one single pursuit without fear of failing, because I loved doing it so much that I couldn't focus on anything else. (It's a miracle I graduated.)

There were also times when people took the Lampoon way too seriously and acted like huge dickheads to each other in the name of comedy. If you told a joke that didn't work, the seniors wouldn't just not laugh—they would look you in the eye and say, "That wasn't funny." (Which is so lame that it now, ironically, makes me laugh.)

I started overthinking things real fast. And I regressed to the childhood me who didn't speak for fear of saying the wrong thing. I also became a lot more closed off emotionally because the culture of the Lampoon was surprisingly stoic and severe. You never let your guard down because you were worried about someone exploiting it for a joke. I know that sounds awful, but at the time I wasn't even aware of it—that's just how everyone operated. (All of these downsides, by the way, are the exact same at SNL and in stand-up comedy. So maybe it was the perfect preparation?)

We all cared deeply about what we were doing, to the point that it alienated us from friends who weren't on the Lampoon. I even missed my grandfather's funeral to turn in my final submission when I was applying, which is so strange and sad in retrospect, but joining the magazine was the most urgent goal in my life and I was terrified of anything getting in the way.

Here's how seriously people took the Lampoon: After I worked my way up from staff writer to a "mid-level position" (I was literally a janitor), I got elected president in my junior year, and the election took *fourteen hours* to decide. That is longer than the election for president of the United States.

But if I hadn't joined a group with that kind of zealotry, I wouldn't have developed as a writer as quickly as I did. That's why whenever someone asks me for advice about how to succeed in comedy,* I tell them: Find other people who care about comedy as much as you do, even to an unhealthy degree. That's why people join Second City in Chicago or the Groundlings in L.A. or Upright Citizens Brigade on either coast. (Or why they make videos online with friends who are also funny

---

* Which is not very often. People are more likely to ask: "Is your hair real?"

and ambitious.) No one in comedy (or any field, really) succeeds in a vacuum. And the faster you find friends who challenge you and sometimes make you jealous, the faster you'll grow as a comedian (and regress as a human).

More than anything, I learned that comedy could be an actual job. Maybe that sounds like a minor revelation, but growing up I had zero exposure to show business. When I watched SNL or Letterman as a kid, I understood that humans were involved in making those shows, but I never thought that *I* could be one of those humans. Everyone in my family was a firefighter or worked for the city. So before the Lampoon, my dream jobs were doctor, lawyer, pizza model, or any city job that had a pension.*

After the Lampoon, there was only one clear path.

I was going to steal the Declaration of Independence.

---

* Even now, my grandfather says that the greatest thing you can have in life is a pension. (My living grandfather, not the grandfather whose funeral I skipped to write jokes.)

Why I Love My Mom

"We do survive every moment, after all, except the last one."

—JOHN UPDIKE

My first day back at college sophomore year was September 11, 2001. I had just left New York the day before and my best friend, Chris, and I were sharing a dorm room. His mother called at 9 A.M., a solid two hours before I planned to wake up.

She called on our landline, which was the only way she could get through since cellphones weren't working. I didn't know we even *had* a landline, let alone what the number was. But mothers are enterprising.

I answered and she said, "Are you watching TV? A plane just flew into the World Trade Center. I want Chris to know I'm okay."

Normally, his mom worked *inside* the World Trade Center. And that day she happened to get assigned to a different location. Which was a miracle.

I handed Chris the phone. Then he turned to me and said: "What about *your* mom?"

My mom, Dr. Kerry Kelly (she kept her maiden name), was chief medical officer for the New York City Fire Department for twenty-four years. She was reappointed by four different mayors—two Democrats and two Republicans—and as far as I can tell from my cursory online research, she was the longest-serving chief of any department in New York City history. (For comparison, Ray Kelly was the longest-serving police commissioner in city history and he did it for a decade less.) She was the first woman to serve as chief medical officer, and the first female doctor to ever join the FDNY.

She joined the fire department, like many do, because her father and grandfather were both firemen (along with her brother Billy, who became an FDNY dispatcher). She said that the fire department felt like home. It was "a tight-knit community," which is also how she described Staten Island. That's why when she got married, she moved into the house next door to her parents and down the street from two of her uncles and three of her cousins—who, yes, were all firemen. It was a *very* tight-knit community.

A big part of her job was responding to major fires in New York and treating first responders who were injured on the scene. When I was growing up, she would come to my bedroom to say good night, and I would ask, "Are you going to bed too, Mom?"

"No, Mommy has to work tonight."

"Where is work?"

"It's at a huge fire in the Bronx. Now sleep tiiiiiight!"

Hearing that your mother is going to a fire in the middle of the night is one of the worst things a child can hear before falling asleep. My greatest fear growing up was that my mom would go to a fire and never come back.

So on September 11th, it would have made total sense for her to respond when the planes hit the Twin Towers. But as we huddled around a TV in our friend's dorm, it was not even 10 A.M. yet, and since my mom would be coming from Staten Island, I made a quick calculation in my head that she couldn't possibly have driven into lower Manhattan that quickly. Then we watched on TV as the South Tower collapsed, and I started getting really scared.

An hour earlier, my mom was at a hospital on Staten Island visiting one of her patients, Mrs. Murray. (In addition to the fire department, my mom also maintained a family medicine practice and visited her patients in the hospital when they were sick.)

She received a message on her beeper (yes, she still used a beeper) that a plane had crashed into the World Trade Center. She didn't want to scare Mrs. Murray, so she told her, "Oh, I've got to run. Have a nice day."

But the patient next to Mrs. Murray had the TV on. She yelled, "Oh my god! A plane just hit the World Trade Center!"

"Oh my goodness," said Mrs. Murray. "All my sons are firefighters!"

"Don't worry," my mom said. "They'll all be fine." Then she ran to her car and drove to Manhattan.

When she arrived one block south of the World Trade Center, her first thought was, *I can't believe I found a parking spot!* A thought that only a New Yorker could have. Then she saw a car parked across the street, and it was charred and smoldering, like it had been consumed by lava. Suddenly the parking spot seemed a lot less lucky.

"Hey! What are you doing here?" a firefighter was yelling at her. She recognized him. It was Captain Hank Cerasoli. "Where's your helmet? There's stuff falling everywhere!"

"I don't have a helmet," she said. Then she looked up and saw pieces of the tower falling. Then she saw bodies falling.

"We need to get you a helmet," he said.

They walked to Ladder 10, the firehouse directly next to the South Tower. She didn't know which tower was which. And she didn't know that a second plane had just crashed. She only saw smoke billowing down and body parts all around her on the street. She told Captain Cerasoli, "I need to get to the command center."

He handed her a helmet and they started walking toward the South Tower. On the way out, she saw on the firehouse television that a third plane had hit the Pentagon. That's when she knew it was a terrorist attack.

When my friends and I saw the third plane hit the Pentagon, suddenly everywhere in America felt vulnerable. It seems really stupid in retrospect, but we genuinely thought there could be an attack at Harvard next, especially since two of the hijacked planes left from Boston. No one knew where to go on campus, and everyone from New York or D.C. was really freaking out.

I kept trying to reach my mom or my dad or my brother on the phone, but nothing was going through. We got an email from the professor in charge of our dorm. It said, "Try to remain calm, but stay in touch with the news." I thought, *Maybe my dad will check his email.* I wrote, "Dad! What's going on?? Are you home? Assuming mom is okay???"

There's a reason people use walkie-talkies in action movies. When her phone and her beeper both failed, my mom used the walkie-talkie feature on her Nextel cellphone for the first time in her life and it actually worked.

"Hello?" It was Deputy Commissioner Lynn Tierney, a friend of my mom's and another woman who had been a pioneer in city government.

"Lynn, it's Dr. Kelly. Where are you? Where's the command center?"

"We're moving out of the North Tower now. We're heading across the street to the World Financial Center."

"Okay, I'll meet you there."

As she hung up, a firefighter ran over and said, "Doc! You gotta help, one of our guys is injured." She walked over and saw Danny Suhr, a fireman who had been setting up at the South Tower when he was hit by a falling body. His skull was crushed and he was bleeding terribly.

She got him into an ambulance and tried to resuscitate him, but there was nothing she could do. "Get him to the hospital," she said.

"Are you coming, too?" the fireman asked.

"I have to stay here," she said. "But a few of you go with him and make sure he gets there."

Danny Suhr, whose nickname was Captain America, was the first firefighter to die on 9/11. But he saved the lives of the firemen who went with him in that ambulance. Because as it pulled away, Captain Cerasoli turned to my mom and said, "The building is falling."

She said: "What building?"

Then she looked up and the first tower was starting to collapse.

He yelled, "RUN!!!"

I've asked my dad what he was thinking that morning. What he thought was happening with Mom. He told me that he never thought my mom could have gotten there before the towers fell. He did the same calculation that I had done. We both had too much faith in New York City traffic to worry about Mom reaching Manhattan in time.

My brother was in high school on Staten Island and could see the smoke from the towers through his classroom window. But he wasn't worried about my mom, he was worried about his classmates whose fathers were firemen and were much more likely to be in danger.

The hardest part of my mom's job was that she had to inform family members when a firefighter died in the line of duty. While I was afraid of her going to a fire and never coming back, she had to actually tell the children of firefighters that their father or mother wasn't coming home. And when a firefighter was seriously burned or injured in a fire, she was there with the family at the hospital, which is how she met the family of Timothy Stackpole.

Tim had been severely burned while putting out a fire in Brooklyn in 1998. The building collapsed and two of his fellow firemen died. Tim was in the burn unit of the hospital for sixty-six days and received skin grafts for burns so severe that you could see the bone.

Almost three years later, in March 2001, he returned to full duty at the fire department. Like my mom, he didn't know a life without it. There's a saying in the department: "twenty and out." Because after twenty years on the job, you can retire and get a pension and do whatever you want with the rest of your life.

Tim used to tell my mom: "Forty and out." Because you're either in for life, or you're not really in.

When the first tower fell, Captain Cerasoli realized they couldn't outrun it. He instinctively grabbed my mom and pushed her against an alcove of the World Financial Center building across the street. They pressed against the wall and everything around them turned black. All they heard was noise and all they felt was debris piling up on top of them. She said that she was waiting to die.

And in that moment, she thought of Tim Stackpole and "forty and out" and how that's always what she planned to do, too. She realized, *I already have twenty years! What the hell am I still doing here?*

Then a few minutes passed, and they were still alive. Then a few minutes more. Then the tower stopped falling and there was suddenly silence. It was pitch black and she thought that even if they survived, they'd be buried alive under all the debris.

Then the air cleared just a little and they saw light.

And Captain Cerasoli said, "We have to get out and find the others."

It was at this moment, as they clawed their way out of the rubble and back to some semblance of a street, that my mother looked down and realized she was still wearing sandals.

They started calling out the names of the firemen they had seen just before the building collapsed, but they couldn't hear anyone and they couldn't see more than a foot or two in front of them. The debris in the air was like a driving snowstorm, only black instead of white. She said it felt like being in a blizzard in the middle of the night.

Then, out of nowhere, she saw her car. Still parked in the same spot and somehow only partially buried. She said to Captain Cerasoli, "I'm changing my shoes."

"What? You're changing them *now*?"

"I just survived death. I've had it. I'm getting out of these sandals."

She pulled sneakers out of the back seat of her car and changed into shorts and a T-shirt, plus the borrowed fire helmet. Then she and Captain Cerasoli walked back toward the second tower, back into the blizzard, in search of someone to help.

The first person they found was a firefighter named Kevin Shea, who had lost his thumb and been hit in the head by falling debris. He was so disoriented or concussed that he didn't even realize the first tower had fallen. He would later find out that every single firefighter in his company who responded to the attacks had died, except for him.

They dragged Kevin out of the debris and into a parking garage one block south of the towers. His neck was badly injured and my mom knew he needed some kind of gurney and an ambulance. Then another firefighter appeared out of the smoke and started helping my mother tend to the wounded and move them into the safety of the garage.

His name was Mike Shepherd, and three years earlier my mother had told him he could never become a fireman, because he had a metal plate in his foot. So Mike went straight to his doctor and said, "Take the plate out of my foot!" Nine weeks later, he was a New York City firefighter.

Mike was a Golden Gloves boxing champion and an iron-worker in his spare time. The morning of September 11th, he was actually off-duty, welding a girder in the basement of Carnegie Hall to earn extra money. When he heard the towers had been hit, he jumped on the back of a passing fire truck and rode to Ground Zero.

Now he and my mom were roaming the streets looking for an ambulance, or at least bandages and supplies. They were about to break into a dentist's office when they heard a deafening noise above them. Mike grabbed my mom's hand and started running.

The second tower was falling.

For the second time in the span of half an hour, a fireman saved my mother's life.

Mike Shepherd pushed her through the revolving door of a lobby as pieces of the second tower exploded past the window.

It was the first of several times Mike would be a hero that day. He spent thirty straight hours at the site, searching and digging for any survivors he could find.

He would see my mom later that day at the new command center near St. Paul's Chapel. My mom gave Mike a hug and said, "You saved my life."

Weeks later, Mike visited the medical office, haunted by all the friends he couldn't save. My mom gave him a hug again and said, "You did everything you could."

In the moments after he rescued her, though, they stood in the dark lobby of an office building, watching the black air swirl around outside the window. And they didn't know what would fall next.

I still have the email that I got from my dad that day at 11:51 A.M.

Date: Tue, 11 Sep 2001 11:51:24 EDT
From: ROAinc@aol.com
To: cjost@fas.harvard.edu
Subject: Re:

Mom's ok !!!! She did get caught in the secondary collapse, but dug herself out and is ok - wow!!

I'll keep in touch

He barely saw my mom for weeks. At some point she came home covered head to toe in white ash. She showered, changed clothes, and went right back to work. She spent each day traveling between Ground Zero and the medical office, treating whoever needed help.

After she survived the second collapse, she said she felt like a medic in a war zone: She would keep bandaging people up, only to realize they had died.

She had gotten Kevin Shea and the other injured firemen from the parking garage into ambulances, and had them evacuated to a hospital. Then she set up a triage center in a Duane Reade down the street, only to be evacuated again when a third building, 7 World Trade Center, was about to collapse. They moved the triage unit to the auditorium at Pace University and waited for the injured to arrive, but no one came.

What arrived instead, in waves, was news of the people who had died. Dear friends of hers like Chief Ganci, who oversaw the entire department that morning from the base of the first tower; Commissioner Feehan, who was the oldest first responder to die that day, at the age of seventy-one; and Father Mychal Judge, their chaplain, who died while administering last rites to a fallen firefighter.

In the family of the fire department, these were her brothers. They were people she loved dearly. And it was now setting in that she would never see them again.

At 9 P.M., a full twelve hours since she'd left Mrs. Murray at the hospital on Staten Island, my mom closed down the triage center. She realized that all the injured first responders she'd expected to arrive were already dead.

In total, 343 firefighters lost their lives, including Scott Davidson, father of my future SNL castmate Pete Davidson, who was only eight years old at the time. And Tim Stackpole, back on the job for less than six months, who had taught my mother the meaning of "forty and out."

The work they did saved thousands of civilian lives, as they evacuated the lower floors of the towers and put out fires that had spread to the surrounding buildings. In the wake of September 11th, more than two thousand new recruits joined the FDNY.

There are many reasons why I love my mom.

I love that while she took care of her fire department family, she never neglected her real family. We never felt like she was absent or not fully present in our lives.

I love her as a role model. Because of her, my brother and I have never thought twice about women doing the same jobs as men or getting the same pay or having completely independent and satisfying lives. If anything, we expect to see it more because that's all we knew.

I love how caring and thoughtful she is toward my dad, and how they rely on each other and help each other get through hard times.

And I love how she wrangles our grandparents and aunts and uncles and cousins to come together for every holiday and birthday and anniversary—even the cousins who aren't firemen.

Most of all, I love how grateful my mom is. She would always tell us, "I have the luckiest job in the world." And somehow she felt that even more after September 11th. I'm so proud of how my mom responded that day, and I'm even more proud of the work she did in the days, months, and years that followed.

She helped modernize the department to prepare for any future attacks. And she put in real time with the families who lost someone that day. She testified before the U.S. Senate and helped secure millions in funding for the long-term care of 9/11 first responders, including a screening process for the types of cancers and lung problems that no one considered when they ran in to save people's lives. And she helped create a counseling unit to help firefighters deal with the psychological effects of having survived when so many of their friends didn't.

She told Congress, "In the department's first one hundred years, we filled a wall with the names of fallen firefighters. On the eleventh of September, we filled a new wall."

She would never say that she was a hero, because she's very humble and because she knows how much firefighters risk every day doing their jobs. But she's been a real, lasting hero for a long time. She protected and improved the lives of thousands of firefighters. And when you talk to them about my mom, you can tell they love her, because they know how much she cares about them.

She retired from the fire department in March 2018.

She did forty and out, to the day.

My mom drove up to visit me at college in late October 2001. It was the first day she had taken off since September 11th. I didn't know she was coming, and I was so happy and surprised to see her.

I said, "What are you doing here?"

And she said, "I needed a hug."

To Russia with Love

"Russia! What is this inscrutable, mysterious force that draws me to you?"

—Nikolai Gogol

"In America you can always find a party. In Russia the party always finds you."

—Yakov Smirnoff

"What did you study in college?" That's a question I've been asked (genuinely) by aspiring comedians and (sarcastically) by my parents.

The answer: The History and Literature of Russia and Britain. Which really just means: "I Read a Bunch of Books and Learned that Stalin Was Maybe Not a Great Guy After All."

My love for Russia started in high school when I took a senior elective called "Great European Novels" and three of them were Russian—*Anna Karenina, Crime and Punishment,* and *Pnin* by Vladimir Nabokov. *Anna Karenina* was rough because I violently procrastinated (as is my style in all aspects of life) and had to read the entire 864-page book in three days. There have been studies that show that "cramming" can work in the short run but doesn't help you retain information in the long run.

This might explain why I cannot tell you a single plot point from *Anna Karenina* or name a single character outside of Anna Karenina. (If she is not actually in the book, that wouldn't surprise me either.)

The other two books were among my favorites of all time and made me want to learn a lot more about Russian literature. So when I arrived at college, I abandoned my stated major—Economics—and instead chose Russian Books (a.k.a. The Opposite of Economics).

For context, jobs available in the field of economics include: all jobs.

Jobs available in the field of Russian literature include: writing Russian literature, teaching Russian literature, and being an extremely well-read homeless gentleman.

This major also required me to learn the Russian language and write a fifty-two-page thesis, entitled "Double Cross: The Double as Delusion in Nabokov's Early Novels *The Eye* and *Despair.*" Not to be confused with my junior year essay: *"Double Team*: How the 1997 Film Starring Jean-Claude Van Damme and Dennis Rodman Was in No Way Connected to Vladimir Nabokov."*

Writing a thesis is a long, mostly unpleasant process, but initially I wanted to make it even harder. I thought, *Maybe, as part of my thesis, I should translate a short story from Russian to*

---

* Why is the title of every college paper disgusting? There's always a pun, then a colon, then a string of nonsense phrases like "literary hyperconsciousness" and "Freudian Postcolonialism." Read more about it in my essay "Over the Overkill: Deconstructing the Constructing of Phraseological Masturbation in College Term Papers."

English that's never been translated before. That's an extremely difficult task, even for a native Russian speaker—let alone a kid from Staten Island who just learned how to say "apple" in Russian. For some reason, my teacher encouraged this and helped me get a grant from the department to go live in Russia for the summer, with the goal of translating a short story.*

My parents, understandably, were a little nervous about me spending the summer alone in Russia. But you can't say no to a grant—it's free money! (Not enough to actually live on, but it's free!) And I reassured my parents that it would be okay because a Russian woman who worked at our school had set me up with her parents in St. Petersburg, who would rent me their extra bedroom for the very reasonable price of all my grant money. (They also requested that I bring "teddy bears wearing Harvard T-shirts" as a "gift," which I'm hoping was a means of transporting drugs because otherwise I don't know what the hell was going on with that. Who sees a teddy bear and thinks, *Pretty cute and all . . . but where'd it go to college?*)

What this Russian woman failed to mention was that her parents were turning ninety years old and didn't speak a word of English. I'm not sure they spoke a word of Russian either. Because they didn't speak a word in any language the entire time.

I arrived alone in St. Petersburg with no directions, only an

---

* For any Russia-heads reading this, it was a short story called "Lower World Tambourine" by one of my favorite contemporary Russian authors, Viktor Pelevin. I highly recommend his book *Omon Ra* (available in English), about a fake expedition to the moon by astronauts who don't know it's fake. It's very "Russian funny."

address,* and found my way in halting Russian to their apartment. They opened the door, nodded at me, took me to my bedroom, nodded at the bedroom, showed me the bathroom, nodded at the bathroom, and then disappeared for three days.

They had a "Soviet era" apartment, and from the looks of it, I'm guessing they weren't higher-ups in the Communist Party. I was honestly afraid to turn the lights on because the light switch hummed when you touched it. It was like the electricity was whispering, *"I'll kill you!"*

When my host family was actually around, they never once invited me to join them for a meal or offered advice on where to go or said anything like, "Hi. My name is [insert name here]." The closest I got to "sharing a meal" was when I went to the kitchen every morning to make breakfast† and the old woman was already sitting there, just staring at the clock—sorry, running out the clock.

She then got up, went to the fridge, and took out the largest carton of sour cream I'd ever seen in my life. Costco would have been jealous. She sat across from me at the table, opened the carton, and started spooning sour cream into her mouth like it was chicken noodle soup. The sound of an elderly woman slurping sour cream at eight in the morning was seared in my brain forever, along with a visual of the sour cream remnants stuck in her very healthy mustache.

After that, I was cool fasting till lunch.

---

* This was before Google Maps or whatever they use in Russia. Gulag Maps?

† "Make breakfast" is a glorified way of saying: I poured some kind of animal's milk over a bowl of off-brand Russian Lucky Charms, where the cartoon leprechaun was threatening children with a switchblade.

I later spoke to other friends who lived abroad and discovered this was not the norm. They all said things like "Oh my god, my host family is like my real family now!" "Oh my god, they fed me the most delicious food every night and we sang songs together by the fireplace!" "Oh my god, they legally adopted me and they're paying off my college debts! Plus, I can name anyone and they'll have them killed!" A real slap in the face after my experience with the couple I came to describe as Sour Cream & Onion.

I had a careful plan laid out for my time in St. Petersburg: I would get to the library by 9 A.M. every morning, translate a few lines of the short story, and then I'd have the afternoons free to savor the many cultural opportunities in the city.

Very quickly I started skipping the library part of the plan, and focused instead on aimlessly wandering the city in a lonely depression. I visited locations such as: an abandoned amusement park, an abandoned zoo, a patch of darkness under a bridge, a staircase that led

into a river, and of course, the Museum of Death. And this was in the summer, by the way. When there were almost twenty-four hours of daylight and warm weather. This was Russia at its *least* depressing. But I was alone and literally had no one to talk to except a street performer who tricked me into holding his pet bear and then demanded two hundred rubles for the photo.

I had no money to eat at restaurants (and no one to eat with anyway). I would go down to the grocery store every couple days and buy some kind of "pasta" that was made from a grain that has been discontinued in the United States. Then I would buy these weird chunks of "cheese." No brand or type—just general cheese. It had the consistency of Gouda and the flavor of wet baking soda. Sometimes it was shaped into triangles, sometimes into rectangles—depending on the cow's mood.

I went so stir-crazy at one point that I wrote a parody of a poem by Aleksandr Pushkin *in Russian*. The original poem begins, *"Ya vas lubil"* ("I loved you"), and mine opened with: *"Ya vas kupil"* ("I bought you") and was a very tender sonnet to a prostitute. So that's where I was at mentally.

After weeks of descending into madness, I thought: *I gotta meet someone. Anyone.*

Now, before I'd left America, my friends from high school said, "Dude! You're gonna meet so many Russian women! Think about Russian mail-order brides! You're gonna meet them without even having to put them in the mail first!"

But the thing about Russian brides is: They're looking for a *better* life. If they saw me walking around St. Petersburg, I guarantee they weren't thinking, *That's my ticket outta here.* They were thinking, *That poor Estonian boy needs a mom.*

I did finally meet a girl, though. Actually, a group of girls. They were visiting from Spain and didn't speak a word of Russian, so I communicated with them via my high school Spanish. They became my closest friends in St. Petersburg, by which I mean we hung out three times. It would have been more, had I not humiliated myself on the third "date."

I met them at a bar and one of them said, "Hey, Kolya!" (This was my name in Russian. And I guess Spanish?) "Do you like absinthe?"

I had never tried absinthe before, so naturally I said, "Oh yeah. Love absinthe. Probably my favorite drink."

Five tall glasses of absinthe later, we were all dancing by the bar when I said, "Could you excuse me for a second? Necessito ir al baño. Solo uno momento!"

I went to the bathroom and immediately threw up all over the walls. Didn't even come close to the toilet. Like a 360-degree fire hose of vomit.

Then, because I was out of my damn mind, I just walked back to the dance floor and started dancing again like nothing had happened. "Whoooo! Nosotros nunca vamos a morir!"

Roughly thirty seconds later, an employee came up to me and said, "Excuse me. Did you just vomit all over our bathroom?" To which I said, "Uhhhh . . . no hablo inglés."

These wonderful, kind women saw that I was profusely sweating and even paler than usual and knew that I was not well. They smoothed the whole thing over with the manager and helped me clean up the bathroom, which is an extremely generous gesture to a guy they met a week before. I was now shivering and starting to see ghosts, so one of the women offered to take me home and even put her coat over me to keep me warm in the taxi.

Fun fact about St. Petersburg: At some point in the middle of the night, all the bridges go up for about an hour, so whichever part of the city you're in, you can't leave. This poor girl and I sat in a Russian taxi for forty-five minutes waiting for the bridge to reopen so she could take me back to the Sour Cream Museum. When we finally arrived at 3 A.M., I took off her coat to give it back to her. But she saw how gross and sick I looked and said, "Uhhh . . . maybe just keep it?"

Weirdly, we never spoke again!

I was so sick, I didn't leave my bed for three days. Even my elderly landlords peeked in and nodded at me sadly as if to ask, "Are you okay? We won't do anything about it either way, but we thought we should ask."

As soon as I recovered, I decided that I needed to go back to America immediately. I had never (and still haven't) felt that homesick in my life. I flew home two days later, with 0.0 percent of the short story translated. As far as I can tell from a ten-second Google search, it remains untranslated, ready for the next brazen college senior to sacrifice joy and health for the sake of Russian literature.

Before I left for the airport, I laid out seven teddy bears in Harvard T-shirts on the bed, as requested. Along with a note in Russian that said, *Thank you for everything. I'll truly never forget our breakfasts together. Sincerely, Kolya.*

I Leave Staten Island and Immediately Get a Job Back on Staten Island

"If a person is not talented enough to be a novelist, not smart enough to be a lawyer, and his hands are too shaky to perform operations, he becomes a journalist."

—NORMAN MAILER

"Americans are always afraid of coming home."

—*Breakfast of Champions*

When I graduated college, I joined the 67 percent of graduating seniors in America who didn't have a job. My first instinct: *What if I created a TV show about college? Then I wouldn't have to leave!*

So fellow Lampoon writer Simon Rich and I came up with an idea for a hidden-camera show called *Admissions Impossible,* which would involve us posing as alumni interviewers or college admissions officers in order to trick high school students into saying awful things during their interviews. This was the description of the show that we wrote in 2004, which I just found on my laptop because, in a digital age, nothing ever disappears except hope that things will disappear:

> **Admissions Impossible** exploits high school seniors at their most vulnerable. We set up fake college interviews under the guise of real, ultra-competitive universities. Instead of chatting with alumni, students will meet actors posing as university representatives. This is a prime opportunity to screw with these kids.

Man, we were *monsters*. But also . . . not a terrible idea for a show! If my agent is still reading this book, maybe we should talk about it?

Sadly, no one wanted to buy it. And by "no one," I mean the one manager who cold-called the Lampoon and told us to "pitch me ideas." (That manager was a man named Trevor Engelson, who later married Meghan Markle before Prince Harry did. What a world!)

So, with no prospects and no skills (again, I majored in *The History and Literature of Russia and Britain*), I got ahead of the millennial curve and moved back to my parents' house and into my childhood bedroom. Which, if you haven't done it, is one of the most humiliating experiences an adult can go through.

At first you think, *No big deal. It's like I'm back in high school, except no curfew and I can drink in front of my parents!* Then you have one drink in front of your parents in your childhood kitchen and you're like, *I'm the saddest boy on Earth.*

There's something about moving back home after college

that eliminates all the respect you accumulated by going away to college. All the bragging your parents did about you going to a good school disappears overnight. You live in their house, yet they dare not speak your name in public, for fear that a friend of theirs with a working child will ask, "And what is Colin doing *now?*"

So you slink around and try to eat alone at odd hours and then go to a movie at 11:45 P.M. on a Tuesday with your one other loser friend who moved back home. Then you go to a diner at 2 A.M. and see your high school girlfriend and she's already married with three kids and you don't understand how that's even physically possible. (Or why she's at a diner at 2 A.M. with three kids at home.) So you ask the diner to make your plate of eggs "to go" to escape the whole scene and now you're eating cold eggs in the basement of your house at 3 A.M., watching Howard Stern tell a porn star to kiss Gary the Retard, because that's easily the most thrilling moment of your day. And pretty soon you're thinking, *Why the* fuck *did I major in the History and Literature of Russia and Britain?*

After a few weeks of extreme depression, I talked to a couple friends from college who were equally miserable and unemployed, and we all decided: *Let's move to Manhattan or Brooklyn or wherever we can get an apartment and just force ourselves to get jobs and become actual adults.*

And my parents were like, "No . . . don't . . ." And then closed the door behind me and locked it.

There were seven of us sharing two apartments on Twentieth Street and Avenue C, in a development known as Stuyvesant

Town, which was later part of a class-action lawsuit because they charged us full price for an apartment that they were claiming was low-income housing. In our case, that description was accurate. The most successful of us, Gena, was a waitress at an Irish bar down the street. Her boyfriend (and my best friend), Chris, was getting paid to participate in scientific "sleep studies," where you couldn't sleep more than fifteen minutes for a period of five days, which might violate the rules of the Geneva Convention. I was living off my winnings from appearing on the game show *The Weakest Link*—unfortunately, I was really bad at *The Weakest Link*,* so my prize was only six thousand dollars (a net of three thousand after California taxes), which has to be a record for the least a winner has ever won. In Manhattan, that was two months' rent.

So a week after I finally escaped Staten Island and moved to the city, I accepted a job at a local newspaper . . . back on Staten Island. Why? Because I had zero other job prospects. Because I majored in *The History and Literature of Russia and Britain*.

The only reason I even got offered the newspaper job was because I had interned at the paper for two summers in high school and wrote articles for the "Teen Section," such as my glowing review of Bernadette Peters in *Annie Get Your Gun* on Broadway, and an essay imploring teens to "admire the classics" with lines like: *While teens should hardly abandon modern trends, they should also recognize the classics in art, music, and literature.* Wow, great insight, Colin. Also, anytime a teenager

---

* Statistically, I was the "weakest link" in three of the four rounds.

refers to his own peers as "teens" or uses the phrase "modern trends," he deserves to get punched. (So . . . right on brand.)

This all makes more sense once you see my official "Teen Correspondent" press photo:

This is also the photo I use on Tinder to attract lesbians over fifty.

That job as a teen reporter led me to become editor in chief of my high school newspaper, *The Owl*, where we published more issues of the paper than any other regime in years—thanks to hard-hitting breaking news like: "Peter Jung Eats Five Big Macs."

That led me to join *The Harvard Crimson's* editorial board, where I wrote such memorable articles as "Habitat for Humanity Offers Up Free Ice Cream," and pointed op-eds like:

PETER JUNG EATS FIVE BIG MACS, "STILL HUNGRY"

"The Army Shouldn't Switch from Regular Caps to Berets." Not sure why that was an issue, but I was *adamant* that it not happen:

> Not only is this change ineffective and impractical, but it's also insane. They've looked for a solution and come up with berets? I'm still hoping that they haven't realized what berets actually look like.

I guess I really hated berets!

Anyway, I had a "background" in journalism, as much as anyone can have at the age of twenty-one. But I never expected to bring that background into the foreground. (See what I did there? Can't stop being a news anchor.)

The paper I worked at, the *Staten Island Advance,* was actually an amazing newspaper with incredibly talented reporters and editors. And at the time, it had a circulation of 100,000, which was roughly one out of every five people on Staten Island. It was also the first publication ever owned by Samuel Irving "S.I." Newhouse, Jr., who became one of the richest men in America by acquiring dozens of newspapers and the entire Condé Nast magazine empire.*

But it all started on Staten Island, and his corporation is still called Advance Publications after his very first paper. That's why he received the greatest honor a Staten Islander can receive: He has a ferryboat named after him. Which is the Staten Island equivalent of the Presidential Medal of Freedom.

---

* He's the *second* richest Staten Islander of all time, behind one of the richest humans in history: Cornelius Vanderbilt, who built a shipping empire with ferries along the New York Harbor and, adjusted for inflation, was richer than Bill Gates and Warren Buffett *combined.*

The job itself was fantastic. I was a "night editor," which meant I did whatever random stuff hadn't been done before the paper went to press: rewriting articles, designing the layout for each section, proofreading every page, and my favorite task—writing headlines.

The *Advance* took a conservative approach to headlines, whereas I came from more of a *New York Post* tradition. If they wrote "Teenager Stabbed in Heroin Bust," I would suggest, "Angel Tot Chopped Up in Smack Smackdown!" It usually ended up a lot closer to their version than mine.

I also had to write stories from scratch if they came in overnight. And occasionally I got sent out in the field as a crime reporter to cover "breaking news" from the gritty streets of Shaolin. One story I remember was a multicar accident where I arrived on the scene just after the paramedics. Luckily no humans were injured in the crash, so the paramedics began resuscitating a raccoon that had gotten hit by a truck. If you think our healthcare system is broken, just wait until you see a raccoon getting CPR.

This being Staten Island, the story made the front page.

As you can see, it was far more important than the

story below it: "Island Priest Pleads Guilty in Sex Abuse Case." Because that story didn't have an adorable picture of a raccoon getting carted away on a stretcher:

RACCOON RESCUE IN CLIFTON

Rescued raccoon receives care from an EMT.

It was a matter of life... and death

Two EMTs provide aid to the injured animal, but city law seals its fate

By COLIN JOST
ADVANCE STAFF WRITER

EMTs Norma Edwards and Che Vinson rush the injured raccoon to a waiting ambulance.

PLEASE SEE RACCOON, PAGE A 4

Island priest pleads guilty in sex abuse case

I'll let you have a moment of feeling warm and fuzzy before I tell you what happened next . . .

The raccoon bit the paramedic's eyes out.

Kidding. What really happened was: They turned the raccoon over to Animal Control, and it was immediately euthanized. Apparently that was the city's policy: Take a raccoon, kill a raccoon. The paramedics, understandably, were like, "What the fuck! We just saved that raccoon's life!"

And that led to a *second* front-page story the next day, about the outrage over raccoon euthanasia on Staten Island. Which of course led to my first Paw-litzer Prize.*

The weirdness of local news on Staten Island was one reason I loved the job. Plus, I learned a ton from the senior editors, who went on to prestigious jobs at the *Star Ledger,* the *Times,* and, of course, the *New York Post.* And shockingly, my job at the *Advance* had an incredible healthcare plan. Full vision

---

* I'm sorry, but I couldn't stop my fingers from typing it.

and dental—things that no working American would ever expect. I thought about getting an extra set of teeth made and keeping them in a drawer until I was eighty.

The downside of the job was that my shift went from 11 P.M. to 8 A.M., plus an hour-and-a-half commute each way. So I would be having dinner with my friends and then get up from the table at 9 P.M. and say, "Time to go to work!" Then I'd walk a mile to an express bus that took me to a local bus on Staten Island, which dropped me half a mile from the newspaper.

And when I left work at 8 A.M. every morning, I was in full New York City rush-hour traffic back into Manhattan. So while other people were having coffee and waking up, I was watching the sunrise from a bus window and slowly losing my mind. I barely slept for the five months I worked there, and I had headaches all day. Turns out that going to bed at 10 A.M. and waking up at 2 P.M. is not a healthy night's sleep. It's an extended nap full of day-mares.

Of course the larger problem was that I wanted to be in comedy, not journalism. I knew this because I spent every free moment at work compiling news stories I could use for stand-up instead. Like when police arrested a man for disorderly conduct and the man's name was Jihad Williams. (So his first name was basically the definition of disorderly conduct.) Or when a guy was accused of attempted murder and his nickname was "Murder Mike." Pretty hard to beat a murder charge when people refer to you as Murder. (The worst part was, he tried to shoot someone but missed on all six shots. So "Murder Mike" was really bad at murder.)

Once I saved up enough money to pay two months' rent (and enough healthcare to buy a second set of eyeballs, just in case), I quit the newspaper and decided to put everything I had into getting a job in comedy.

And I don't want to brag, but since I left that newspaper, all newspapers have plummeted in circulation. You might say, "Yeah, you idiot. That's because of the Internet." But I'd like to think it's because the *Staten Island Advance* lost its swag.

I Apply to Every TV Show in America

"A good many young writers make the mistake of including a stamped, self-addressed envelope, big enough for the manuscript to come back in. That is too much of a temptation to the editor."

—RING LARDNER

While I was working the overnight shift at my local newspaper, I spent my days applying to every television show I could think of—except *Saturday Night Live*.

That would have been my dream job, but I never let myself consider it a real possibility. I knew that getting a job anywhere in comedy was a crapshoot, and I wanted to get a bunch of rejections under my belt before I could face applying for SNL.

Plus, I had no idea how to actually apply.

I didn't have an agent or a manager, so I just looked up the mailing addresses for all these shows and wrote a cover letter begging them to read my submission. Which is like sending a résumé to Goldman Sachs with a note that says, "Wanna do finance together?"

I applied to the *Late Show with David Letterman, Late Night with Conan O'Brien, The Daily Show* with Jon Stewart, *Whatever*

Carson Daly's Show Was Called at That Time with Carson Daly, and *Goofin' Around!* with Tito Puente.*

I also wrote a "spec script" (short for "spectacular-failure-of-a script") for the show *Arrested Development*—my favorite TV show at the time—not realizing that the show had already been canceled, which meant that my script was about as useful as a spec script for *The Cosby Show* in 2020.

Then I wrote a pilot with my friend Chris for a show called *The Back Room;* it was basically *Reno 911!* but for the New York Fire Department. (At a firehouse, the "back room" is where firefighters hang out, eat dinner, and share stories about which single mom on the block they're sleeping with.) My dad, who for some reason had a strong opinion about this show, kept telling me that it should be like *Barney Miller,* but I had never seen *Barney Miller* and thought it sounded like a department store.

The problem with writing a pilot as an unknown writer (beyond the fact that it probably sucked) was that I had nowhere to send it. I couldn't just mail it to HBO in an envelope marked: "OPEN ONLY IF YOU WANT TO CHANGE TELEVISION FOREVER. P.S. IT'S LIKE *RENO 911!* MEETS *BARNEY MILLER.* DOES HBO DO STUFF LIKE THAT? IF NOT COULD YOU FORWARD TO STARZ?"

So my friend Chris and I rewrote the pilot a few times, then emailed it to a couple friends who were like, "Cool! Nothing we can do with this!" and then we just moved on. (Chris is now a doctor. *Thanks, HBO.*)

At this point, I was so desperate to write anything for any

---

* Possibly fake.

outlet that I started inventing fake anecdotes and mailing them (in the physical mail) to *Reader's Digest* for their "Life's Like That" section. They were supposed to be true, first-person, humorous stories—except my life wasn't that interesting or humorous, so I had to make them up. (Strong evidence that my life wasn't interesting: I was reading *Reader's Digest*.)

Here's one "amusing anecdote" that I sent in:*

> **My ex-wife was getting remarried, so I decided to attend the wedding as a sign of friendship.** [Note: Already so, so crazy. I was attending my *ex-wife's wedding*??]
>
> **Since the ceremony was right around Easter** [what?], **I drove down to her hometown a few days early** [a few extra days in my ex-wife's hometown, sure] **to avoid the holiday traffic** [Easter traffic?] **and enjoy a little extra vacation.**
>
> **I was driving a little too fast** [so much use of "little"] **through my ex-wife's neighborhood** [her *childhood* neighborhood, *days* before I was supposed to arrive], **when suddenly a policeman pulled me over.** [Incredible plot twist.]
>
> **Hoping to avoid a ticket, I made up a quick excuse: "I'm late for a meeting with my ex-wife, Officer. She's annoying enough as it is, so I wanted to keep her happy, you know?"**

---

* This is further proof that nothing on computers ever disappears. I opened a search window on my laptop, typed "digest," and this document from fifteen years ago appeared instantly.

"I *should* know," the cop said after examining my license. "I'm the guy she's gonna marry!"

Okay, couple things:

1. I was attending my ex-wife's wedding, but I didn't know who she was marrying or the fact that he was a police officer?
2. My excuse for speeding was "I'm late for a *meeting* with my ex-wife." If that doesn't sound like I'm about to murder my ex-wife, I don't know what does.
3. Why did I suddenly become a Catskills comedian from the 1950s? "Ex-wives, am I right?! So annoying! Yap, yap, yap! It's like, didn't I already divorce you??"

And here's one more anecdote I sent to *Reader's Digest*. (Because I can't help myself, and this is all part of the healing process.) Critics take note: This anecdote should prove beyond a shadow of a doubt that I can write just as well for female characters.

> For my senior prom, I wanted to wear a very tight, low-cut evening gown I recently saw at the mall. [I'm already sweating just from cutting and pasting this sentence.] But I knew my father would have problems with his little baby girl [oh my god] going to prom in a revealing dress. So I planned to describe my outfit in the nicest way possible. I would tell him it was "a lovely strapless evening gown and very sensible." [This might be the same setup as *Carrie*.]

When I approached my father, though, I quickly went into a panic. Glaring at me, he asked, "So what are you wearing exactly?"

"A gownless evening strap and it's very sensual!" I blurted out.

Needless to say, I didn't get to wear it.

Wow. So I truly apologize to every woman in history. As well as to the concept of humor. And I'd like to thank and bless the great people of *Reader's Digest* for being smart enough to burn that submission.

That way I was free to submit it to *Penthouse* instead.

Finally, I applied to SNL in November, which I later found out was the exact wrong time to apply. Apparently SNL only looked at writer submissions in the summer when the show was on hiatus, so I had to wait until June to resubmit.

In the meantime, out of all the shows I had applied to, only one responded. But the one that responded was *The Late Show with David Letterman*.

This was particularly exciting for me because Letterman was a hero of mine and when I was in sixth grade, I had convinced our teacher, Mrs. Purij, to let us re-create *The Late Show* at the beginning of every history class.* I played the role of David Letterman, and I would read several of his Top Ten lists

---

* I've often wondered why she let us do that, but I guess teachers are looking for a way out, too.

from one of four full books of Top Ten lists that I forced my dad to buy me.

We would then reenact our favorite SNL sketches, like Chris Farley's Motivational Speaker or Will Ferrell's "I DRIVE A DODGE STRATUS!" Or we would perform musical numbers and skits from Adam Sandler's comedy albums, which were decidedly *not* appropriate for a Catholic middle school. Mrs. Purij had to cut us off when we launched into Sandler's audio game show: "Is This Man Having Sex or Just Working Out?" (Spoiler: Every one of the men is having loud, graphic sex.)

Our show was so popular within the sixth-grade community that Mrs. Purij moved us to a school-wide assembly in the gymnasium. (It was by far my finest hour in that gymnasium.) The event, as far as I can remember, was a hit. Mostly because it featured zero original material. But that didn't stop us from celebrating afterward with a round of Ecto Coolers.*

So when the head writers at Letterman's show actually liked my submission, I thought, *Wow. Those books of Top Ten lists really paid off!*

They told me to submit a second packet that should be "similar to the first one you did, but better." And I got to work, still thinking it was an extreme long shot.

I didn't know this at the time, but Letterman had a history of hiring random people who sent in submissions, even if they were untested or mentally unstable. For example, I later found out that Will Forte, as a then-fledgling writer (and then-mild lunatic), had mailed a series of intentionally dumb cartoons to the Letterman offices, which the writers were passing around

* The green *Ghostbusters*-themed Hi-C drink, discontinued in 1997.

because they looked like drawings done by a slow-witted child. Then Letterman himself passed by, saw the cartoons, and said, "Hire that guy."

Which made me love Letterman even more.

So I put together a second submission and they liked it enough that I got called in for an interview with the head writers, Justin and Eric Stangel,* who were very welcoming when they could have been intimidating jerks. I could also tell how stressful and exhausting it was to work on a nightly show like that, because every five minutes someone would knock and walk in with a piece of paper that probably said, *ALL THESE IDEAS ARE BAD. Love, Dave,* and I'd watch the Stangel brothers pull clumps of hair out of their heads, then turn back to me and say, "So why do you want to work here?"

I did not get the job. But I do still receive a Christmas card from the Stangel brothers every year, which was well worth the rejection.

---

* They were brothers. Probably still are.

.   .   .

A couple months later, I took a job writing for a now-defunct animation company called Animation Collective. Myself and three of my friends were hired to write twenty-six half-hour episodes of a brand-new animated show for Nickelodeon called *Kappa Mikey*. (It eventually aired on Nicktoons, which was like the MTV6 of Nickelodeon.)

The premise of the show was (stay with me here): A cocky American pop-art-style teenage boy named Mikey gets cast in a Japanese *anime sitcom* and has to move to Tokyo and become friends with his new castmates: Mitsuki (a human Japanese girl), Guano (a "fuzzy purple creature with many insecurities"), and Gonard (a "tall husky dim-witted man," who is also purple for some reason even though he's human). Pretty straightforward, right? Oh, and the title *Kappa Mikey* was a play on *kappamaki,* which is apparently a type of sushi. You know, a kids' show!

Of course, my friends and I were very grateful to have a writing job of any kind, even though we endured what in retrospect were illegal working conditions on many levels. First of all, our office was also our boss's apartment. I just googled "Can my boss live in our office?" and Google seems to think the answer is "No." The artwork on the walls included vintage photographs of Ukrainian boys in sailor outfits.* We'd find condoms on the floor and have to pretend not to see them. And certain employees would have to take

---

* Our target audience?

breaks from work so our boss could dress them up in old-timey costumes and have them pose for a photo shoot on the roof.

I really liked our boss, even though he was at times a maniac. His previous company was an online toy business, which, I kid you not, was ranked the No. 2 most promising company in America by *Businessweek* in 2001. No. 1 on that list? Enron.

The good news was: We had technically become professional writers, even though I was making a lower hourly wage than when I was lifeguarding at age fifteen. When you're starting out, any credit is a good credit. You can tell people you're working in entertainment, even though you're actually working on a madman's fever dream.*

Then I got a call from one of the associate producers at SNL, after I finally (properly) submitted a sketch packet. He said, "We want you to come to the office next week. You're going to meet with Tina Fey and Andrew Steele, our two head writers. And then you *might* meet with Lorne Michaels." Which is like hearing "You're going to meet with St. Peter and the Virgin Mary. And then you *might* hang out with God. So just mentally prepare for both scenarios."

Like any seasoned pro, my first question was: "What should I wear?"

.   .   .

---

* And not to brag, but *Variety* called *Kappa Mikey* "a cacophony of sights, sounds and animation interspersed with some relatively clever writing." They also falsely predicted that it would become "a cult hit."

Meeting with Tina and Steele was actually more intimidating than meeting with Lorne, because I sensed that they were the ones actually making decisions about which writers to hire. My instinct was to wear a suit because I thought that was what adults wore to job interviews, but luckily my friends convinced me that would look desperate, so I wore jeans and a button-down shirt and tried to act "normal."

I later found out they weren't expecting me to be funny during the interview. They were just trying to make sure I wasn't a crazy person.* Like when they asked, "Where are you from?" I just had to avoid bursting into tears and yelling, "I DON'T REMEMBER ANYTHING AFTER THE ACCIDENT!"

I managed to survive the interview without doing that, and was told by one of Lorne's assistants that Lorne would like to see me too. So could I hang out at the office for a few more hours? I looked at my wrist, which didn't have a watch. "No problem!"

While I waited, I met Andy Samberg, Akiva Schaffer, and Jorma Taccone from The Lonely Island, who had gotten hired the week before, and Bryan Tucker, who had just come to SNL after working at *Chappelle's Show*. I also found out they were putting Andy and a guy named Bill Hader in the cast. And that Jason Sudeikis, who had been a writer, would be joining the cast as well. (A few weeks later, they hired Kristen Wiig.)

---

* "Don't be crazy" sounds like simple advice, yet at least one or two people each year interview at SNL and act full crazy. They'll show up drunk for a 2 P.M. interview. Or you'll ask, "How are you?" and they'll say, "Honestly, *not good*." Or they'll use the word "we" when talking about SNL, like they already work there. "I think we need to get the sketches shorter, but we also need better endings. By the way, do we still do cocaine here?"

I didn't know it at the time, but that would be the group I started with and would spend eighty hours a week with for most of the next decade.

Six hours later, I met with Lorne Michaels. (I would have waited six days.) When I entered, he was on his computer, presumably conducting high-end talent negotiations, though I now know with 100-percent certainty that he was playing *Snood*.

We sat in two chairs facing each other, and he just asked me questions about my life and about my experience as a viewer of SNL. He asked me which cast I watched the most growing up, and I told him it was Farley, Sandler, Chris Rock, David Spade, Jan Hooks, Tim Meadows, Mike Myers, Kevin Nealon, and Phil Hartman.

"And Dana?" he asked, almost worried.

"Oh, and Dana! He was the best!"

Now I was terrified that I had blown the entire interview because I forgot to mention my genuine love of Dana Carvey.

We spoke for another five minutes and then Lorne paused. He said, "So, do you have any questions for me?"

Somehow I was not prepared for this most basic of interview questions.

He had been asking me where I was from, so I just panicked and asked him, "Where are *you* from?"

That was my one question for Lorne Michaels. "Where are you from?"

That's like asking a genie, "Can you make sandwiches?"

Lorne said, "Well, I'm from Canada. And then I came to New York to start the show."

And I was like, *Right, right, right. So like the very first informa-tion that comes up when you google "Lorne Michaels"? Very cool.*

Then he said, "Okay, it was good meeting you, Colin. I'll be seeing you around." And the interview was over.

I didn't know whether "I'll be seeing you around" meant "You're hired," or if he just hoped to "see me around the streets of New York." None of Lorne's assistants or the pro-ducers of SNL knew what Lorne meant by that either, so they quarantined me in one of the writers' offices while they fig-ured it out. A half hour later, the phone in the office rang and I sensed that I should pick it up. (Proof that I *was* a crazy per-son after all!)

It was producers Mike Shoemaker and Steve Higgins, and they said, "Congratulations. You're hired."

I was so happy, I didn't even process how weird it was that I was *at* SNL but somehow hired *over the phone.*

"When can you start?" Mike asked.

I had completely forgotten about my current job dodging condoms at Animation Collective.

"Well, I guess I should give my boss two weeks' notice . . ."

"What about you start tomorrow?"

"Tomorrow works, too."

Being a Staff Writer at SNL
Was the Most Fun I'll Ever
Have in My Life

"Look for the job you'd take if you didn't need a job."

—Warren Buffett

"The banquet is in the first bite."

—Michael Pollan

I was twenty-two when I got hired at SNL. My first show was Steve Carell as the host and Kanye West as the musical guest. As far as first shows go, that's a pretty outstanding lineup. Especially since the previous season had featured host Paris Hilton and musical guest Ashlee Simpson, who got caught lip-syncing and just . . . walked off the stage. (Kanye would also walk off the stage, but that was just at dress rehearsal when he got into a screaming match with our ninety-five-year-old lighting designer.*)

---

* I'm guessing Kanye was right. I still love Kanye despite all of his everything.

There's no "ramping up" when you start at our show. My very first day of work was pitching sketch ideas to Steve Carell in front of Lorne, the entire cast, and all the other writers. You very quickly have to convince yourself that this is normal in order to survive. (This has been a theme throughout my life: Pretend I belong somewhere until eventually I do.)

It didn't help that the walls at SNL are covered with photos from some of the best sketches in the show's history. So while I wrote a terrible scene about a "cocky gas station attendant," I had to look up and see a framed portrait of Chevy Chase as the Land Shark. It's like if you were an artist and you had to paint *inside* the Museum of Modern Art. Halfway through painting a haystack you'd look up and think, *Dammit. I think Monet's might be better.*

Of course, when you're starting out, you're not trying to write a "great" sketch. You're just hoping to get something funny on TV and not get fired. My first week, I pitched an idea about a real news story, where a JetBlue plane had to make an emergency landing and the passengers were watching coverage of their own plane crash on the JetBlue TV screens (luckily the plane landed safely). People around the office seemed to like the idea, so I wrote it with Bill Hader and Erik Kenward, and somehow the sketch made it onto the show. Not only that, it was the first sketch after the monologue. So I had written the first sketch of my first show at SNL, which, I didn't realize at the time, is extremely rare. In fact, in the fifteen years I've written at the show, I've only had the first sketch after the monologue a handful of times. Liz Cackowski, one of the senior writers, warned me: "Don't let it get to your head. Last year, a new writer got *two* sketches on his first show and by the end of the year he was fired." I thought, *Jesus. Was he putting cameras in the women's bathroom?*

I took Liz's advice to heart and completely let go of any joy I derived from my first sketch. It's a Puritanical pattern I would follow for the rest of my career at SNL: If I had a great week, I would enjoy it on Sunday, then forget about it by Monday. And if I had a bad week, I would fall asleep on a pizza on Sunday, then forget about it by Monday.* It might not be the healthiest approach emotionally, but you need that mentality to survive the extreme highs and lows of an SNL season. It's so rare that you experience unbridled success, where your sketch goes well and there isn't a technical problem or a flubbed line or a joke you wished you had changed or a note that you forgot to tell a performer. You have to stay levelheaded because it's a long season and it's a live show, so a lot of elements are out of your control. (For example, when Bruce Willis walked out halfway through a sketch because he thought the sketch was over. And then . . . it was just over. Because he couldn't walk back in and say, "Oh wait, guys, there's more sketch!")

That doesn't mean I'm always calm and even-keeled, mind you. There have been many, many nights when I opened a Word document and wrote, "I FUCKING HATE THIS PLACE. I'M QUITTING AFTER THIS SEASON. CLEARLY NO ONE WANTS ME HERE OR LIKES ANYTHING I WRITE. I'M MOVING TO PUERTO RICO AND WRITING MY FAN-TASY NOVEL!" (For some reason, all my empty threats end with me moving to Puerto Rico and writing a fantasy novel. *That'll show 'em!*)

---

* To this day I've never rewatched an episode.

But even when I was angry or felt like I sucked and couldn't get a sketch on the show, I was still deeply grateful to work at SNL. It's not for everyone, and there are clearly funny people who fail at it and then go on to tremendous success. (See "Larry David.") But it's an incredible opportunity, and whether you flourish or explode in flames, you leave there a tougher, more capable comedian. It was an opportunity I never took for granted.

Even in my first season writing, agents would come to the after-party and ask, "Do you want to be *on the show* someday?" Like, "Writing's cute and all, but do you want to be someone who *I actually care about talking to?*"

In truth, when I got hired to be a writer, writing was all I thought about. That's *plenty* to worry about without also angling to be in the cast.

Also, I loved writing for other people. I still do.

It's liberating to write in other people's voices, and it's inspiring to see great actors elevate your material in ways you couldn't imagine. Clearly, there are things Kenan Thompson or Kate McKinnon or Leslie Jones (especially Leslie) can do that I will never be able to do. And to write a character or even a joke that they score with still gives me a huge rush. Plus, you get to write for a different host every week, including people I grew up idolizing, like Jim Carrey, Will Ferrell, Julia Louis-Dreyfus, and Adam Sandler. People you want to impress and write something great for.

All the senior writers and cast members looked out for us, too. Seth Meyers would help me rewrite any stupid sketch I brought him, which I appreciate even more now that I understand how little free time a head writer has. Andrew Steele, Emily Spivey, and T. Sean Shannon would encourage me to keep writing in my own voice even after one of my weirder sketches bombed at the table. Erik Kenward and Matt Murray would make every sketch I wrote funnier and make sure I wasn't depressed when I went four shows in a row with nothing on the air. Paula Pell would pitch me a joke that ended up being the biggest laugh in the piece, just because she liked making other people's sketches better. And Amy Poehler would say, "Hey, Jost! Want to write something together?" which was a very kind gesture from a senior cast member to a brand-new writer. (I would then sit there and type while Amy improvised way funnier lines than I could ever come up with.) I started collaborating with Rob Klein, John Solomon, and Kent Sublette, who have each written some of the best sketches of the past decade and made anything we wrote together ten times funnier. And I had the wisdom, guidance, and occasional Irish fury of our producer Erin Doyle, who fought for me with Lorne but also called me out when I was, to quote the NBA on TNT, "Shaqtin' a fool."

And I was lucky that a bunch of really funny writers came in over the next few years—like John Mulaney, Simon Rich, Marika Sawyer, Zach Kanin, Sarah Schneider, and Chris Kelly—because they were immediately writing great sketches and it made me think, *Oh shit, I need to keep getting better at this job and keep reinventing how I write.*

Plus, we had insanely talented performers who were writing at the show, like Tim Robinson, Mike O'Brien, Jillian Bell, Hannibal Burress, and J. B. Smoove. So I was surrounded by really funny people all the time. And what you realize years later is that so much of your career is driven by your peers. Lorne always says, "You never want to be the smartest person in the room," because you always want to challenge yourself and try to get to the level of the people you admire. I was fortunate to be around a lot of people who I still admire and still want to catch up to.

SNL is probably the least routine job in the world. Monday is the pitch meeting, where you have to make your coworkers (and ideally the host) laugh. Tuesday you're writing all day and night. Wednesday is the table read, followed by meetings with all the heads of production (if your sketch got picked) and heavy drinking (regardless of whether your sketch got picked). Thursday you're at a rewrite table with the other writers, pitching jokes and eating a pound of candy and donuts to relieve your hangover. Friday you're either rehearsing in the studio or filming a pretaped piece on location somewhere. And then Saturday is the show, followed by two parties.* That's a lot of variety, even for a variety show. And it's why I haven't gotten bored, even after fifteen seasons of writing.

For my first few years at the show, I essentially lived at work (and actually slept there one or two nights every week), because there was nowhere else I wanted to be. I owned two pairs of jeans, ten T-shirts, and three pairs of New Balance

---

* What other job in America has two parties at the end of every workweek?

sneakers. My only expenses were a thousand dollars a month in rent* (which in New York was somehow "a steal") and eighty dollars for a monthly subway card (the train, not the sandwiches—though I did eat at Subway four or five times a week). The rest I saved in case I got fired or sued by a celebrity for defaming them in a sketch.†

More than anything, I wrote as much as I physically could. I'd submit five or six sketches every week in hopes of developing as quickly as possible. (In terms of page count, I was writing the equivalent of half a screenplay every Tuesday night.) And even though 90 percent of what I wrote never made the show, I could look back at the end of the year and see that I was improving. (And that I had destroyed half a forest with the number of scripts I printed out.)

But I wasn't just developing my skills as a writer, I was developing a knowledge and an awareness of every single element of show business. Because at SNL, unlike at most shows, the writer is also the producer for any sketches that get picked. For better or worse, the ultimate decision on staging, costumes, hair, set design, and special effects rests with the writer.

Now, that doesn't mean the writer has any *clue* how those things actually work. It just means you have to communicate your vision for the sketch to all the different department heads—who are all exceptional at what they do—and then you have to have a real conversation about how (and if) that vision

---

* I had two roommates for my first five years at the show. Our hours . . . did not line up well.

† I got a Prism Award for a sketch about steroid use in baseball, but I'm guessing Barry Bonds didn't love it.

is achievable in a matter of forty-eight hours. Because eventually, when you're watching the sketch at dress rehearsal next to Lorne, *you* are the one he'll turn to and say, "What the hell is going on with Awkwafina's wig?" And it's not because Jodi Mancuso, head of our hair department, made a bad wig.* It's because you, the writer, asked her to "make the wig look insane."

If I've learned one thing at this job, it's to never ask for a wig that's "insane."†

I got eight sketches on the show my first year, including one cold open and a parody of MTV's *My Super Sweet Sixteen*, starring first-time host Scarlett Johansson. She had just turned twenty and I was twenty-three, but in terms of status and maturity, she was here [holds hand above head] and I was here [holds hand one inch off ground].

She claims that she remembers thinking I was "cute," but I know what I looked like and that's not the word I would have used. ("Shaggy" would have been generous. "Slovenly," more accurate.)

I remember her being beautiful, smart, sweet, and intimidatingly sophisticated. And she had a grace and a smile that I've still never seen in any other human.

---

* If you've ever seen SNL, you know the wigs are maybe the most impressive part.
† My favorite wig-related story at our show involves a host who was bald but wore a toupee. Rather than admit he was wearing a toupee, he had the hair department put a bald cap *over* his toupee, and then a wig over the bald cap. So the layers were: his own bald head, then fake hair, then a fake bald head, then more fake hair. I'm sweating just imagining how hot his scalp must have been.

The only line I remember from the sketch is when Scarlett's bratty character says, "This party is *literally* worse than the Holocaust."

That was my Shakespearean sonnet for the woman I would one day fall in love with.

It was a memorable season for hosts, and not just because I would end up dating one of them. (Antonio Banderas.)

These were the pairings of hosts and musical guests:

The aforementioned Steve Carell and Kanye West
Jack Black and Neil Young
Lindsay Lohan and Pearl Jam
Steve Martin and *Prince*

And maybe my favorite show of the year:

Tom Hanks and the Red Hot Chili Peppers

That was everything I grew up loving in one show. *Plus*, the Red Hot Chili Peppers played "Give It Away" for their second song, because they were supposed to play it the first time they appeared on SNL in 1993, but the show ran out of time and it got cut. (1993's loss was 2005's gain.)

And, like in any season of SNL, there were some very odd combinations too, such as:

Jon Heder and Ashlee Simpson (again)
Eva Longoria and Korn
Matt Dillon and Arctic Monkeys

And, of course, the classic duo of:

Kevin Spacey and Nelly Furtado

That's one of the underrated aspects of the show to me—how it becomes a strange time capsule of fame at that moment in time. Every year has some real home runs and some real question marks. (Just like each episode has—hopefully—a home run or two and then maybe a double, a couple singles, and one or two times when the batter lets go of the bat and it flies into the stands and hits a kid.)

There are still giant old VHS tapes outside Lorne's office with labels of the hosts and musical guests from the '80s and '90s, and it's like joke combinations you would see on a *Family Guy* parody of SNL:

Charlton Heston and Wynton Marsalis
John Larroquette and Timbuk 3
Sylvester Stallone and Jamiroquai
Jackie Chan and Kid Rock

And my favorite combo of all time:

Charles Barkley and Nirvana

When Barkley came back to host years later, he said he had no idea who Nirvana was at the time. He was backstage listening to them rehearse, and he turned to our producer and said, "Are those guys saying 'Rape Me'? Because it sounds like they're saying 'Rape Me.'"

And that's pretty much SNL in a nutshell: one of the greatest basketball players in history asking why one of the best bands in history was saying, "Rape Me."

Why would I want to work anywhere else?

Oops, I Fell Asleep in a Graveyard

"Peculiar travel suggestions are like dancing lessons from
God."

—Kurt Vonnegut

"Colin, why are you bleeding?"

—A concerned Danish citizen

In August 2007, I got a call from Andy Samberg around eight
o'clock at night. He told me that he, Seth Meyers, and two
other SNL writers, Akiva Schaffer and Liz Cackowski, were all
going to Scandinavia for the week. The plan was: Copenhagen,
Helsinki, Estonia, and Amsterdam. Would I like to come?

Me: "Soooo, when would I fly to Copenhagen?"

Samberg: "I don't know. I guess tomorrow morning?"

Me: "Um . . . Okay, sure!"

(This is how little I had going on in my life beyond work.)

I packed whatever clothes I needed for August in Scandinavia (shorts and a Viking helmet?) and flew to Denmark with no
hotel reservation or transportation booked beyond that. I just
arrived alone at the Copenhagen airport and asked, "Is there a
train that goes to my friends?"

This was after my first two seasons writing at SNL, so I had saved a little money, but I never liked spending it because I was always terrified it would disappear. When I met up with everyone, they were killing time in this high-end men's clothing store near the hotel. Seth and Andy were looking at these fancy European shirts and they were like, "You should get one!"

Now, up until this point, I had never spent more than 40 dollars on a shirt. I just didn't believe in spending money on clothing because a 40-dollar shirt served the same practical function as an 80-dollar shirt (it covered your torso and the top of your pants). This store sold 250-dollar shirts.

I tried on a slim-cut, white button-down shirt and a really thin black tie,* and Seth and Andy were like, "That looks great! Get them both!" And they gave me an earnest talk about how it would be okay and how I could spend 250 dollars on a shirt and it wouldn't be the end of the world or derail my life or prevent my future children from going to college, so why not get the shirt! (And the tie!)

So the first thing I did in Copenhagen was blow 400 dollars on a white button-down shirt and a really thin black tie that I still had to wear with my 29-dollar American Eagle jeans from college.

After I paid, I asked Seth and Andy, "What are you guys buying?" And they said, "Oh, nothing." *You sons of bitches!* How'd I get peer-pressured into doing something my peers didn't even do?! That's like a friend passing you a joint and after you take a hit and pass it back, he's like, "I don't touch the stuff!" *Then why did you even have it?!*

---

* Apparently I was auditioning for the Hives.

That night, I put on my brand-new shirt and tie, and we all got on bicycles we had rented to cruise around the city. Biking at night in a strange city + drinking Danish liquors = what could go wrong!

Liz's sister Jeanett actually lived in Copenhagen and she was a doctor (this will become relevant later on), so she led our group on bicycles and took us to dinner and then to a Danish nightclub. On the way to the club, we were biking past a skate park with a huge quarter-pipe for skateboarding tricks and Seth said, "Watch this!" He biked really fast toward the quarter-pipe and everyone was like, "Holy shit! Seth's gonna do it!" Then, right before the jump, he skidded to a halt and everyone laughed because of course he wasn't gonna really do the jump on a Schwinn bicycle. That would be dumb.

Then *I* was like, "Watch *THIS!*" I started biking really fast toward the jump, unaware that (a) everyone else had started biking away already, (b) the jump was really steep, and (c) bikes aren't the same as skateboards.

I hit the jump at full speed, but instead of "jumping," the bike clipped the top of the ramp and violently flipped me forward onto the concrete. I ripped open my 250-dollar shirt and was now bleeding through my white shirt onto my 150-dollar tie (which was too thin to use as a tourniquet). And the worst part was, *no one even saw it*. I was just lying on the pavement waiting for my friends to be like, "That was *awesome*! We never knew you were such a *cool idiot!*" Instead they were two blocks ahead, confused that I had disappeared.

Now, one thing you should know about me is that I hate disrupting a good time. So after I stood up and saw that I was bleeding, my first thought was: *Play it cool*. I got back on my (now dented) bike and caught up to the group like nothing had happened. "Oh hey, guys!"

"Wait, why are you bleeding, Colin?"

"Oh, who knows? It might have been this ramp-jump thing I did on my bicycle. Or maybe it's just that time of the month! Hahahaha, ow my ribs."

"Maybe we should go back to the hotel."

"No no no no no! I'm totally fine, let's definitely still go to the club and keep having fun!"

As mentioned earlier (classic foreshadowing), Liz's sister Jeanett is a doctor and she offered to find a first aid kit at the club and bandage me up, which was very kind of her. So my first experience in a Danish nightclub was getting Steri-Strips on my wounds in the bathroom while we did shots of Gammel Dansk—an even more disgusting version of Jägermeister—which was the closest thing they had to Advil.

Once I was patched up, being a twenty-four-year-old single man, my thoughts naturally shifted from: *I'm bleeding in the bathroom of a club* to: *Where da ladies at?*

I met a cute Danish girl at the bar and we started talking and then dancing, and at some point we started making out. And I thought, *Maybe this 250-dollar, blood-soaked shirt was worth it after all!* I said to her, "You want to go back to my place?"

Now, the question "You want to go back to my place?" is a lot more complicated when (a) it's not "your" place—it's a hotel room with two twin beds that you're sharing with your coworker, and (b) the ride back to "your place" is on a bicycle.

She was like, "Yeah! Let's do it!"

So about an hour after I was bleeding next to a skateboard ramp, I was back on my bicycle, only this time I was pedaling standing up while a Danish girl I just met was seated behind me, holding on for dear life.

It was a full half-hour bike ride.

By the time we arrived at my hotel, I could already sense her enthusiasm waning. (Weird, right?) I went to open the front door of the hotel, but it was locked, which I had never experienced at a hotel before. The Danish girl was like, "Are you sure this is your hotel?" I was like, "I'm 76-percent certain."

I noticed a sign that said: AFTER HOURS, RING BELL FOR DOORMAN. So I rang the bell. And rang it again. And again.

You know how they say that every time a bell rings, an angel gets its wings? Well, every time my hotel doorbell rang, I got further away from having sex.

Finally, after what was probably ten minutes but felt like two weeks, we heard a loud FLUSH and the doorman walked out of the lobby bathroom with a newspaper under his arm and unlocked the front door. And that was pretty much the icing on the cake, mood-wise.

The Danish girl had (understandably) lost interest in anything remotely romantic, so I said, ". . . Should we go back to the club?"

I can tell you, the second half-hour-long bike ride felt a lot slower than the first half-hour-long bike ride (when sex was still a possibility). By the time we arrived, I was exhausted and stone cold sober. We said good night, and I went back into the club and found all my friends still drinking and dancing, so I figured, *I better start drinking and dancing again too!*

And, still being a twenty-four-year-old single man, my thoughts once again shifted from: *Why did I just bike an hour to and from my hotel with a random Danish girl?* to: *Where da ladies at?*

I go to the bar, and I meet a *second* Danish girl. And I usually have no game whatsoever, but this bloody, "wow, he must have gotten injured in a bar fight or some non-bicycle-related incident" shirt was giving me irrational confidence.

The second Danish girl and I started talking, and then dancing, and later on we started kissing. And I'm thinking, *How do I get a bicycle inside a taxi . . .* When all of a sudden, the *first* Danish girl walks up to us and says, "What the hell are you doing?"

And I say, "Oh! Hey! Sorry, I thought you went home and didn't want anything to do with me . . ."

And she says, "What is wrong with you?! *That's my sister!*"

So . . . that was Copenhagen!

Our next stop was Helsinki, Finland. And the real reason we chose Helsinki (beyond their "boulevards made for strolling" and the fact that they "eat reindeer") was that Seth was running the Helsinki marathon, which I wasn't even aware of until he casually mentioned it on the flight from Denmark. Like, "Oh, and while we're in Finland, I'm gonna run a full 26.2-mile marathon just for fun." (Clearly, he and I have different ideas of fun.)

The day after the marathon, the plan was to take a ferry to Estonia, where Seth could celebrate with a traditional Estonian feast of sauerkraut, jellied meat, and blood sausage. But you know what they say: "The best-laid plans of mice and men don't matter when the men drink way too much of a Finnish liquor made from pine tar."

But I'm getting ahead of myself. First came the marathon.

It was a very exciting day in Helsinki. All the Finnish celebrities had showed up, from the blond guy to the blond woman. The mayor or president or town bear yelled, *"Juosta pää kolmantena jalkana!"* which means, "Run using your head as a third leg!" And they were off!

Andy and I waited around the 15-mile mark to cheer Seth on when he passed. We ran into the street and jogged along with him for about 1,000 feet before we patted him on the back, already winded from a fifteen-second jog. As Seth continued to the finish line, Andy and I walked up to the water station where they were giving marathoners cups of water, and we each grabbed a cup because we were so thirsty from having run 1,000 feet.

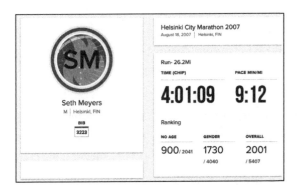

That night we all went out to celebrate Seth's 1,730th-place finish in classic Scandinavian style—by drinking to the point of near-death.

Seth's brother, Josh, had come to meet us in Helsinki to support his bro, and at the bar that night, Josh was talking to a charming Finnish woman, so I decided to be his "wingman." I walked up and said to the Finnish woman: "Do you know who this guy is? This is *Gerald Ford, Jr.*!"

Why I chose Gerald Ford, Jr., I'll never know. Nor do I know to this day whether a person named Gerald Ford, Jr., actually exists. But in that moment, I was absolutely sure that telling this Finnish woman that she was talking to Gerald Ford, Jr., would "seal the deal" for Seth's brother.*

It had the opposite effect.

She actually *believed* that he was Gerald Ford, Jr., and she proceeded to launch into an angry diatribe against the state of American politics, which she somehow blamed entirely on Gerald Ford, Jr.

HER: How dare you invade Iraq!

JOSH: I'm not Gerald Ford, Jr.

HER: Your arrogance in foreign policy is a disgrace to Western civilization!

JOSH: I'm not Gerald Ford, Jr.

HER: How do you sleep at night!

JOSH: In a bed that does not belong to Gerald Ford, Jr.

This continued for quite some time. As usual, I accepted full responsibility for the trouble I had caused by tiptoeing away and Irish exiting from the Finnish bar so I could stop drinking. (I do this a lot for self-preservation.) I didn't tell anyone I was leaving. I just wandered off alone and decided to walk all the

---

* (Who I later found out had no interest in pursuing this woman.)

way back to the hotel at 2 A.M., through a city I'd never been to before, with street signs in a language I couldn't read.

Then, about halfway to the hotel, I got really sleepy. And I'm the kind of person who, once he gets sleepy, cannot stop himself from falling asleep on whatever surface or food is next to me.* So I started looking around for a viable "mattress" and saw a nearby park with grass that seemed ideal for a 2 A.M. nap. I lay down in the park with my jacket as a pillow and fell asleep to the distant, soothing sounds of Finns throwing up brambleberry schnapps.

About an hour later, I woke up and took "A Closer Look" (™ Seth Meyers) at the park I was sleeping in, and noticed that it contained a number of tombstone-shaped granite slabs sticking out of the ground all around me—a detail I missed upon entering the "park," which was, in fact, a Finnish graveyard. (R.I.P. my nap.)

I reacted to this newfound information with classic Colin Jost grace—by running full speed out of the graveyard while slapping myself as though I were covered in spiders. (Because that's how you chase ghosts away.)

I ran the rest of the way to the hotel, went up to Josh's room, and knocked on the door. He opened it and I said, "You've got to help me! I was just asleep in a graveyard for six hours!"

Again, why I thought I had slept there for six hours, I'll never know. But Josh, expertly sensing that I was still in "Ger-

---

* I've twice fallen asleep cradling a tray of buffalo wings like a body pillow. And during my first year as a writer at SNL, I went out with the cast to a diner at 7 A.M. (*after* the after-after-party) and fell asleep at the table with my face on a hamburger, earning me the nickname "Burger Jost."

ald Ford, Jr." mode, let me into his room and spent the next five minutes lovingly building me a bed on the floor using pillows and blankets from his own bed. I then proceeded to fall asleep on the bare floor *next to* the bed he had built for me.

In the morning, I was awoken by Seth, who shook me by the shoulder and said, "Are you ready to take a boat to Estonia?" That's when he saw that my skin was green and quickly realized we were not getting on a boat to Estonia. We were getting on a much later flight, to Amsterdam, where I would spend the next three days lying in bed in a feverish semi-coma, while Seth and Andy hung out with friends from the Boom Chicago theater troupe, which Seth had performed in after college.

They asked Seth, "What's with your other friend who stays in bed all day shivering and throwing up?"

And Seth said, "Oh, that's Colin. His body's been taken over by Finnish ghosts."

Top Banana

"With great power comes overwhelming neurosis."
—Spider-Man, to his therapist

"Try to relax, you're just having serious heart palpitations."
—The NBC doctor

After my first season or two as a writer (once I felt semi-confident that I wouldn't be fired immediately), I had a couple years of unmitigated joy at the show. At that point, I was twenty-four or twenty-five, and I was getting sketches on the air regularly, but I didn't have any serious responsibility yet. I could write whatever I wanted, even flights of fancy, like a sketch where Jason Sudeikis was the first caveman to ever dance (set to the Darude song "Sandstorm"). Or a sketch I wrote with Rob Klein about a combination emergency room/BBQ restaurant where they kept switching the bags of blood with barbecue sauce. Or a game show sketch for Bradley Cooper called "I'm Gonna Have Sex with Your Wife!"

I never had to worry about scrambling to write the cold open at midnight on a Friday. I rarely had to figure out a monologue for the host. I could just write whatever dumb idea came

into my brain that week, like a sketch where Jonah Hill sur-
prises his wife, Kristen Wiig, with an orchestra for their anniversary, but the orchestra starts playing "C U When U Get
There" by Coolio while Jonah raps along. Or a talk show called
Two First Names where every one of the celebrity guests has
two first names, like Neil Patrick Harris and David Lee Roth
(played by Fred Armisen with puppet legs that kick in the air).
True fever dreams that somehow made it onto the show.

And most of the cast and writers were young enough that
the crazy hours of the show never bothered us. I didn't miss a
single after-party or after-after-party for at least my first five
years. We would all stay out until 9 A.M. every night after the
show, then go to bed (or have a casual breakfast), sleep for
most of Sunday, and start all over again at work Monday morning. I wasn't even doing any drugs!* I was awake on pure adrenaline from working at the show I always wanted to work at
and hanging out with really funny friends who were all single
and didn't want to go home to their tiny, barely furnished New
York apartments.

Then I had to screw it up and become "responsible."

Being the head writer at SNL is like being an assistant zookeeper at a zoo where you used to be a monkey. Being a monkey is really fun. You eat bananas all day, you throw feces at
humans, you have sex with frogs (at least according to You-
Tube), and sometimes a guy gets too close to the cage and you
rip his nuts off. It's a great life.

---

* Unless you count alcohol as a drug. Which I guess "scientists" do.

Now, imagine if the owner of the zoo took you out of the monkey cage, put a uniform on you, and said, "Get those other monkeys in line!" After a few weeks, you'd think, *Can't I just be a monkey again?*

I remember when I found out I was becoming head writer because it was one of my proudest achievements and it happened to involve one of my closest friends. It was the summer of 2013 and we were at 30 Rock because Lorne was holding auditions for new cast members. Seth Meyers called me into his office and said, "So, I have something I want to ask you."

"Just tell me a name. And they're dead," I told him.

"No, not that. I took care of that already. The police will never find the body. Not after what I did to it. Besides, the police are too stupid to catch me. I dare them to try, even six or seven years from now."

"Wow, I was joking, but you sound serious, Seth."

"I am serious, Colin. I've taken a man's life. And for what? A few ha'pennies and a cheap thrill?"

"Hay-pennies?"

"That's right. They're halfpennies."

"Huh. Guess I never realized that's what 'ha'penny' meant."

"Well, you learn something every day, Colin."

"Great point, Seth. Anyway, you were saying?"

"Oh right, the real part. Lorne wants to know if you would join me as head writer this season."

And then he surprised me with the gift of a really expensive fountain pen—the only pen I've ever owned that wasn't free from a hotel room. (I'm still too scared to use it.) He gave me a big hug and said, "I'm so happy we get to do this together."

And if I weren't already getting nervous about the job, I probably would have cried.

The idea of being head writer was always a distant goal of mine, even though plenty of successful writers at the show never become head writer (or never want to). The list of people who had done it before me was extremely intimidating: Jim Downey, Tina Fey, Adam McKay, Seth Meyers, Michael O'Donoghue, Paula Pell, Dennis McNicholas, and, way back in season one, Lorne Michaels. Being in company like that was the cool part of getting the job. But then came the *job* part of the job, and that proved overwhelming in ways I didn't expect.

Let's go back to my award-winning zoo analogy.* The fundamental frustration of being head writer at SNL—like being the assistant zookeeper—is that it's not *your* zoo. You can influence the way the zoo is run, but only so much. You can raise your hand at a meeting and say, "Hey, I think one of the anacondas ate a baby." But it's still up to the head zookeeper to agree to let you slice the anaconda open and take the baby out.

This puts you in the very stressful position of trying to address your boss's concerns about the show while also defending your colleagues/friends and *their* vision for the sketches they wrote. It's a more delicate situation than you might think. For example, say there's a first-year writer at the show and she writes a sketch about Hitler Jr., and Lorne doesn't like it. Maybe I think it's funny and I say to Lorne: "I think we should do the Hitler Jr., sketch." If Lorne relents and puts the sketch on the show, and he still hates it afterward (which he almost

---

* Oddly, it won a Tony Award.

certainly will), then he won't just be angry at me (that part I don't really care about anymore)—he'll be angry at the first-year writer, and that writer could lose her job at the end of the year. So you're always making these weird calculations about what is best for the show, what is best for the individual writer, and what you think is genuinely the funniest version of a sketch.

Maybe some people are good at ignoring people's feelings and not taking on the stress of decisions like that, but I am not. Each of those decisions weighs heavily on my conscience, and as head writer I have to make fifty of those decisions a week. I can easily get overwhelmed by guilt, and there's no time to feel guilty at SNL. The week moves too quickly. So I experience this strange cycle of guilt, then repressed guilt, then guilt that I was *able* to repress the guilt. HAVE I MENTIONED I WAS RAISED CATHOLIC? IT'S ALMOST LIKE THERE'S A SUBTLE THEME EMERGING IN THIS BOOK.

Here's how overwhelmed I got:

One Wednesday after a table read, I got called into Lorne's office to discuss which sketches would get picked for dress rehearsal, and on the way there I suddenly felt like I was having a heart attack. My heart was racing and skipping beats and I didn't know what to do. I lay down on the couch outside Lorne's office and his assistant brought me water and called for a doctor. I remember thinking, *If I die, will they mention me in the show on Saturday? Which sketch of mine would they show? Should I have chosen the clip ahead of time? What if they pick a really dumb one like the Update feature I wrote with Andy called "Liam, the Boy Who Just Woke Up"? Or the ad I wrote for Baby Toupees? Or the sketch where Dwayne Johnson brings Kristen Wiig*

back to his apartment, but his apartment is a lighthouse, so when he
turns out the lights to set the mood, a ship immediately hits the rocks
below and Will Forte is a sea captain who starts screaming up at
them for help—what if that's the clip they show? Is that how people
will remember me??

It turned out that I had serious heart palpitations that were
brought on by a combination of stress and staying awake forty
hours straight every week, subsisting only on pizza and bulk
candy. My doctor's advice was: "Don't stay up forty hours
straight every week, eating only pizza and bulk candy. Because
if you do, your heart will try to walk out of your chest.

"Oh, and try to relax."

What I eventually realized is: A lot of the show is completely
out of my control. Even if I wanted to change it, I probably
couldn't. So why not focus on what I *can* control and let the
producers (and other writers and head writers) figure out the
rest? I just wrote the sketches I wanted to write, and wrote
the best cold open I could think of that week (if needed), and
tried to encourage the newer writers and cast members to
work really hard on the sketches they cared about most. If I
fought for a sketch and Lorne didn't pick it, I didn't let it bother
me anymore.

The reality is: If there are great writers on staff (and a great
cast), you're gonna look like a great head writer. If the writers
are only so-so, then you better find new writers fast or they're
gonna find a new you.

The only other thing you can do is lead by example. If you
want the staff to write smart sketches, then you have to write
smart sketches yourself (and occasionally some really dumb
sketches to keep them honest).

I have a feeling it's the hardest job I'll ever have. Not hard like manual-labor-in-a-gulag hard, but existentially it's extremely stressful.

I was head writer for three years, then I took two years off to basically survive on Weekend Update (more on that next!), and then Lorne asked Michael Che and me to be head writers with Kent Sublette, and we've done that together for the past three seasons.* So, six years in total as head writer. Just typing that sentence gives me anxiety.

When I got re-promoted with Che, I asked my agent, "Do I get more money now?"

"Nope."

"If the show wins an Emmy, do I get an Emmy?"

"Nope."

"And if the show is reviewed poorly by critics, who do you think they'll blame?"

"Almost certainly you."

"So . . . why am I doing this again?"

"Frankly, I have no idea."

---

* With Anna Drezen, Streeter Seidell, Sudi Green, and Fran Gillespie doing really brilliant work as writing supervisors. (I was once a writing supervisor and still don't know exactly what that title means. It sounds like you'd be overseeing an assembly line of scripts and saying, "Good. Good. *Very* good. Oooh, this one is bad." But in reality you're just trying to write funny sketches and not freak out when Lorne asks you a direct question.)

Okay, So Maybe I've Shit My Pants a Couple Times

Note: Please feel free to skip this chapter if you are: my fiancée, my parents, my grandparents, any of my "older" (above thirty) relatives, a former girlfriend who might have been present on one or more of these occasions, an active police officer, a retired police officer who still "has pull" and can get the department to "revive a cold case," any future employer, or anyone in the "fashion" or "glamour" industries who might one day consider hiring me as a watch model— except that it's contingent on me having never shit my pants as a full adult.

The rest of you, you're welcome.

I remember when I was twenty-seven, I reflected on the five years I'd been out of college and thought, *Wow, since I graduated, I've only shit my pants like five times.* I felt a genuine sense of pride in that moment. Not an Edison-level achievement, but surely something I could hang my hat on, or at least hang my pants on to air out.

Then I shared that information with a close friend and he had, you might say, the opposite reaction.

HIM: *Only* five times? You're an adult.
ME: Yeah, but things happen!
HIM: No they don't. They honestly don't.
ME: Well, how many times have *you* shit your pants in the last five years?
HIM: *Zero!*

Well *la-di-da*! Must be nice, Mr. My Intestines Function Properly!

Anyway, cut to: I'm thirty-four. I've been cruising along at a "Shit My Pants Once Every Year or Two" kind of pace. Not gonna make the Shit Olympics, but I'm definitely invited to the U.S. Time Trials. I'm out in Long Island and my buddy calls me up and says, "I'm playing some golf with a colleague of mine from work. Want to join us?"

I say, "I'll put on my brand-new light blue golf shorts and I'll be right over!"

This was my (verbatim, unedited) text exchange with my friend John Solomon after I completed that golf round:

ME: Just shit my pants on a golf course so we good
JOHN: Please tell me that's real
ME: So real
JOHN: Fuck yes
      Might be my fav thing about u
ME: The details are pretty great
      And upsetting

JOHN: Give me one

ME: This sounds like it would defy physics but I shit the front of my pants

JOHN: Whaaaaaaat????

ME: Basically I had to run into the woods (implying to my playing partners that I just had to pee) then pulled my shorts down and let loose in the woods. Only problem was the shorts weren't fully off and it coated the front of my shorts

JOHN: Hahahahahahahaha
       Then what happened?????
       Fuck

ME: Then I used my underwear as toilet paper
     So at that point I was only wearing a polo shirt and golf cleats. Otherwise fully nude

JOHN: That's not true

ME: Yup. All while a beautiful deer was 5 feet away watching me. Even he knew how wrong this was

JOHN: Wait u threw shorts in woods?
       No

ME: Had to take shorts off to get underwear off
     This is all while my playing partners were 15 feet away teeing off on the next hole

JOHN: Wait but then u got back on the course in shorts with a shit stain?

ME: Correct

JOHN: WHAT
       Did they see it?

ME: I put them back on without realizing
     Thought I had "gotten away with it"

Then halfway to the next green I look down and
saw a clump of shit on the front of my pants

JOHN: Hahahaha

Godfuckingdamnit

Fuck

ME: Then I tried to spit on my hand and wipe it off which
did NOT work

JOHN: This is the one we waited for

ME: It then looked like I had pissed my pants to disguise
the shit

JOHN: This is Kundun

ME: Extremely noticeable

For my playing partners

JOHN: What did they say?

ME: They DEFINITELY noticed and basically stopped
talking altogether. We played the last four holes in
silence

JOHN: Fuck

ME: So if you see a deer wearing blue Ralph Lauren boxer
briefs covered in human feces, tell him 'Sup

JOHN: Ur the king

Now, again, I wish this were "an isolated incident." A "rare
occurrence" on an otherwise "spotless record." I wish you
could interview my neighbors and hear, "We never saw this
coming! He was a nice kid. Kept mostly to himself. We just as-
sumed he could make it to a toilet."

But as you can tell from John's initial response—"Might be
my fav thing about u"—this wasn't my first rodeo.

I've shit my pants in: a college classroom, the offices of *Sat-*

urday Night Live at 30 Rockefeller Center, a car on the way to the airport, a movie theater during a first date, a comedy club right after I performed, a comedy club right *before* I performed, and—perhaps most impressively—in my own home. Can you take a moment to marvel at that, please? I didn't make it to the bathroom in *my own home*. And this was a New York City apartment, mind you. I wasn't trapped in the wrong wing of my Foxcatcher estate.

I'll probably have to write a second book focusing solely on these stories. (I'll call it *Everybody Poops, But Not Like This.*) So for now, I'll just tell you about the first time it happened to me as an adult. My superhero "origin story," if you will.

I was a summer intern at my local newspaper, the *Staten Island Advance*, and the event we looked forward to all summer was the Intern Party, when real reporters and editors at the paper threw a "secret" (i.e., actually illegal) party for us interns where we could drink booze and feel cool for two and a half hours.

And who knows, maybe I could ask out that cute girl Jessica I've always had my eye— Oh, what's that? She's already hooking up with the forty-five-year-old crime reporter? Got it.

So I go to the Intern Party and start nervously pounding Stoli Ohranj like I had a vitamin C deficiency. By a strange (cruel?) twist of fate, the reporter who's throwing the party lives down the street from my parents. In fact, he's one of the few non-relatives who lives on our block. I clock that immediately but don't really think much of it.

Fast-forward an hour or two, and I'm the drunkest I've ever been. Which is realistically four drinks deep. I've technically eaten a full ohranj. The good news: I ain't getting scurvy. The bad news: I'm about to puke everywhere. So I do what any self-respecting Staten Islander would do: I go outside and puke all over the lawn.

Now, if you've ever gotten really sick, or if you've ever been me for a full calendar year, you know that when things are coming out of the Holland Tunnel, odds are something's coming out of the Lincoln Tunnel, too. For clarity, the Lincoln Tunnel is the butt. Joke about Log Cabin Republicans TBD.

So I'm on my coworker's lawn with a full diaper, staring down a garden gnome that's covered in the ravioli I ate for lunch, when I hatch an ingenious plan: I'll go home to my parents' place for, like, forty-five minutes, shower and change my clothes, maybe sneak in a quick nap, then be back at the party before Jessica even notices.

My plan wound up working perfectly. EXCEPT that instead of showering and changing my clothes and going back to the party, I took my soiled pants off, put them in my parents' washing machine, FORGOT TO PRESS START, then fell asleep on their couch for eight hours.

I know, I'm pretty good at life.

Let's just say that Jessica is kicking herself right now. (For not marrying that crime reporter, who is now a senior citizen and probably has a sweet pension!)

The next morning, I was so hungover that I honestly forgot about the pants altogether. I chugged some Tropicana Ohranj, showered, and went downstairs like I had just qualified for *The Great Escapes of World War II*.

Then my mom called from the living room and said: "Colin, could you come in here for a minute?"

I was like, "If it's for a high five, can I owe you one? My arms are super tired from all the journalism I was writing last night."

And my dad was like, "Get in here. *Now.*"

I came into the living room like Lucy entering Narnia for the first time—full of curiosity yet wary of some unspeakable evil that lay ahead.

Even worse, my mom had also called in my younger brother, who was way more confused than I was.

She told him: "I want you to be here for this too." (Side note: WHY?!?!)

There was a long disappointed pause, then my mom said: "Do you want to tell us what happened last night?"

Immediately my brother, Casey, was *thrilled.* This was his greatest dream come true. He always got in trouble at school, and I always escaped trouble at school (mainly because my grades were good, unlike my brother, who has literally read one book in his entire life and I'm not sure he actually finished it. If you're curious, it's a book of Greek myths).

Casey smiled at me like the White Witch with a box of Turkish Delight and said, "Now, what is this all about?"

Then my dad said: "Look, we know . . . 'accidents' happen. People don't always . . . 'make it' to the bathroom."

At which point my brother slapped his forehead and his eyes turned to cartoon dollar signs. "WHAT is this ABOUT?"

MY MOM: We . . . found your pants. In the washing machine.

ME: Fuuuuuuuuuuuuuuuuuuuuuuuuuuh.

MY DAD: Again, people make "mistakes." They have "episodes." We just want to make sure this isn't a medical issue.

My mom: Colin, do you think this is a medical issue?

My brother: [does the Maury "I'm not the father" dance]

I had to reassure (lie to) my own parents and tell them this was a "one-time deal" and that "it wouldn't happen again" and that "I'll use my reporter income to buy you a new washing machine."

Thankfully, we never spoke of the Sisterhood of the Troubling Pants again. Except for my brother, who brings it up every year at Christmas, as a gift to himself.

Now if you'll excuse me, I'm going to cut and paste this entire chapter into Web MD and try to figure out what the hell is wrong with me.

Night School

"Stand-up comedy is a very hard thing on the spirit. There are people who transcend it, like Jack Benny and Steve Martin, but in its essence, it's soul-destroying."

—MIKE NICHOLS

"It's in my will: I am not to be revived unless I can do an hour of stand-up."

—JOAN RIVERS

The reason I started doing stand-up was because of a club in the East Village called Rififi. I went to see shows there when I first moved to New York after college, and it was the first time I saw young comics who were really funny, really smart, and weren't afraid to try weird material and fail. It was John Mulaney, Nick Kroll, Jenny Slate, Eugene Mirman, and also guests like Zach Galifianakis, Sarah Silverman, Demetri Martin, and Todd Barry. You could see a ridiculously talented group of people for five dollars and drink troublingly cheap beer while you did it. I saw those comics perform and thought, *That's what I want to do.*

Before that moment, I had loved watching stand-up, but all the comedians I looked up to—particularly Seinfeld and Chris Rock—seemed of a different generation and also way more polished. I never looked at them and thought, *I could do that,* because it seemed impossibly hard to get to that level. Whereas at Rififi, there were comedians who just read aloud from a diner menu and described what kind of fart went with each item of food. And I thought, *Oh, I could definitely do* that . . .

It's telling about stand-up as a vocation that I've been doing it for sixteen years—performing thousands of shows across all fifty states at all hours of day and night—and yet I still barely feel like a stand-up. It's like saying you're a surfer. You might surf *a lot* and be pretty good at it, but unless you've been doing it every single day since you were young, you don't feel totally legit calling yourself a surfer. (Remember, I surfed one wave in New Jersey and needed stitches on my face.)

There were years at SNL where even during show weeks, I was performing stand-up four nights a week. Which is nothing for a full-time comedian, but when you're one of the senior writers at SNL, four nights a week on top of your normal job is *a lot.* I would leave work on my "early" nights—Monday, Wednesday, and Thursday—and do a show at 11 P.M. or midnight. And on my one night off—Sunday—I'd do at least one, sometimes three or four shows. (You know who loved this schedule? My girlfriend!)

One question you get asked a lot as a stand-up is: "What was your worst show ever?"

Sometimes the answer is truly horrible, like when my friend Steve made fun of an audience member, so the audience member called him a "chink," hit him in the back of the skull with a barstool, and Steve had to get staples in his head. Fortunately, I've never been physically assaulted while performing comedy. Though, oddly, I was called a "chink" by a guy in Boston once. (He was *really* drunk. And *really* Boston.)

One of my worst shows took place at noon (as touring comics call it, "a nooner") on a random Tuesday at Finger Lakes Community College in Canandaigua, a five-hour drive north of New York City. (The Finger Lakes region is where Kristen Wiig's character with tiny hands is from.)

I was told the show would take place in the cafeteria, but when they led me to the "stage," I saw it wasn't in the cafeteria at all. It was in a weird empty room adjacent to the cafeteria with ten folding chairs, a plastic table, and a microphone. I wondered, *What is the table for . . .*

The person organizing the show waved in about seven students, who clearly had agreed to attend last-minute out of pity. Then he introduced me: "Hey, guys, this is Colon Jast, and he's gonna do some improvs for you! Oh, and we're putting out pizza on this table directly in front of the microphone, so whenever you want to come up and take a slice, just go for it. All right, sweet! Now give a big Finger Lakes welcome to . . . Colon!"

I entered to zero applause. Just some whispered conversation about what type of pizza they would be serving.

As promised, five minutes into my set, fifteen pizzas* were brought in and placed on the table in front of me. There was a thirty-second grace period where the audience calculated how rude it would be to grab a slice while I was talking. Then the

---

* They were clearly expecting more of a crowd.

first dude decided, *Fuck it, I'm not laughing anyway,* and took a slice. That opened the floodgates.

In fairness, most of the kids looked morally conflicted about interrupting my train of thought to get pizza. One girl grabbed a slice and whispered to me, "Hang in there, it'll be over soon." Little did she know I had forty-five minutes left.

The worst part was that the room had a giant window looking into the actual cafeteria, which was packed. So after a while, the bustling cafeteria (which had no interest in seeing me do stand-up) noticed the presence of pizza. (And except for sex and drugs, pizza is the only thing a college student truly cares about.) This led to a steady stream of football and lacrosse bros peeking into the room, asking each other, "What is this shit?" (re: me), then walking in front of me and digging through pizza boxes until they found the pepperoni.

I did an hour of stand-up for an audience where the pizza outnumbered the humans. It felt like three and a half days. And it only got worse as students came to the front, found no pizza left, and looked at me like I had tricked them with empty boxes. A lot of my jokes ended with, "Sorry . . ."

After about five years of doing mostly "bar shows" downtown, I started making inroads at some of the more mainstream clubs in the city: Carolines, Gotham, the Comic Strip, Stand Up NY, and the Comedy Cellar, which was the most exclusive and also the most intimidating. When I went to see shows at the Cellar, I saw comics like Nick Di Paolo, Colin Quinn, Keith Robinson, Dave Attell, and Jim Norton—guys who were not only ten times funnier than me but also looked like they could physically kick the shit out of me.

What I loved about the Cellar was the intensity of it. The ceilings are like six feet high, it's always packed, and everyone who performs there—from the comic doing his first set to Kevin Hart—wants to kill. It's the club where you know your peers are watching and judging you, and it feels like every set matters. If you do "medium" at the Cellar, you feel like an asshole.

The best comics there could overpower and dominate any crowd. It was the exact opposite of the "alternative" rooms where jokes were generally more cerebral and writerly. The Cellar was energy and power. At Rififi, a joke might bomb and you'd get a laugh from commenting on how badly the joke just bombed. At the Cellar, comics would MAKE you laugh. Like you didn't have a choice. And if you still weren't laughing, they'd physically get in your face and say, "Fuck you." And then you'd laugh out of fear.

My goal from early on was to succeed in both those worlds. I always thought that a great comedian should be able to kill at a random bar show and also kill at the best club in the city.

Around this time, I met a comic named Steve Byrne, who would help me a ton in my stand-up career, as he has done for many other comics. He was doing shows at Gotham Comedy Club that weekend, and he told me to stop by if I wanted to do a set. I did, and afterward he said, "Hey, I liked your set. Want to come on the road and open for me in Hollywood next month?"

I was like, "Whoa. I'm going to Hollywood?"

"That's right, Colin. Hollywood, Florida."

Now, the outskirts of Fort Lauderdale are not everyone's idea of a good time. But I can tell you in all honesty that our weekend at the Seminole Hard Rock Hotel and Casino was one of the greatest weekends of my life.

There were six shows. One Thursday, two Friday, two Saturday, and one Sunday. I was the emcee, Neal Brennan was the feature act, and Steve Byrne was the headliner. I probably made two hundred dollars for the entire weekend, which didn't even cover the cost of the flight and the hotel. But it was worth it.

After the very first show I ever did on the road—the 7 p.m. Thursday show, where I did eight minutes of stand-up to scattered laughter—I was waiting outside the club when two extremely pretty girls walked out and said, "Weren't you just onstage?" I said, "Yes . . ." Then they linked arms with me and asked, "Where to?" Sensing I might never have this opportunity again, I said, "I don't know . . . my hotel room?" They said: "Let's do it." Fort Lauderdale, baby!

Now, I am not one to discuss my love life, even with friends, but I needed to share that story with you because: (a) It was the most insane thing that could ever happen after your *first show* on the road. And (b) because fifteen years later, it has never happened again.

That's correct, I peaked after my first show. I thought, *Whoa . . .* this *is stand-up comedy on the road???* When in fact, my next four years on the road were me sleeping alone in a derelict comedy club "condo" and transitioning into being a headliner who could barely sell tickets.

But I'll always have Fort Lauderdale!

. . .

My next two goals were getting "passed" at the Cellar (which means the owner, Estee, thinks you're good enough to perform there*) and getting chosen for the New Faces showcase at the Montreal Comedy Festival. After being rejected by the festival three years in a row, I finally got a callback. It was at the Broadway Comedy Club at 10 P.M. on a Wednesday and the audience was all drunk foreign tourists. I told myself, *Just do your set the way you want to do it, and don't care about how the audience reacts. Don't get thrown if they don't laugh and they just cough or occasionally burp.*

I thought it went terribly. Then I talked to the other comics, and they thought it went even worse. Turns out that the bookers from the festival were intentionally testing us to see who could survive a hostile crowd. Sticking to the set I wanted to do and not getting thrown was at least half the battle. (There was a second callback that went way better.)

I got chosen for New Faces, along with Fortune Feimster, Jack Whitehall, Mike Lawrence, James Adomian, and my future SNL castmate Melissa Villaseñor. In the '90s, being chosen for New Faces meant getting a sitcom on a major network six months later. For us, it meant meeting the other New Faces and that was pretty much it. But it gave me my first real "credit" as a comedian. After that, when I was introduced to a crowd, they didn't just say, "This guy tells jokes all over town!" They said, "This guy was a 'New Face' at the prestigious Montreal Comedy Festival!" And the crowd went, "Ooooo!" or at least,

---

* I still feel like I'm auditioning every time I go to the Cellar.

"Oh." And later that year, it helped me land my first-ever television appearance on *Late Night with Jimmy Fallon*.

Standing behind the curtain, about to go out on national TV, was one of the most exhilarating panic attacks I've ever had. For the first time ever, I thought, *What if I forget everything I was going to say? What if I walk out and just . . . freeze. What would happen? Would they have to reintroduce me and try it again? Would my career officially end in that one horrible moment?* That was honestly all I could think of before I walked out.

Then the curtain opened and I let go and didn't think about a single thing until it was over. It was like I blacked out until Jimmy was shaking my hand and yelling, "Colin Jost, everyone!"

Years later, I would have the same nervous feeling before I opened for Dave Chappelle at Radio City (one of the coolest moments of my career). I would feel it the first time I ever did Weekend Update. I would feel it before Che and I hosted the Emmys.

Tiger Woods said that he's always nervous before a big tournament because if you're not nervous, it means you don't care. I'm still at least a little nervous before every set I do, even a ten-minute spot at a bar downtown for twenty-five people and zero money. Because I care very deeply about doing a set I'm proud of and that I stand behind. (And I'm always worried that someone will put pizza boxes in front of the stage and derail my entire set.)

.   .   .

I still do about fifty to a hundred shows a year—from theaters around the country to colleges, corporate gigs, casinos, and sometimes just a random show in New York. Stand-up is unlike any other type of performing. You don't have to rely on anyone other than yourself. It's you and a microphone and, beyond that, it can go in any direction you take it.

That's extremely liberating, especially in an industry where so much depends on forces that feel out of your control. If you're funny onstage, it's undeniable. And when you're killing, there's nothing else in the world you'd rather be doing.

I used to write out every single word that I would say onstage, because I was that anal-retentive.* I've since abandoned that practice, but I still make a "set list" for every show that looks like a militia leader outlining his manifesto:

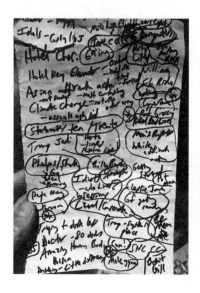 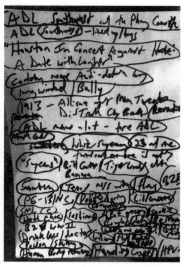

---

* Well . . . anal-retentive about anything that doesn't actually come out of my anus. (See previous chapter.)

Sometimes I'm on an airplane traveling home from a weekend of shows and I'll be looking over seven set lists at once, which looks like this:

And the woman sitting next to me on the plane will be visibly worried.

She'll ask, "So . . . are you . . . a writer?"

"Yes," I'll say. "I'm writing the blueprint for a new humanity."

And that's how you get a whole row to yourself!

Hand Job

"It ain't about how hard you hit. It's about how hard you can *get hit* and keep moving forward."

—ROCKY BALBOA

"Dude . . . have you ever thrown a punch before?"

—DAVE BOLLAND, CHICAGO BLACKHAWKS, TO ME, AGE THIRTY

The year was 2012. Mitt Romney had just secured the Republican nomination for president, Honey Boo Boo was teaching us new words like "redneckognize," and Psy's "Gangnam Style" was on its way to *3.5 billion* views on YouTube. (That is half the population of Earth.)

In more personal news, I had been invited to the Just for Laughs comedy festival in Chicago to tape a fifteen-minute stand-up set that would air on TBS. As someone who had barely appeared on television before, this was a big deal and something I wanted to prepare for intensely.

The only problem was, my friend Steve was getting married the night before my taping—also in Chicago—and his bachelor party was the night before the wedding.

So my weekend schedule was:

Friday—raging bachelor party
Saturday—wedding and after-party till 5 A.M.
Sunday—achieve important career goal

Notice any potential trouble spots?

I should also point out that among Steve's friends were several members of the Chicago Blackhawks hockey team. Ordinarily they would be recognizable figures around the city, and people in bars would buy them drinks because they were famous hometown athletes. (Chicago loves hockey more than almost any other American city.) But this was not an ordinary time. The Blackhawks had just won their first Stanley Cup in *forty-nine years,* which was the longest active drought in the entire league.

So people in Chicago were *really* excited to see the Blackhawks. And the Blackhawks were *really* excited to drink.

Now, I am not a professional hockey player. Therefore I do not have a gigantic super-body capable of absorbing gallons of alcohol in a single sitting. But that didn't stop me from trying! Because even though I'm not athletic, I'm fiercely competitive.

So the bachelor party gets under way at a steakhouse in Chicago.* And I'm attempting to keep pace with a group of much larger men with way fewer inhibitions. We leave dinner, where the group has already consumed approximately 140 bottles of red wine, and waiting outside the restaurant is a Chicago Police Department paddy wagon. I think, *Oh shit. We're* already *arrested?*

---

* I probably could have written "restaurant in Chicago" and you would have known it was a steakhouse.

Then a cop opens the back of the van and says, "Hop in. I'm taking you boys out drinking tonight!"

Now, I realize that is a particularly *white* experience to have in any city: a group of adult men being chaperoned by the police as they drink their way through increasingly sketchy bars across town. But again, this was Chicago. And we were with the World Champion* Chicago Blackhawks. I wasn't going to stop the party and inquire about whether this "special treatment" violated police protocol. (I'm not *that* punchable.)

We proceeded to visit four different dive bars, each time rolling out of a police van as the patrons inside watched and wondered why criminals were allowed to stop for drinks on their way to prison.

Four hours later, we arrived at our final stop: a large warehouse on the side of an expressway, labeled CHICAGO WHIRLYBALL. For those of you who have not had the honor of playing Whirlyball, it's basically bumper cars plus lacrosse sticks plus basketball hoops minus sobriety. You ride around in the bumper cars attempting to ram the other team before they can use their plastic rackets to throw a Wiffle ball into the goal.

As the Whirlyball website explains: "Agility. Speed. Strength. None of these qualities will be of any use in the highly competitive world of Whirlyball."

Athleticism not required? Suddenly, I'm in my element.

We play game after game of Whirlyball and somehow I'm really good at it. I'm scoring goals, I'm setting up teammates, and I'm forcing opponents to leave the game with serious back pain. I've finally found my calling and its name is Whirlyball.

---

* (Really just America and Canada, though . . .)

I'm paired with a bunch of the Blackhawks, so as we keep winning games, I start to think, *Wow. Maybe I* am *a pro athlete after all.* And as I'm gaining this newfound tequila-fueled confidence, one of the Blackhawks yells, "Hey! They have a punching bag over here!"

He's referring to an arcade game where you put coins in the slot and a punching bag descends for the player to hit as hard as he possibly can while the machine measures how hard you can throw a punch. Now, again, I'm among *hockey players.* The only thing they're better at than drinking is punching. But I have now decided that I can "hang" and try to punch as hard as they punch, while continuing to drink as hard as they drink.

I'll pause again, *Dora the Explorer* style, to see if you notice any signs of danger.

¿Notas algún problema?

We take turns punching this arcade game like we're Liam Neeson and the game knows where they've taken our daughter. Just *unloading* on a child's-size punching bag. If the range of scores is between zero and 1,000, the hockey players are punching 900s and I'm punching a 32.

Dave Bolland, who would score the winning goal in the Stanley Cup finals one year later, watches me hit the bag and says, "Dude . . . have you ever thrown a punch before? You have to keep your hand straight and use the weight of your body. Otherwise you're gonna destroy your wrist."

Not wanting to show weakness, I respond, "Uh, I think I know what I'm doing." And I go back to punching with the same terrible form—only harder. And because I've been drinking at a professional hockey level, I cannot feel pain. My fists are rocks and I am the destroyer of worlds. I am like Super Mario after grabbing a star—invincible and also blinking a lot.

I get back to my hotel room at 3 A.M. and crawl into bed with my girlfriend, who must have really appreciated how late it was and how bad I smelled. I whisper (probably at full volume), "Good night, honey! Can't wait to spend the day together tomorrow!" And I fall asleep with all my clothes on.

Two hours later, I wake up. And guess what? I can feel pain again!

In fact, it's the most excruciating pain I've ever felt. *What the hell happened to my hand?* I wonder. *Is there something I did that might have injured it somehow??*

After fifteen minutes of hearing "Ow ow ow ow ow ow ow ow ow ow," my girlfriend is kind enough to escort me to the hospital, where a doctor takes an X-ray and informs me that I've broken my hand.

Me: 32. Punching Bag: 1,000.

We get home at 8 A.M., sleep for a couple hours, and then roll over to the wedding, which is taking place at the Lincoln Park Zoo.

As we arrive at the cocktail hour overlooking the park, my friend Steve and his bride are taking photos in a garden down below. Steve looks up and sees that I have a giant cast on my arm. And he proceeds to laugh so hard, they have to stop taking pictures. We don't even get to talk about it for the first hour. He just occasionally notices me from across the room and starts laughing again.

The Blackhawks players look like they've been partying straight through the night, so in terms of being a hungover derelict, I'm somehow not in the worst shape. I have a broken hand, but they have the thousand-yard stare of a soldier whose mission is to destroy every bottle of alcohol in Illinois. A sensible person would have quit while he was behind and left the reception early to nurse his wounds and prepare for his television appearance the next evening.

But by this point in the book, you must realize that I am not a sensible person. I'm a creature driven by a combination of guilt and FOMO, which often overrides any sense of self-preservation. My thought process was: *I can't half-celebrate my friend's wedding. I need to really go for it. After all, statistically speaking, Steve will only get married two or three more times in his life.* So I ignore my broken hand and my impending stand-up performance, and I give myself over to the night.

This is how it ends:

It's 5 A.M. We've ended up at the apartment of one of the Blackhawks. I'm playing *Big Buck Hunter* (with my good hand) and marveling that a person can have a full Buck Hunter arcade game in their living room. As I'm justifying the night to myself, thinking, *I can use all of this in my act! Besides, when you're in comedy, alcohol is almost a performance-enhancing drug!* Steve brings me a can of PBR. We toast and he tells me, "I'm so glad you're here. I couldn't imagine doing all of this without you."

It was a moment that made the pain and the hospital and the eventual physical therapy worth it. I could almost hear Dionne Warwick singing "THAT'S WHAT FRIENDS ARE FOR—" Then suddenly, there's a loud banging on the door and three cops bust in wearing full riot gear.

Everyone freezes. I become a scared high school student again, and throw my beer on the floor, even though it's perfectly legal for a thirty-year-old man to drink a beer in a private home.

"LISTEN UP!" one of the cops yells. Everyone braces for what's coming next. In my mind, I already have those plastic riot handcuffs on my wrists.

But instead of saying, "YOU'RE ALL UNDER ARREST!" the cop yells, "WHERE THE HELL IS *MY* BEER?"

Everyone cheers. A hockey player throws a cold beer to a cop in full uniform.

How is Chicago really this Chicago?

The next night I filmed my set for TBS, and as you can see from this photo, the cast features prominently! (And the giant Ace bandage *over* the cast makes it look like I'm 5 percent of the way through transforming into a mummy.)

When I recently rewatched the video, I noticed that I'm speaking way too fast and my eyes are darting back and forth

like a maniac. Perhaps because I'd only slept five of the previous sixty hours.

It was not the "career springboard" I had hoped for. In fact, it might be my worst recorded performance. But I did use my experience from the weekend in my set. I pointed out that I had broken my hand in the nerdiest way possible: I got beat up by a video game.

And I learned the hard way that for someone who is very punchable, I am very bad at punching.

SNL Sketchbook

"These are a few of my favorite things."

—Rodgers & Hammerstein

"Eventually, all our graves go unattended."

—Conan O'Brien

There's a reason they're called sketches and not "oil paintings." They're never really finished. They just go on the air because we run out of time to make them better. The show is live and mistakes are made—by actors, directors, camera operators, puppeteers, even sometimes by writers. (Though we would never admit that.)

I've almost never said which sketches I write for the show because, again, I'm Irish Catholic and pride is a sin. But also, I think there's something cool about not knowing who wrote what at SNL. It lets you experiment a little more without the pressure of having something in the show every week, or the stress of people critiquing you directly. You lose the individual glory of being the "credited writer," but hopefully that will come later in life. For now, there is safety in numbers. So you might as well take a big, weird swing.

Another reason I never talk about the sketches I've written is that I truly forget about them within a few days. People ask, "What did you have on the show last week?" And it's like someone asked, "What did you eat for lunch on July 8, 1997?" The next week of work is so daunting that you instantly forget about the previous week. (Unless you wrote a clear hit for the show; then you might savor it for a week or two.)

I've now written more than five hundred sketches that have aired on SNL (along with thousands more that were thrown in the trash). Here are a few that I remember fondly, for various reasons:

Will Ferrell's "Goodnight Saigon" Finale

In Staten Island, Billy Joel's music had a strange, mythical power that danced in our blood and drew our souls together as if seduced by a tribal drumbeat. You could play "Piano Man" in any bar in the tristate area and grown men would sing every word through a veil of tears, as they recalled the lives they could have led, the high school girlfriends they might have married, and that one golden opportunity they would never see again.

Will Ferrell was hosting the season finale, and I wanted to write a farewell sketch that captured that Billy Joel energy in the weirdest way possible. I always kept a playlist of songs that might be useful in a sketch someday, and for reasons I don't fully understand, "Goodnight Saigon" was at the top of that list. It wasn't one of Billy Joel's most popular songs, but it might be his most melodramatic. And I really liked the idea of someone casually mentioning a vacation in Vietnam and then Will Ferrell standing up, with a faraway look in his eyes, and launching into "Goodnight Saigon."

It wasn't picked after the table read, but to Will's credit, he called Lorne late Wednesday night and said, "I think we should try that Billy Joel sketch." And even though it was the very last sketch in the show, Lorne made sure it snuck on the air.

At dress rehearsal, the entire cast went up for the final chorus. And since so many former cast members and hosts were backstage to watch Will, we asked if they wanted to grab a random instrument and walk onstage for the live ending. It ended up being Amy Poehler, Maya Rudolph, Tom Hanks, Anne Hathaway, Elisabeth Moss, Paul Rudd, and Norm Macdonald, who grabbed Artie Lange and brought him onstage, too.

By far the most surreal part of the performance was seeing Artie Lange standing at the end, with no idea what the hell was happening or why he was suddenly a part of this sketch. As far as I know, it's the only time he's appeared on SNL. And when it ends, you can hear an audience member yell, "Hey, Artie!" I don't remember ever hearing an audience member yell something on camera, before or since.

It was also Darrell Hammond's last show after fifteen seasons and he had the last line in the sketch, which was: "Why do we always fall for that?" Kind of a great last thing to say at SNL.

"Red Flag Perfume"

I wrote a farewell sketch for Kristen Wiig when she left the show, but this commercial was as much a tribute to her power on SNL as that farewell was. It was a perfume for women who present a lot of "red flags," like how she "lived in Vegas for eleven years" and "one of her pinky nails is waaaaay longer than the rest." It's a premise that could have worked for a lot of different actors, but Kristen's performance and the way our director Rhys Thomas shot her elevated it to something special.

It was the first thing that aired after the monologue during the season premiere, and I still have the perfume bottle, which was just a Chanel No. 5 bottle with a RED FLAG logo taped over it.

Drunk Uncle

It's a testament to how great a performer Bobby Moynihan is that he could say some truly awful things and still get huge laughs.

Drunk Uncle embodied what I loved the most about writing with cast members on the show: getting to fully develop a character with his own world and his own defined set of values, and then leaving enough space between jokes for the cast member to just perform. Bobby had real power. He could yell, cry, whimper, burp, giggle, fall asleep, and make you laugh doing all of it. He was fully in that character in a way that's especially hard on a live show.

We did it thirteen times, but over the course of five years because we didn't want people to get sick of it. Every time it aired, my actual uncle asked, "We good?"

"George W. Bush Returns Cold Open"

After a year of writing for Trump, writing for George W. Bush again seemed so much sillier and happier. You might think W. was a terrible president, but it's hard to argue that he's not a decent man who cares a lot more about America than our current president. And using him to put Trump in perspective was a lot of fun.

Will is so precise and so at ease at the same time. For every joke you write for him, he makes it a joke and a half. He obviously has a complete command of that character, and it was almost like fantasy camp getting to write for him. My favorite line was about the Iraqi reporter who threw two shoes at him during a press conference: "Shoe me once, shoe's on you. Shoe me twice . . . I'm keeping those shoes."

I also felt a sense of things coming full circle with this sketch, because in the writing packet I submitted to SNL in 2005, one of the sketches was a speech from George W. Bush, and it was really satisfying to do it for real fourteen years later.

"Can I Play That? Game Show"

I had been trying to figure out some version of this sketch for weeks but couldn't quite crack it. There were so many actors getting burned for doing parts they "shouldn't do" that I started wondering how far it would go. Bryan Cranston got shit for playing a character in a wheelchair because he wasn't in a wheelchair in real life. Will Smith was told he shouldn't play the father of Venus and Serena Williams because "he wasn't black enough." It seemed like the fundamental definition of acting was changing, so I came up with a game show called *Can I Play That?* where the host described a role and the actor-contestants had to decide if it was a role they were allowed to play.

You could sum up the entire sketch with this exchange between Kenan and our host, Idris Elba:

> IDRIS: Isn't that what acting is about? Becoming someone you're not?
>
> KENAN: Not anymore. Now it's about becoming yourself, but with a different haircut.

"Trick-or-Treat"

The premise of this sketch was: What if a convicted sex offender went door to door on Halloween and said his costume was "sex offender" and then had people sign a paper acknowledging that he was a sex offender "as part of his costume."

I had tried it the year before with host Brian Williams, oddly enough, but it got cut. Then we performed it at the SNL Strike Show at Upright Citizens Brigade during the writers' strike in 2008 and thought, *Maybe we should try this again.* (When it's a holiday-themed sketch, you really only get one shot a year.)

I just rewatched it for the first time in ten years and the ending is a real roller coaster.

Will Forte says: "If I'm guilty of *anything* . . . it's the crime of sexually assaulting five teenagers."

(Audience reacts with horror.)

Will: "Now, this is gonna sound like a terrible segue, but are you guys looking for a babysitter?"

Then Will turns to camera and says, "Happy Halloween! *Whaaaaat?*"

And it freezes on his face as text appears: "Happy Halloween from SNL."

If that's not an ending, I don't know what is.

The Girl You Wish You Hadn't Started a Conversation with at a Party

Even fans of this character have no idea what the character's official name is.

Che's mom calls her "The Girl Who Gets Everything Wrong."

Cecily Strong and I sat in her office during her first week at

SNL and wrote this in probably an hour because, once she had the voice, it felt like writing downhill. We all know someone like this who is insanely strident with almost zero understanding of the facts:

"There are homeless people out there who can't even pay their mortgages."

"People who are orphans are twice as likely to not have parents."

"There are high school students who can't even point out India on a map of Africa."

"People with Ebola aren't even sick of the Ebola. They're sick of the hypocrisy."

Cecily is a real genius and it was pure joy to write these together.

"Diner Lobster"

Here is the header for the script we submitted in 2010 with host Zach Galifianakis:

```
(JOST/MULANEY)(FIRST DRAFT — March 3, 2010)                    1


DINER LOBSTER ~ Zach/Fred/Will/Andy/Jason/Kenan/Kristen/Bobby/
                Extras
```

And here is the one that aired in 2018:

```
(JOST/MULANEY) (SECOND DRAFT - APRIL 11, 2018)

DINER LOBSTER ~ JOHN/KENAN/PETE/CHRIS/KATE/CECILY/LUKE/MIKEY
```

Kenan was the only cast member remaining from our first attempt (when it bombed at the table read), but this time we wisely switched Kenan to the role of Jean Valjean. And the rest, as they say, is lobster-y.

This sketch stemmed from two religious beliefs that John Mulaney and I shared: (1) that *Les Miz* is the greatest musical of all time, and (2) that lobster only appears on diner menus as a joke.

We did a sequel a year later called "Bodega Bathroom." And if I had to guess, the next one will be called "Airport Sushi."

Porn Stars

The hosts we did this recurring sketch with were Justin Timberlake, Tina Fey, Jonah Hill, Jamie Foxx, James Franco, Andy Samberg, Ben Affleck, Chris Hemsworth, and Donald Trump. That's a pretty insane combination of people to be in a sketch about two porn stars selling merchandise they can't pronounce. Vanessa Bayer and Cecily are amazing on their own, and together they had a perfect rhythm and a dark, dead-eyed confidence.

I remember when Leslie Jones started at the show as a writer, she had never seen them perform this sketch before. We read through the script at the rewrite table and Leslie said, "Oh my god. This isn't funny! These women's lives are so sad!"

Then I looked at the script and saw Vanessa's line: "One time I banged a quiet guy, but it turned out it was a corpse. I was like, 'Hey, it's your funeral!' And his family was like, 'Yes it is, now get out of the coffin.'"

I thought, *That is pretty sad . . .*

But then I saw Cecily's line: "One time I thought I banged E.T., but it was just an old Chinese man on a bike."

And that made me happy again.

The first brand they talked about was Swarovski crystals and Swarovski sent them free jewelry. We thought, *Whoa, we better do one about Lamborghinis next time!* We did. And then we did eleven more luxury brands after that. Never got a single free thing again. You'd think Hermès would have been more grateful that we called them "Herpes."

"Yo! Where Jackie Chan at Right Now?"

Kenan and I shared an office for *eight years* at the show. We wrote a lot of truly dumb sketches together, like a talk show that Barry White hosted from heaven, a sketch for Gabourey Sidibe called "Crazy Woman Yelling Out a Window," and a commercial parody called "Bathroom Businessman," where Kenan tries to set up an entire office inside a bathroom stall, then gets trapped behind the desk and shits his pants. (I clearly drew on my own experience for that one.)

But "Yo! Where Jackie Chan at Right Now?" is maybe my

favorite one we ever wrote together, because the entire sketch is just Kenan and Tracy Morgan asking ten different guests, "Where Jackie Chan at?"

By the time Sasheer Zamata shows up as the woman from *Carmen Sandiego*—in a sketch about Jackie Chan—you know the sketch is off the rails. *Then* Pete Davidson appears as "Young Osama bin Laden" holding a skateboard. And someone pointed out, "Hey . . . maybe you should ask Pete about that because Osama bin Laden killed his dad on 9/11 . . ." So I talked to Pete and apologized and he said, "Oh dude, I'm doing it. It's fucking hilarious."

Not sure what the audience thought about any of it.

"Bidet"

Okay, this is a sketch about a bidet, but I stand by it. John Solomon and I went on a surf trip together to Puerto Rico and there was an old fancy hotel in Rincón called the Horned Dorset. We went to look at the rooms, which were way too expen-

sive for us, and every bathroom had a bidet. The person showing us the rooms kept pointing out the bidet like it was the most important thing in the room and we thought, *That could be a sketch* . . .

It's Andy Samberg as a hotel employee giving a tour to a wealthy couple, Zach Galifianakis and Kristen Wiig, but the couple's only questions are about the bidet. "Is there . . . a sturdiness to the bidet?" "Could the water pressure to the bidet be . . . increased substantially?" "Is there a . . . hospital nearby? For bidet-related injuries?"

They all play it perfectly straight, and it almost seems like a "British sketch," even though I don't quite know what that means.

"Brett Kavanaugh Cold Open"

This one was tricky. It was a super delicate subject that was painful for a lot of people, and I wasn't sure we should write

about it at all—until I watched Brett Kavanaugh's testimony in response to Dr. Christine Blasey Ford's allegations of sexual assault. Kavanaugh came out so aggressively and with such conspiratorial anger at "the Clintons" and a left-wing "circus" that I thought, on a basic level, *How is this person going to be an impartial judge?* What other Supreme Court nominee used their testimony to call out their enemies and say things like "What goes around, comes around"?

I sat down to write with Kent Sublette the next day, on Friday night around 8 P.M., and finished around 4 A.M. Lindsay Shookus, who runs our talent department, reached out to Matt Damon around midnight and, despite the fact that he was in California and hadn't seen a script yet, he said yes and got on a plane an hour later.

He landed in New York Saturday morning, slept for about forty-five minutes, drank one beer to get into character, and delivered an incredible performance. PJ, Squee, and Donkey Dong Doug would have been proud.

"The Real Housewives of Disney"

I wrote "The Real Housewives of Disney" with Marika Sawyer, because we thought the casting for all the women on our show would line up perfectly with the Disney princesses. As the child of two Disney fanatics, this sketch was very much in my vocabulary. Then Marika caught me up on the real *Real Housewives* and my mind was blown.

My favorite moments are when Jasmine confesses that she slept with Iago the parrot because it was dark and he was mimicking Aladdin's voice; and when Snow White holds up her hand after bad-mouthing Cinderella and seven dwarf hands reach into frame to give her a high-five.

Plus, anytime you have Lindsay Lohan as Rapunzel getting her weave torn off, you're in a good spot.

"Under-Underground Festival"

DJ SUPERSOAK

Mike O'Brien (who later created *A.P. Bio*) had the idea of doing a promo for a festival like Insane Clown Posse's Gathering of the Juggalos, and at 2 A.M. on a writing night he said to me, "You want to brainstorm some acts that would appear at the festival?"

It ended up being one of our favorite things to write, because where else on television do you hear phrases like:

"Come play Farmville with Khalid Sheikh Mohammed!"
"Or see stand-up comedy from the Menendez Brothers!"
"Plus, a live sex show by the green M&M!"
"And former surgeon general C. Everett Koop challenges
    you to a mayonnaise fight!"

Each sketch is only two minutes long, yet there are four recurring characters—Jason Sudeikis as DJ Supersoak, Nasim

Pedrad as Lil' Blaster, Bobby Moynihan as "Ass Dan" (who dies in every episode), and Jay Pharoah as "MC George Costanza," who is missing most of his teeth and makes dolphin noises after everything he says.

It has to be one of the strangest things that's ever aired on our show, and definitely the strangest thing that aired five separate times.

"Everyone. Gets. A pitchfork!"

"Schoolhouse Rock Cold Open"

It was hard to write cold opens in the Obama era because he wasn't on television every day attacking American companies or re-tweeting white supremacists. But he did use an executive order to circumvent Congress on immigration, and it seemed like "Schoolhouse Rock" was a way to make that subject a little more bearable. (With cold opens, anything that's not a president talking at a desk is a win in my book.)

First Kenan appears as a cartoon "Bill" that is working its way through Congress. Then President Obama pushes the bill down the Capitol steps and introduces "An Executive Order."

Bobby walks in smoking, and his only line was: "I'M AN EXECUTIVE ORDER/AND I PRETTY MUCH JUST HAPPEN!"

The whole sketch was three and a half minutes long and it was one of the only clean hits on Obama that entire season.

"Sean Spicer Press Conference"

Kent Sublette, Rob Klein, and I wrote the three Sean Spicer sketches for Melissa McCarthy, who gave one of the most powerful performances ever on the show, especially for a political sketch.

The first one was my favorite because the audience had no idea what was coming. It wasn't even the cold open. It was, like, the fifth sketch in the show. Melissa walked out to the podium as the White House press secretary. The audience laughed and cheered in anticipation of a Sean Spicer send-up. Then, after a few seconds, they realized: *Holy shit, that's Melissa McCarthy under there!* And there's a whole second wave of applause and cheering.

Then Melissa just *attacked* for six minutes—vocally, physically, with props and puppets, and with the podium itself. It was like an entire one-woman show in a single sketch. The only break was when Kate McKinnon appeared as Secretary of Education Betsy DeVos and said, "I think there should be school."

"Election Night"

Neal Brennan (who was guest-writing for the Chappelle episode) was in my office on election night and we were talking about what to write, but all the ideas were based on Hillary Clinton winning. We were thinking about a version of *Training Day*, where Chappelle as Obama took Kate as Hillary on a ride-along for her first day in office.

The election results started coming in. The first one was a deep-red state like Alabama. And we joked that if Hillary couldn't win Alabama, it was over! Then she won New York and California, and she was already halfway there. It didn't

seem demographically possible that she would lose. People forget, but newscasters at the time were saying things like, "This is the end of the Republican Party! Statistically, they can never win again!"

Then you got to states like Michigan, Wisconsin, and Pennsylvania, and we thought, *She can't lose* all *of those states . . . right?*

Once it became clear that Trump had won, all our previous ideas became sad garbage. And we said, "Maybe we should just try to write about how the night unfolded in real time. And then Dave Chappelle's character can be the only one who sees it coming from a mile away."

There was an extra line at dress rehearsal: "Who did you really think white women were going to vote for? A rich guy, or a woman who's more successful than them?"

The audience was *not* ready to hear that!

Screen Test Sketches

This format was done long before I got to SNL (see the *Star Wars* screen tests from 1997), but bringing it back for *Top Gun* and *Back to the Future* was really fun because it meant getting to write for Bill Hader as Alan Alda, Al Pacino, and Harvey Fierstein, all of which were historically great impressions. Plus, Kenan as Sinbad, Jon Hamm as Robin Williams, and Alec Baldwin as a whole different era of Al Pacino. Fred Armisen also destroys as Prince—twice—without saying a word. Because sometimes writing means not writing at all.

More than anything, these are a testament to our wardrobe and hair departments. They prepared multiple looks for almost every single cast member in less than twenty-four hours. (Including a look for me as an '80s production assistant. Probably my first appearance on camera.)

"Mom Celebrity Translator"

This was one of my first commercial parodies on the show—
a pocket translator that interpreted the name of a celebrity

that your mom was at-
tempting to pronounce
correctly, but butchering.

This was 100-percent
based on my own mother,
who is incapable of pro-
nouncing the name of
any celebrity. Even names
like "Kate Hudson" she
will find a way to butcher.
("Is it Cart Hummus?")

The more troubling part is that my mom is a doctor and
writes prescriptions and I can't imagine she is pronouncing the
names of drugs properly either. So if you need Valtrex, she
might give you Viagra. And then the problem will only get
worse.

And last (and least?): "Sloths!"

This is a stop-motion short film about wildly aggressive rock
'n' roll sloths.

Jorma Taccone deserves the real credit for animating this
entire piece, along with our graphics coordinator, Tara Don-
nelly, who had to find two thousand usable images of sloths.
But Jorma, Andy, Jason, and I wrote this fever dream over the
course of a week when we had nothing else going on in the

show. Lorne had no idea we were working on it. Then on Saturday we said, "Hey . . . we got this thing about sloths . . . if you want to try it at dress rehearsal . . ." And somehow it snuck on the show.

Thank god Jorma and Andy had a microphone in their office so no one else had to hear us record lines like *"Shank your mom with a pterodactyl dick bone!"* or *"Eat cocaine off America's gravestone!"* You know, sloth stuff.

I got to do my first ever voiceover at the beginning of the sketch, and I name-dropped my hometown Staten Island Zoo (New York City's third best zoo!). Jorma and I went on to write several other non-hits together, including a sketch for Shia LaBeouf where his parents tell him, "You need to settle down, mister! No more monkey business!" And then Shia walks into his bedroom and there are six monkeys operating a business, making phone calls and closing deals. The sketch got cut, but none of the monkeys ripped off anyone's face or genitals, so we considered that a win.

Honorable Mention:

"Big Papi" David Ortiz on Weekend Update

"Don Draper's Guide to Picking Up Women"

"*CSI: Sarasota*" with Betty White

"*The Miley Cyrus Show*" (with Vanessa Bayer and Rob Klein)

And a sketch about the film *Black Swan* that John Solomon and I wrote for Jim Carrey, who screamed so loudly in the scene that he accidentally pooped his leotard. *That's* commitment.

Weekend Update, Part I

Am I Destroying a Beloved Franchise?

"If you don't want to be great, then step aside and let someone else be great."

—ANTHONY DAVIS, LOS ANGELES LAKERS

"On your first Update, whatever you do, don't take an awkward moment to introduce yourself."

—JIMMY FALLON, A WEEK BEFORE I STARTED UPDATE

The very first thing I did on Weekend Update was take an awkward moment to introduce myself.

I said something to the effect of "Wow-wee! This is a dream come true and I really hope I don't screw it up! Aw, shucks!" Something truly humiliating. I'm not sure of the exact phrasing because I've never rewatched it—I'm afraid I might puke.

It wasn't even my idea. In fact, at dress rehearsal I didn't introduce myself at all, we just went right into jokes. And that would have been *so much better*. But one of the writers said, "You have to introduce yourself. Otherwise it's weird." And in that moment, fifteen minutes before I went on live TV for the first time ever in front of ten million people, I forgot Jimmy's advice, and I introduced myself because I thought I *needed to*.

That's two lessons I learned very quickly: (1) You don't *need* to do anything in life—if it feels wrong or unnatural, it probably is. And (2) I had no one but myself to blame for not trusting my own instincts and pushing back when I felt something was wrong.

When I started doing Update, I was operating purely out of fear. I had spent the last eight years doing stand-up to be prepared in case this moment ever happened, but that entire time I had also been a writer at SNL. So within the walls of 30 Rock, that was my identity: a writer. That was how most people at work thought of me. That was how I earned most of my money. That's where I derived all of my self-esteem. That's what I wrote on my tax returns under *Occupation:* "Writer." [And then, under *Marital Status,* I wrote, "I never kiss and tell. ;-)"]

With Weekend Update, I was about to start a very different job but in the same exact place, which is strange. Think about it. If you were working at McDonald's for eight years and your job was making Big Macs, it would be a little jarring if one day you showed up dressed as a clown and announced that your new job title was Ronald McDonald. Your coworkers would probably think, *Why does this jackass get to be Ronald McDonald?* And you're like, "Well, I've actually been doing some light clowning on the side . . ." I was terrified about ruining both my writing and performing careers at once. Because if you get promoted to Ronald McDonald and then you, say, touch a kid, they don't let you go back to making Big Macs.

I also had a larger fear: *Can I do this job? Or will I try to do what* *the people I looked up to did and fail miserably and then I guess just . . . combust?* Basically, I was terrified of fucking it up. And that might be the single worst instinct to have when you're trying to make something your own. The existing structure of Weekend Update was defined by Chevy Chase (and immediately before us by Seth Meyers), and I was so worried about messing that up that I didn't even think about changing it. My goal was maintenance, not reinvention.*

The first eight Updates I did with Cecily Strong from March to May of 2014 were like getting hit by a truck, and then the truck transformed into Optimus Prime and started kicking the shit out of me. I would drink a glass of bourbon before dress rehearsal, another between dress and air, and a third before I went on. And I never felt drunk once. The fear and the adrenaline burned it right off. Those eight shows are a complete blur and I couldn't tell you a single joke I told or a single moment I remember. It was a three-month-long, out-of-body experience.

What I do remember—quite vividly in fact—were the reviews. And to say that they were "negative" would be like saying Pol Pot received negative reviews. If I had a Yelp page, it would have been a thousand 1-star all-caps tirades with the words "Closed Permanently" under my name.

I'm paraphrasing from memory, but here are a few samples:

"Why are my eyes and ears bleeding? Oh, it's because Colin Jost is on camera. That makes sense now." —*The New York Newspaper*

---

* Of course I only realized this in retrospect. At the time, my goal was simply: Don't physically die on camera.

"I rarely use the word 'hate' and I rarely put words in bold-face and underline them and italicize them, but I **<u>hate</u>** Colin Jost." —*USA Tomorrow*

"I'm finding out where Colin Jost lives and I'm going to murder him." —*That Stalker Who Came to My House and Tried to Murder Me*

"Two Stars." —*My Aunt in Her Annual Christmas Letter*

So the press was not great, but at least the ratings were . . . immediately worse. The moment we debuted on Update, SNL lost 1.5 million viewers. Right after I told my first joke, the Nielsen company reported "seismic activity" from so many people changing the channel at the same time. It was the loudest America had ever said "No thank you" since the Dustin Diamond sex tape.

Here's the thing: Until you're on TV, you never think, *I wonder how America will perceive me?* I was just me. I didn't over-think it. And I was thirty! So I'd had a long time being me. Then suddenly, when I was on camera, I panicked and thought, *WHO AM I????* Then people at work, who were trying to give helpful advice, would say things like "Hold your head this way" or "Don't smile too much, but also don't *not* smile." To the point where suddenly I was not only questioning who I was on camera but also who I was in real life. I started worrying, *Do I smile weird in real life or something?* (Answer: Probably.)

And when you're unsure of yourself, people give you even *more* advice, because they want to help. And that confused me even further. Here's just a sample of the actual advice I got from producers, writers, and former anchors when I started doing Update:

"Be yourself."

"Be a newscaster first and foremost."

"You need a persona that's not quite you and not quite a newscaster."

"Treat it like you're entering church and the desk is the altar."

"Relax and have fun."

"Never look like you're having fun out there."

"Look at the camera like it's your best friend."

"Look at the camera like it's a girl you want to fuck."

"Seduce the cue cards."

"Let your mouth hang open, but not *open* open."

"Don't move your hands like you're Italian."

"Could your chair be higher and your hair be lower?"

"Could your voice not sound like Kermit the Frog's?"

And my favorite:

"Maybe you could just be a straight man?"

It's my fault for allowing all these different voices into my head. As a result, I never felt physically present at all. I would get nervous and my reaction was to smile or laugh on camera, which was unnatural and probably came across as smug or overconfident even though I had zero confidence and was acting out of pure fear.

The other thing is: If you're a regular cast member on SNL, people might hate a *character* you do or might criticize your *impression* of, say, JonBenét Ramsey. But when you're on Update, people hate *you*. There's no hiding behind a different per-sona or an accent. Plus, if you're a regular cast member and you're new on the show, you might only appear briefly on your first couple episodes as a waiter or, say, JonBenét Ramsey, just to get your feet wet. Whereas with Update, the first time I was ever on camera was for *ten minutes straight*. And when you're new and bad, that feels like an eternity.

It didn't help that I was following Seth, whom most people really liked. Now Seth was gone, and most people essentially hated me. I like to quote Gilbert Gottfried, who was part of the second SNL cast, which took over from the original group in 1980. Gilbert said, "Imagine! At the height of Beatlemania! If they took away the Beatles and replaced them with . . . *a whole new bunch of Beatles!*"

And that happens a lot with SNL. When a certain cast exits, it takes a while for the show to adjust and find a new voice. I started as a writer with Kristen Wiig, Andy Samberg, Bill Hader, and Jason Sudeikis, which is one of the strongest casts to start together in the history of the show. And they had time to adjust because they blended in really well with the existing cast—Amy Poehler, Maya Rudolph, Fred Armisen, Will Forte, and baby Kenan Thompson. After that, Bobby Moynihan was the only new cast member hired for three or four years, so ev-eryone gelled into a real unit.

But when that whole group departed, the show struggled for a while because the cast was suddenly new and unfamiliar. And I was squarely in the middle of those growing pains (™ Kirk Cameron), both as a head writer and as the new guy on Update. I was also just depressed that a huge group of my friends were suddenly gone, and I felt like the kid who's still stuck in high school when all his friends have graduated and started cooking meth.

But with all the criticism, I never felt bad for myself because (a) I deserved a lot of it early on, and (b) that's what I signed up for! Any promotion or opportunity you get in life comes with increased exposure and increased criticism. The more people want your job, the more shit you're gonna get for not doing it well. And the more famous you get, the more people are gonna hate you.

But everything is motivation. You get punched and it snaps you into focus. And the reviews definitely felt like a punch. (Several critics would have physically punched me if they could have.) As with most punches, it hurt a lot. I took all the criticism to heart and I was really, really sad for about two full years of my life. I felt like I sucked at the thing I most wanted to do in the world, and that is *not* a pleasant feeling.* I actually thought about quitting many times. I thought, *Shit, I'm trying my best and people really don't like me. Maybe I should just quit so everyone on Earth can celebrate.*

Then I got angry and thought: *Fuck you, dickheads. You didn't work all your life to achieve this. I did. And I'm gonna do it—and do it my way—until someone pulls me off this desk.*

And the person who helped me come to that realization was Michael Che.

---

* I also started feeling like I was a bad *person* because some people viscerally hated me so much. That's such a dumb, irrational mind-set but I couldn't help it.

Weekend Update, Interlude

Am I Still Doing Weekend Update?

"When you go to auditions and you fail to prepare, prepare to fail."

—Paula Abdul

After those rough first eight episodes on Weekend Update, the season ended and the most confusing summer of my life began. I had no idea whether I would be doing Update in the fall. I had no idea if I would get rehired as a writer. I didn't know whether to move to L.A. and start looking for a job, or move to Puerto Rico and start living off the grid in a rain forest.

That's actually where my mind goes when work is terrible: *I could always disappear and move to Rincón and write erotic thrillers under a pseudonym like "Madame Z." I could build a log cabin in the forest, cease all communication with friends and family, and let my mind descend into madness like Kurtz in* Heart of Darkness. I think this at least once a month. (The main obstacle: I have no idea how to build a log cabin.)

Instead I spent the summer touring and doing stand-up, and I decided that whatever happened with Update, I wanted to get better as a performer. I didn't know how, exactly, outside of getting onstage every night, so I started meeting with an acting coach. This was something I hesitated about doing for a long time because I was embarrassed. Isn't that dumb? I was embarrassed about getting help. And I was embarrassed about *trying*. I was scared to put myself out there and commit to getting better, because if I committed and failed then I would have no one to blame but myself. (This probably described my approach to all my relationships up to that point, too.)

What I realized was: I might never have this chance again. In fact, I almost certainly would never have this chance again. Did I really want to look back and think: I *could* have done more, but I was afraid people would think I was lame for trying too hard?

I decided to try really hard.

Well, I should clarify that, because I was already trying really hard, but at several different things simultaneously. I was a head writer at SNL, I was a headlining stand-up comedian who toured around the country, and I was filming a movie for Paramount. I decided to narrow it down to the one thing I cared about most: Weekend Update. I stepped down as head writer. I stopped going on the road to do stand-up during off weeks. And I let the director and the studio edit the movie I wrote. I wanted to succeed at one thing instead of failing at four.

The only problem was, I didn't know if I still had the one job I wanted most.

In August, I got a call from Lorne's office: They were going to hold auditions for Weekend Update.

So I was going to *audition* for the job I already had. Call me crazy, but that didn't sound very promising.

I would be auditioning with Vanessa Bayer, Leslie Jones, Chris Kelly (who was a writer at SNL at the time), Sasheer Zamata, and Michael Che. We all met up for a few days before the auditions and wrote jokes together and picked other jokes written by the Update staff. It was actually a great process, because everyone who auditioned was really funny. It was like figuring out five different versions of Weekend Update that could have all worked in different ways. I temporarily forgot the stress of potentially losing my job and just enjoyed this weird moment where we were all trying random stuff we thought could work. That was the good part.

The frustrating part was the actual auditions. We were all supposed to rehearse once in the studio, then do it for real on camera with Lorne and all the producers sitting in chairs watching us like they do for cast member auditions. Instead, Lorne decided at the last second to scrap the run-through and do it directly on camera.

So there was zero rehearsal for what was probably one of the most important moments in all of our lives. I remember that halfway through the auditions, I was so angry at Lorne for not letting us rehearse that I actually got better. My skills were sharpened by rage, like Mel Gibson in *Braveheart,* or Mel Gibson in *The Patriot,* or Mel Gibson during a routine traffic stop. It snapped me back into the moment and I stopped overthinking any one joke. That might have saved my audition.

But it was still a demoralizing exercise and, if anything, I felt further from keeping my job than I had before. To this day, I don't know what Lorne and the producers wanted from those auditions, or what they learned from them. I just know that I felt like I'd failed.

The other unknown in this whole process was Cecily. We had done eight episodes together and she had done another twelve episodes or so with Seth before he left. Cecily was unquestionably a better performer than I was, but I didn't know if she wanted to keep doing Update or go back to doing Update Features again, like Girl at a Party and a bunch of other characters that were huge hits for her. Or maybe she wanted to do Update with someone else. I had no clue what she or Lorne was thinking.

One of the reasons we did Update together in the first place was because Cecily and I wrote together a lot. She's one of the funniest performers in the history of our show, and also one of the best writers.

When we wrote "The Girl You Wish You Hadn't Started a Conversation with at a Party," it was Cecily's *first show ever* on SNL. I was so excited about it that I didn't want to jinx it, because a cast member's first show is so stressful that you never know if something will go horribly wrong. We had no idea if it would even air on the show, let alone work in front of a live audience.

I remember watching Cecily in the studio live, and she hit every single beat perfectly. It was really incredible for someone's first time on national TV. I talked to Seth right after and both of us were blown away. She had an ease and rhythm to her performance that seemed like she had been in the cast for five years already. It was a very special moment that doesn't happen as often as you would think.

I'm guessing that's why Lorne wanted her to do characters again on Update rather than being an anchor. But I didn't know what Lorne or the producers were thinking, because everyone at SNL stopped talking to me. It was like your family stopped returning your calls. I was already jumping ahead to what I would do next: Audition for movies? Write a YA fantasy novel? Accept my destiny and become a New York City firefighter? (My mom definitely floated this idea.)

A week later, I got a call from my manager at the time. "Hey . . . so . . . congrats?"

That was "congrats" with a question mark.

Which was an extremely confusing thing to hear.

"Congrats about what?" I asked. "Are you telling me that I'm doing Weekend Update?"

"Oh. Uh . . . I don't know. Are you not?"

"What the hell is going on?"

"Oh. Uh . . . don't say anything . . . but I think maybe you and Che are gonna do it?"

"You *think*? Where is this coming from?"

"Oh. Uh . . . I don't know. Forget I said anything. Okay, good luck."

Good luck?!?!

Five minutes later, I got an angry call from one of the producers at SNL: "DID YOU TELL YOUR MANAGER THAT YOU GOT WEEKEND UPDATE???"

To which I replied: "WHAT THE HELL ARE YOU TALK-ING ABOUT???? *AM I EVEN DOING WEEKEND UPDATE???* NO ONE HAS TALKED TO ME IN A WEEK. HOW WOULD I TELL MY MANAGER INFORMATION THAT NO ONE HAS TOLD ME? I HAVEN'T TOLD MY MANAGER A SIN-GLE THING IN FIVE YEARS. I DON'T TELL MY THERA-PIST MAJOR THINGS THAT HAPPEN IN MY LIFE. SERIOUSLY WHAT THE FUCK IS HAPPENING?"

To which the producer said: "Lorne is really mad about this. I don't know what's going to happen now."

Suddenly it seemed like I *did* get the job, but then immedi-ately *lost it* because of something my manager said. Which was mind-boggling to me because (a) I didn't think Lorne even knew who my manager was, and (b) I HADN'T TOLD MY MANAGER A SINGLE THING IN FIVE YEARS.

The whole exchange was so disturbing, I thought: *At this point, I don't even care if I get Update!* But of course I did care, very deeply. I was just behaving like the '90s emo teen I se-cretly dreamed of becoming.

I don't remember how I found out that my manager's creepy information was somehow accurate. But he was right: Michael Che and I were doing Weekend Update together—question mark. Because until you're actually on the air, you have no idea if Lorne will change his mind and give it to someone else.

So, to recap: It could have been about twenty different com-binations of anchors for Weekend Update. I disappointed most of America by being part of the winning combo. And I was extremely motivated to prove that I could do it.

The entire process was like an Eastern European roller

coaster where a couple people fall off at every turn and if you're still alive at the end, they hand you a chicken.

Michael and I had chickens. Now it was up to us to murder them and eat them.

And don't worry, I can say that. I've won a PETA Award.

Weekend Update, Part II

Figuring Shit Out

"Sometimes it takes a long time to learn how to play like yourself."

—MILES DAVIS

"Oh my god, please do not quote Miles Davis."

—LESLIE JONES

At the end of my second season on Update, I ran into Chris Rock in the hallway of 30 Rock and he said, "Hey! You're still here!"

Not *Good job!* Not *You've made it, kid!* Just "You're still here!" Like, "They haven't kicked you out of the building yet!" And that's exactly how I felt: I was still there. After two years of grinding and feeling completely lost, still having the job actually felt like a huge accomplishment. But I didn't have any confidence.

One of the reasons I was still there was Leslie Jones. She helped me a lot early on. I was so in my head, overthinking every joke—but when Leslie came on Update, she would literally shake me out of my head and into my body. She forced me to be present in the moment with her, the same way she forced the audience to sit up and pay attention. I'll always be grateful to Leslie for making me better, especially when a lot of Update felt like a work in progress. And by "work in progress" I mean an empty lot with a pile of loose bricks and a detached toilet seat.

Every summer for the first three years of doing Update, I was convinced I was getting fired. Then I turned a corner and thought, *If I'm gonna get fired, I might as well get fired doing what I believe in.* And after that moment, I never tried a joke unless I wanted to try it. I never went along with a bit I thought was lame just to appease someone else. And I truly didn't care about getting fired. I wanted to tell jokes and write sketches that I cared about and not really worry about anything that was out of my control. Everything I'd been concerned about as a head writer—keeping people happy, managing Lorne's notes, anticipating problems with the network—I just didn't care about any of it anymore. It wasn't my show, but whatever part of it I could control, I would. The rest was someone else's problem.

The thing I learned about Weekend Update, and about SNL in general, is that no one (including Lorne) actually knows what they want until they see it succeed. They might say, "The last thing we need is a sketch about an actress in a gay porn film who's worried about her character's motivation." Then Julio Torres and James Anderson wrote exactly that sketch for Emma Stone and it was great, even though it barely snuck onto the show. Of course, *afterward* everyone will say, "That was exactly what we needed!" but that's just a reaction to the sketch succeeding.

In the process, I learned to do what I think is funny and either it works or it doesn't. And it was Michael Che who helped me learn to trust my instincts. (Except when they're terrible, which Che is happy to point out.) He's the perfect foil for me, because I'm terrible at saying no and I'm constantly worried about disappointing people. It's almost like I'm controlled by a crippling guilt or something. COULD THIS AGAIN RELATE TO MY CATHOLICISM? WHO KNOWS FOR SURE!

Che got me to think about Update in a different way. He taught me that if you try to do something you love *and* something someone else wants you to do, they both suffer, and the thing you love might disappear entirely. (It might disappear anyway if the audience hates it, but at least you gave it your best shot.)

I've learned to eliminate any joke I wouldn't be excited to say on the air, even if it seems like a "safe" joke that "will work." (I now hate the phrase "That will work." It's such a mediocre goal to set for yourself.)

I've also learned that if a joke makes us laugh in our office on Friday night, it's probably worth trying even if the audience doesn't like it. Because why not? Even if the joke bombs at dress rehearsal, at least I can turn to Che and say, "Remember when we thought that was funny?"

My first year on Update, Jason Sudeikis told me, "Try at least one thing on Update every week that's totally *your* voice. That only *you* would write." Four years later, that advice finally made sense.

And once we started defining our voices, the Update writers (Pete, Josh, Katie, and Megan, who are all incredible at their jobs) could take more chances because they had a clearer sense of the "characters" they were writing for.

Che also deserves a lot of credit for questioning every step of the process and asking, "Why would we do it that way?" If the answer was: "Because that's the way we've always done it," he knew that wasn't a good enough reason. That was super helpful for me because I had been at the show so long, I had started to lose any perspective outside of the existing system.

That's how Che and I started showing up on camera a lot more like we were in real life—both as individuals and as a unit. Our sensibility started coming through more, because we weren't watering it down with peripheral stuff we didn't actually care about. And what started out as genuinely terrifying has become—most weeks—extremely fun. I have no idea what our "legacy" will be on Weekend Update and I don't really care. I'm just grateful that we had time to improve before they threw us out of the building. And I'm very grateful I got to do Update with Michael Che, because I never would have survived without him.

As my grandmother told me when I first got the job, "Who knows? Maybe this could lead to a job as a real news anchor someday!"

Baby Colin trying to put his fat fingers straight into an electrical outlet. The sign above my head was so Child Services could identify me.

Me in my mom's fire department car. She made me drive her everywhere.

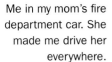

My brother and I appropriating ninja culture. Embarrassingly, we both chose Donatello.

First day of school. Photo taken by a bully for his records.

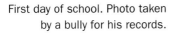

My parents and my grandpa at the Grand Canyon, circa 1993, when bolo ties were super popular.

My brother and I shoveling snow outside our house during the Blizzard of '96, the worst snowstorm in forty-eight years. Luckily we had layers of fat to keep us warm.

Me and my crew playing basketball on a hoop we lowered to eight feet so we could all dunk. As you can probably guess from my jean shorts, I was on the verge of turning pro.

Eighth grade graduation. No one chose the same camera to look at.

My high school ID from freshman year. Why did they make us display our social security numbers??? "Dear criminals, here's all the information you need to steal my identity or kidnap me after school. Sincerely,

Colin Jost

Me in my best Tom Wolfe look outside the Harvard Lampoon building, sophomore year of college.

Celebrating my grandparents' sixtieth wedding anniversary with our cousins Meg, Bridget, and Colleen.

This was taken by producer Mike Shoemaker at the end-of-the-year party after my first season as a writer at SNL. I'm thinking, *Wowwee, what a fun year!* And Lorne is thinking, *Can we hurry this up?*

Steve Higgins, Seth Meyers, Mike Shoemaker, Will Forte, and Teen Wolf at the annual Writers Party, circa 2007.

John Mulaney, myself, John Lutz, and Kenan Thompson spoofing the jazz-fusion group Weather Report for a short film by Noah Baumbach. Somehow this was my actual hair and not a wig.

Leslie Jones after she, Kyle Mooney, Tiffany Haddish, and Lorne Michaels all punched me in the face.

My first headshot as a stand-up comedian. This was before I understood insider Hollywood stuff like "grooming" or "styling" or "having one female friend tell you not to look like this."

This was my second headshot, from 2010, when I was auditioning for the role of "Seductive Teacher" on *Riverdale*.

Erin Doyle, Michael Che, and I at the former club Number 8 after the Museum of Natural History gala in 2014 (when we still went to clubs).

The author at his apartment in the West Village during a holiday party. I perhaps overdid it with the ice. Otherwise everything makes sense.

One of the first times I met Scarlett, as part of a series of cheesy Long Island commercials I worked on with Fred Armisen called "Marble Columns," "Porcelain Fountains," and "Ceramic Busts."

One of my favorite photos of me and Che from a *Variety* Emmy spread. (Before *Variety* called it "the worst Emmys ever.")

Pete Davidson and me discussing how a reporter from Staten Island wrote, "Hey, Pete, keep talking like that and you may end up sleeping with the fishes." So . . . a death threat.

Che and me performing at a benefit for the NYC Housing Authority at Irving Plaza. We also hosted "Gringo Bingo" together to raise money for Puerto Rico after Hurricane Maria. Che always tells people I have a secret second family in Puerto Rico.

Che and me with Opera Man. One of my favorite moments ever on Update.

Dave Chappelle, Leslie Jones, Pete Davidson, Michael Che, Donnell Rawlings, Wyl Sylvince, and moi after performing at Radio City Music Hall.

WWE star Braun Strowman hurls me out of the ring and into the stands at WrestleMania 35. I've never felt more alive and more dead at the same time.

Scarlett and I at our friend's wedding in Wyoming. Seconds later, we were attacked by wolves.

The Time Jimmy Buffett Saved My Life

(And I Don't Just Mean with His Music)

"Show me a hero and I will write you a tragedy."

—F. Scott Fitzgerald

"If life gives you limes, make margaritas."

—Jimmy Buffett

The truth is, I don't know Jimmy Buffett's music that well. The songs I know, I'm always happy to hear. Who wouldn't want to live inside a margarita? Who wouldn't want to arrive in paradise and get handed a cheeseburger? Who doesn't want to get "Too Drunk to Karaoke"? (I just discovered that song title, but it sounds amazing.)

In fact, now that I'm googling his music, every song sounds incredible. "Pencil Thin Mustache." "Why Don't We Get Drunk." "A Pirate Looks at Forty." "Math Suks" (sic). Why am I only *now* looking up these songs? "Jamaica Mistaica"?!?! Okay, enough.

So the year is 2014. About to be 2015. My girlfriend at the time was a very talented writer for *The Wall Street Journal* named Carmel Lobello. And a fun fact about her was that her Twitter handle was very similar to Carmelo Anthony of the New York Knicks, so she would occasionally get tweets that were intended for the NBA basketball player and not for the Wall Street Journalist. My favorite one was after the Knicks lost on Martin Luther King Day, and someone tweeted, "Hey @carmellobello, way to shit the bed on #MLKDay! Great way to honor Dr. King's legacy!" When I first saw that, I thought, *Jesus, Carmel, what did you do?* Then she explained that it was meant for Carmelo Anthony, which made me laugh really hard because in that person's mind the Knicks were *pro*–Martin Luther King and the other team was trying to destroy his legacy.

I can't imagine the DMs she got.

Anyway, through her connections in journalism (or by posing as an NBA athlete), Carmel was invited by the good people at *Vice* to join them for New Year's in St. Barts, which can also be written "St. Barths" or "$t. Bart$." This worked out perfectly since (a) I had made zero plans for New Year's and (b) we would be staying for free on the most expensive island in the Caribbean. For some perspective, the villa we stayed in cost $150,000 to rent for a *week*. For that kind of money, you could go to high school in Manhattan for almost two full years!

For every meal, *Vice* either rented out an entire restaurant or had a catered dinner at someone's house, where you'd end up meeting a really strange cross-section of artists, musicians, writers, and blood-diamond enthusiasts. The second night of our trip, I was randomly seated next to this older gentleman and I basically asked him, "So what's up with you?" And he started talking about surfing and how great the surf was in St. Barts. And I started talking about how much *I* love surfing and we really hit it off. *What a nice guy!* I thought.

I remember at one point, maybe twenty minutes into our conversation, he said something like, "Yeah, I always try to schedule it so I can spend a few days surfing wherever we open a new Margaritaville."

Now, you'll never believe it, but hearing the word "Margaritaville" made me start to suspect that I might be talking to Jimmy Buffett. I know. Call it idiot's intuition, but I had a sneaking suspicion that this wasn't just *any* Margaritaville restaurateur.

Many times in my life, I've ended up talking to someone wildly famous without realizing it until way too late in the conversation. Like I remember meeting Josh Groban backstage at a comedy club in New York and thinking, *What a nice guy!* (I guess I think that a lot.) Then Josh got onstage to play piano along with one of the comedians and I thought, *This guy should really go into music full-time!* At which point my friend pointed out that Josh *was* in fact "doing music full-time," in the sense that he's sold about thirty million records. But also a nice guy!

From then on, whenever I was unsure of the person I was talking to, I tried to listen very carefully for "context clues," like "When I first became senator of Arizona . . ." or "In the early days of Microsoft . . ." or "I'm Shaq."

And "Margaritaville" was a pretty juicy context clue. Also (and this might be the craziest part of the story), I *love* Margaritaville restaurants. I enjoy the original song as well, but my true passion is the dining experience. In fact, I would argue that Margaritaville is the best restaurant ever based on a song.

Way better than Billy Joel's whimsical "Allentown" diners, where every dish is "sprinkled with coal dust!"*

I've been to the Margaritaville in Atlantic City at least five times. Once it was so crowded that I had to flag down the manager and shamefully whisper that I was headlining at the Borgata casino in order to secure a table. *At Margaritaville.* That's like name-dropping Frank Sinatra to get into a Chili's.

This is all to say that I might not be the only person in the world who wouldn't recognize Jimmy Buffett, but I'm *definitely* the only person in the world who knows Jimmy Buffett's restaurants better than they know his music.

But can you blame me? Just look at the menu! For breakfast (YES, MARGARITAVILLE SERVES BREAKFAST), you can choose between a "Cheese Omelet in Paradise" and something called "Boatmeal," which I'm guessing is oatmeal with a slight "nautical" edge (chunks of seagull).

And if you're drinking at breakfast—which I certainly hope you are—might I suggest the "Grand Slam Trio"? I'll let it introduce itself:

> Start with a chilled shot of Jameson Irish Whiskey and butterscotch schnapps, served with a slice of bacon. Follow it with a side of orange juice and finish with an ice cold Landshark Lager chaser.

This is still breakfast, by the way.

For lunch, there's obviously an entire section labeled "Burgers in Paradise." And for dinner, they feature a "Key West

---

* I'm sorry to inform you this restaurant is fake.

Chicken Quesadilla" (all the chickens are read a Hemingway short story right before they're killed), as well as "Jimmy's Jammin' Jambalaya," which—sorry, copycats!—is a registered trademark. And the menu also points out that they have "Pibb Xtra" on tap. Which is a form of Pibb I never could have conceived of.

The scary part is, I didn't have to look up this information. Because I love the restaurant.

Okay, back to the story.

So this older gentleman I'm sitting next to at dinner graciously invites me to go surfing the next day and offers to lend me a surfboard and show me an amazing secluded beach where we might be the only two people surfing and I'm thinking, *Is Jimmy Buffett really inviting me to go surfing*??

Incidentally, "Surfing with Jimmy Buffett" sounds like it could be a song by Jimmy Buffett.

So I say, "Oh. Yeah. Sure. That'd be cool. NO BIG DEAL." (Real cool and casual.)

The next day, I drive across the entire island to this dirt parking lot in the middle of nowhere. And I wander out toward the ocean and come upon this beautiful little shack full of surfboards. And there's Jimmy Buffett and his children getting ready to surf. But when he sees me, I'm not sure he even registers that we've met before, let alone that he invited me here to surf less than twelve hours ago.

So now I'm terrified that I've made a weird social error, and that he "invited me" but I wasn't supposed to actually show up, and now I'm imposing on this special family bonding moment, like someone pouring Pibb Xtra all over a Jammin' Jambalaya. But he and his children are very kind and take pity on me and give me a surfboard and pretend I'm not desperate, and we all paddle out to this incredible left-breaking wave, with no one else in sight.

Now, again, I'm a *decent* surfer. I can be out in most conditions and not make a fool of myself. But I'm always nervous when I surf a new spot, let alone when I'm surfing a new spot on a new board with my new best friend in the whole world, Jimmy Buffett. (And his family.)

Plus, he doesn't know that I'm a decent surfer, so he's being extra careful and giving me advice about this particular wave, and he says something like, "By the way, watch out for those rocks when you get close to shore." And I remember acting nonchalant and saying, "Oh yeah. Rocks. Haha. Totally." And then I immediately forgot what he had just told me.

Pretty soon the waves start rolling in and they're four or five feet high—nothing overwhelming but enough to get a really fun ride. They're shaped perfectly. The sun is shining. We all look around at each other and think, *Yup. Every one of us belongs here. We'll have this family memory forever.*

I let the Buffetts lead the way and they start catching waves in succession and cheering each other on. And I'm just watching them and enjoying the scene. They're having so much fun!

Then, after they've found a real groove, I decide to finally grab a wave of my own. The first one is always a little nerve-wracking for me, but I paddle hard and jump up and catch my first wave of the day. *Whoooo! See? I can kinda surf, Jimmy! We have so much in common!*

So I'm riding this wave and looking back for their approval

and they're not really paying attention to me because, again, they're having an emotionally fulfilling family adventure. And I ride the wave all the way in, almost to the rocks, and then I hop off the board and turn to paddle back out, and suddenly I realize that I can't move. Like, I'm paddling, but the board isn't going anywhere. I look down and see that my leash is stuck under one of those famous rocks Jimmy warned me about. ("On the Rocks"—also a great name for a Jimmy Buffett song.)

My first instinct is: *Don't panic. You're fine. Just reach down and pull the leash out of the rocks.* Which sounds pretty straightforward, but when you add in the additional element of four-to-five-foot waves breaking on top of you every few seconds, the physics get complicated really fast.

After a few more waves hit me, I start to get *slightly* worried. Because it's hard to tread water when there are sharp rocks directly below your feet. And is it just me, or are the waves getting bigger?

At some point, Jimmy (Buffett) notices that I'm hanging around by the rocks for a strange amount of time and he calls out, "You okay over there?"

And my first priority, obviously, is looking cool, so I yell back, "Oh yeah! Everything's amazing!"

But the truth is, it's far from amazing. In fact, I'm beginning to realize how easily I could drown in the next five minutes. I try to reach down and undo my leash, but I can't get it off while also bracing for the waves and staying shallow enough to not hit a rock. And I can't use my surfboard to float on because the waves have now pinned it three feet behind me. Still my mind is thinking: *Don't blow it in front of Jimmy!*

Luckily, Jimmy Buffett can spot an idiot from fifty feet away.

He starts paddling in to see what's going on, and then looks horrified when he sees me pinned against the rocks by my own leash. "What are you doing?! I told you about the rocks!"

"Oh yeah! Haha, the rocks!" I say, but he can barely hear me because my mouth is full of seawater. Also, I'm struggling to tread water and I'm now bleeding because I sliced my foot open on a rock.

"Don't move!" he says. And he paddles over to my board and takes out a KNIFE (which, how awesome is it that Jimmy Buffett swims with a knife?) and he cuts the leash off my surfboard so it comes loose and he tells me to unhook my end of the leash. And I say, "No way! I gotta save the leash!" To which Jimmy replies, "Are you a moron? It's a ten-dollar leash!"

And I think, *Ohhhhhh, right. Cuz ten dollars is not as valuable as my own life.* So I unhook the leash and swim back through the breaking waves with my bleeding foot, and Jimmy Buffett is waiting outside the waves with my surfboard, and I'm super apologetic for not only interrupting his family vacation, but also for destroying his leash and forcing a seventy-one-year-old man to endanger his own life to save mine.

Jimmy hands me the board and points to a gentler section of waves to the right and says, "That might be more your speed over there."

And as he swam back to join his family, I knew that Jimmy Buffett would never respect my surfing the way I respected his restaurants. And I remember thinking: *Man, I could really use a chilled shot of Jameson and butterscotch schnapps served with a slice of bacon right about now. Then I could follow it with a side of orange juice and finish it all off with an ice-cold Landshark Lager chaser.*

.   .   .

The next day, I went to a local surf shop and purchased a leash to replace the one I lost in the rocks, for the reasonable St. Barts price of 75 dollars. (I also wandered into an art gallery where the manager told me, "I regret to inform you that all of Harmony Korine's paintings have already been sold." To which I responded, ". . . what?")

I took the leash and drove back to the surf spot that Mr. Buffett had shown me the day before, but he was nowhere to be found. The waves had disappeared too, as though ashamed to see my face again. There was only a solitary man who cared for the surf shack. I presented him with the leash and asked if Mr. Buffett was around so I could apologize and say thank you for showing me the surf break.

But the man told me, "Sorry, amigo. Jimmy flew himself to Nevis to play golf for the day."

I guess Jimmy Buffett said it best in "God Don't Own a Car" (1976):

I have been out wanderin'
I have traveled far
One conclusion I have made
Is that God don't own a car

That doesn't really pertain to the story I just told, but it does make you think.

Thank you, Jimmy Buffett.

SNL FAQs

"What time does the three-o'clock parade start?"
—The most frequently asked question at Disney World

Here are the questions I am most frequently asked as a person who works at *Saturday Night Live*. I'm providing these answers mainly for the family members of the SNL cast, crew, and writing staff, so they won't have to answer them at Thanksgiving. Instead, your family can jump straight into politics.

You're welcome.

"When does *Saturday Night Live* tape?"

The word "live" in the name of the show indicates that it's live. This is somehow very confusing to people, even though all the information you need is right there in the title—*Saturday Night* (when it happens) and *Live* (the fact that it's live). It's like how the name "Shark Week" implies that over the course of a week, you will see sharks.

"But is it *live* live?"

Why do you think we're trying to trick you?

Yes, every episode is broadcast as it's happening—*live*—in our studio in Rockefeller Center in New York.

I think there's an FCC law that you can't call something "live" unless it's actually airing live. And you can't call something "breaking news" unless you're CNN and you want every tiny story to feel like it's the start of World War Three.

So yes, "live" means it's actually live.

Unless it's a rerun.

"Is this week's episode live or a rerun?"

That's really more of a question for *TV Guide*. (Or whatever replaced *TV Guide*. I'm guessing "Bing's Television Goings-On.") A good rule of thumb is: If you see a current cast member at, say, a bar on a Saturday night, then that week is a rerun. (Or that cast member is having a really bad show.) Also, if you're watching SNL and it's a rerun, it will say at the beginning of the show: "The following is a rebroadcast of a previously aired episode," and you'll notice subtle differences, like how Jessica Simpson and Nick Lachey are the hosts and Captain Beefheart is the musical guest.

"Who was your *least* favorite host?"

Why do random strangers think I will answer this question?

"Oh, thank god you asked! I've been waiting to open up to

someone about this. *Helen Mirren pantsed me in front of the entire crew.*"

The actual truth is that I don't have a least favorite host. I have *three* least favorite hosts, because they were all so bad that I can't pick just one.

And if you can correctly guess all three, I'll send you a personally autographed SNL T-shirt worth approximately three dollars less than a non-autographed SNL T-shirt.

"Okay, then who was your *favorite* host?"

This is usually asked begrudgingly after I won't answer the previous question. Like someone will sigh and be like, "Fine, bitch, if you don't want to give me any of the good shit, then feed me some lame-ass line about which host is 'your hero' and we can all move on."

My hero and favorite host is Will Ferrell.

"Who's your least favorite cast member?"

Again, what version of society do you live in? That's like asking someone, "Who's your least favorite friend?" Even asking someone at an office, "Who's your least favorite coworker?" is a crazy, presumptuous question.

That said, it's Aidy Bryant. WE. ARE. BITTER. ENEMIES.

"Who's your *favorite* cast member?"

Michael Che. (Awwwww.)

J/k though, it's Kenan.

"Does Lorne still, like, come to work?"

Never before 4 P.M., but yes! Every damn day.

"Do you ever have zero funny ideas?"

Quite often! Actually, it's rare that I have *zero* ideas, but most weeks I have no idea whether my ideas are actually funny or will end up getting on the show. You don't really know whether a sketch "works" until it airs in front of an audience on Saturday night. There are ideas that kill in the pitch meeting and sketches that kill at the table read and they *still* might die a horrible death in front of a live audience.

Also, sometimes a host is just challenging to write for and you have no idea how to use them effectively. Like when Lance Armstrong hosted (before he was a villain), I pitched him an idea where he would do a public service announcement that his yellow Livestrong bracelets actually cause wrist cancer. He said, and I quote, "No fucking way, dude." And then I had zero more ideas!

"What do you do if it's writing night and you have zero ideas?"

It's a lot like *Mad Men,* where having a glass of bourbon and falling asleep on your couch can sometimes yield great results! And other times, you wake up hungover, soaked in panic sweat, still with zero ideas, but now you need to change your shirt and maybe your pants.

One time my first year, I fell asleep at 6 A.M. on the floor of the hallway of 30 Rock, which had accumulated about thirty-six seasons' worth of dirt and drugs before I got there, and when I woke up at 6:30 A.M., I thought: *Maybe a sketch about a guy who marries a hot dog?* Then I wrote that sketch and it aired on the show. And they spent, like, ten thousand dollars on the hot dog costumes!

"How much of the show is improvised?"

For some reason, people think the answer is "100 percent" (which seems particularly insulting to the writers) when it's really more like 5 percent. There's no room built in for improvising because it's a live show, which means (a) if someone blurts out a random line, they might not even be on camera, and (b) the show is timed very carefully to end up at exactly ninety minutes (minus commercials), so if someone starts "riffing" then it better be pretty fucking funny because chances are you just got your castmate's sketch cut at the end of the show. Most of the "improv" in our show is the result of people screwing up on-air and having to improvise to react or recover.

"Why do you use cue cards?"

Because the cue card guys are in a union and you don't fuck with guys in a union.

"I've heard it's really cutthroat and competitive at SNL. Is that true?"

Honestly, not really. It's certainly competitive in the sense that everyone wants to get his or her own sketch on the show. And when your sketch doesn't get on, you're really bummed out and sometimes pissed off that someone else's got on instead of yours. But that's pretty standard workplace competition.

And you might say something like—just to use a random name—"Aidy Bryant's whack-ass sketch is getting on?! She wouldn't know what was funny if it kicked her in her dumb clown mouth!" But you wouldn't really wish any harm on anyone.

And sure, sometimes you might do things like go into the folder where people turn in their sketches and delete one that Aidy Bryant wrote so yours has a better chance of getting picked; but in fairness, the way you delete something on a computer is by dragging it into the trash, and that's where Aidy's sketches belong.

And yeah, sometimes you'll buy a bunch of snakes that are a hybrid of a cobra and a rattlesnake (so they have the head of a cobra and the tail of a rattlesnake), and you'll put a few of them in Aidy Bryant's desk where she keeps her Advil. And then you'll play trance music really loud next door for hours until Aidy's headache gets so intense that she reaches for her Advil but instead finds six to ten cobrattlers and then she freaks out and can't finish her sketch, thereby improving the odds of *my* sketch getting on.

But in general, no, it's not that competitive.

I like to quote the Olive Garden: "When you're here, you're breadsticks."

"There was a sketch on SNL that was just like a sketch my comedy troupe Diapers for Algernon performed five years ago in rural Mexico. Why did you steal our idea?"

Believe it or not, our sketch writers are not scouring local comedy theaters for material to steal. Not infrequently, there is a sketch or a joke that was similar to something posted on You-

Tube/Twitter/Grindr/whitehouse.gov. I assure you, no one at our show saw that sketch or joke and then stole it. Lots of people are generating comedy and some of those ideas are bound to be similar.

"How do I become a cast member for SNL?"

The real answer is: You have to prove to someone who already works at SNL that you're funny.

This can happen in lots of ways. For some people—like, say, Kristen Wiig or Bobby Moynihan or Cecily Strong—you spend years honing your skills at established comedy institutions like the Groundlings, Upright Citizens Brigade, Second City, or the ImprovOlympic, and you prove yourself there, so you can impress the SNL producers when they come to see a showcase.

For others, like Pete Davidson or Chris Rock or Sarah Silverman, you start as a stand-up comedian in clubs around New York or L.A. and someone from our talent department goes to see you, and if they like you, they force Lorne to see you too.

Or, in the case of Andy Samberg, Kyle Mooney, or Bowen Yang, you make videos with your friends and hope they gain traction until someone from SNL sees them and recommends you.

Others are more random, like how Megan Mullally saw Bill Hader perform at a small club in L.A. and called Lorne directly to tell him how funny she thought Bill was. Then Bill came in, wowed everyone at his audition, performed oral sex on Lorne Michaels, and got the job.

Sometimes, SNL cast members recommend people they

used to perform with, like how Tina Fey recommended Amy Poehler, and Nasim Pedrad recommended Mikey Day, and way back in the day, Chevy Chase recommended John Belushi.

And then, once in a while, there's a huge backlash against the show for not hiring any black women, so SNL holds an entire audition for black women, and Chris Rock calls Lorne and says, "You know who's super funny is Leslie Jones," and then Leslie Jones gets her first SNL audition at age forty-seven and blows everyone away.

"How do I become a *writer* for SNL?"

There is an annual gathering of trolls. The trolls select one among them who will write down the exploits of the handsome, charming human actors. That troll then abandons the bridge or crude stone byway where they reside and journeys to a dim, gaseous land called "The Writers Room." In exchange for his toils, the troll is provided healthcare through the Troll Guild, which also collects *hundreds of cents* in Internet residuals.

"Why does your show have to do so many sketches with potty words and bathroom humor?"

In fairness, this is only the most frequently asked question by my grandmother, who just turned 103 years old and is perhaps more sensitive to bathroom humor than, say, the under-100 demographic.

But I'll tell you guys the same thing I always tell her: Michael Che writes those sketches, and I can only stop one or two a week.

"Do you guys just laugh all the time?"

Yes, we've lost our minds.

Lorne has been laughing continuously for forty-five years, except for the five years he left the show when he did not laugh once because he was working at the DMV.

"Do you guys do drugs all the time?"

You know when an actor calls offstage and says, "Line!"? At SNL that means, "Give me the goddamn cocaine!"

But seriously, some people smoke weed and some probably do a little cocaine or take some edibles and maybe if it's an off week they'll take some mushrooms or some MDMA or some horse tranquilizers or they'll chew that Somali pirate drug khat or pound some krokodil or some Foxy Methoxy or snort a whole tabletop of angel dust. But in my experience, they're almost never mainlining heroin.

"When do you think you'll leave the show?"

Who are you, my agent? Or my therapist? Or my family and friends?

Listen to me: I WILL LEAVE THE SHOW. WHEN IT'S TIME.

"And when will it be time, Colin?"

(Sigh.) Look, I owe a lot of people a lot of money. Okay? Do you have a better way for me to make 450 dollars a week?

"Seriously though, how much money do cast members make at SNL?"

People are gonna be pissed that I'm spilling the beans on this one, but SNL cast members make somewhere between a hundred thousand and a hundred million dollars a year. There, it's out there. Are you happy now, you vultures?

"Are you and Michael Che really friends?"

"Yes." "Sure we are." I "love" him. What a "great" "guy."

"Are you and Aidy Bryant really enemies?"

Aidy is not my enemy because I don't make enemies with *clowns*.

Hey, Aidy, the garbage truck called. It wants your sketches back.

What's that? You need, like, two years to write a comeback book? Yeah, I thought so.

Clowns.com/AidyBryant

"Where do I send complaints about the show?"

Mike.Pence@whitehouse.gov

"Where do I send all my valuable gold?"

Cash 4 Gold
C/o Weekend Update
30 Rockefeller Plaza
New York, NY 10112

(And my lawyer is asking me to note that we do not send back cash.)

And finally: "What's Lorne *really* like?"

Solid build. 6'2". Jet-black hair. Has an accent you can never quite place. Hands that have clearly seen the handle of an axe.

He's a quiet man. He lets his eyes do the talking. And his mouth.

Every single evening, he watches the sun kiss the horizon. And every single morning he wakes up at 11:45 A.M.

He hasn't touched paper money since 1954. One time I mentioned the subway and he said, "Really? I'm more of a Quiznos guy."

6'5". 6'5½".

Hates raisins. If you even mention raisins in a sketch, he'll leave the read-through and the whole season is just over.

Not afraid to pull out a gun during an HR meeting, that's for sure.

Lorne's the kind of guy who gives you a Christmas present in July and says, "Oops. I guess Santa's losing his widdle mind!"

A kind man. A generous man. In fact, I once saw him donate his most expensive knife to the belly of a vagrant. Said, "Watch this," and just plunged it right in. Afterward he laughed for almost ten blocks. Then we ate ice cream and went figure skating.

Once told me out of nowhere: "Liberace couldn't suck a lemon seed through a roll of toilet paper." Not sure what that was all about.

He's at least 7'8" and he's still growing.

Lorne would never admit this, but he won the Presidential Medal of Freedom and he wears it around his neck twenty-four hours a day. He has a small light above it, like you would put above a painting. And when you say "hello," he waves the medal at you. Because he wants you to say a second, smaller hello to the medal.

Lorne is truly a paradox. Half parade, half ox.

And he's the only real father any of us have ever known.

Maybe that's why we all call him "Unkie Lorne."

And Your Host . . . Donald Trump!

"Even the unusual must have its limits."

—FRANZ KAFKA

As some of you might recall, Donald Trump hosted SNL on November 7, 2015, while he was pursuing the Republican nomination for president.

And the musical guest was Sia!

Kate's expression in this photo really says it all.

It's strange to look back at that moment in our show's history and try to remember what it felt like to work there that week. Fortunately I took notes, James Comey–style, so I'd remember what the experience was like.

Keep in mind, I had worked at SNL for ten years at this point, and I had written for presidential candidates like John McCain, Barack Obama, and Kanye West. I was also there when Sarah Palin came on the show, and Tina refused to appear on camera with her because she didn't want a photo of the two of them chumming it up.*

SNL is also a really disorienting place to work in general. Where else would I get to write a *song* for Larry David and *comedy* for Nicki Minaj? What other show has the real Michael Phelps and the real Jared from Subway in the *same sketch*? Where else would Andy Samberg play Hugh Jackman while Hugh Jackman plays Daniel Radcliffe? (Perhaps the worst casting in history?)

It's the kind of place where Lorne will call you into his office in the middle of the day and say, "Mick Jagger's about to go onstage in Prague and he needs a joke to open the show. Any ideas?" (Because when you see the Rolling Stones in Prague, you're thinking, *These guys better have jokes!*)

I had experienced pretty much every bizarre show business moment there was. I had seen LeBron James dance in a '70s golden cape. I had seen Peyton Manning dance to a janky '60s

---

* Afterward people asked, "Was Sarah Palin *crazy?*" No. She was extremely polite and friendly and seemed exactly like my fun aunt (or "Funt," to quote Maya Rudolph). She's also like my aunt in that neither of them should be vice president.

funk song. But I never thought I'd see Donald Trump dance to the Drake "Hotline Bling" video.

It turned out that the Trump episode would be the most surreal week I ever experienced at SNL. And that includes the Jim Carrey episode when he walked in on Monday and said: "For my monologue, I want to dress up as 'Hellvis' [Elvis in Hell] and I want to sing a four-minute song about pecan pie." And then that just . . . happened. (Coincidentally, Jim and Donald have since become dear friends!)

And that week seems even more surreal in retrospect. Because exactly one year later, Trump was elected president of the United States.

The first thing that Donald Trump said to me when he walked into my office was: "I like you. You got that good face."

Say what you will about the man, but he knows how to make an entrance.

I had never heard the term "good face" before, but it was a uniquely Trumpian compliment: an overly simple adjective that made no sense with the noun it described. Like "tall car" or "long Pope."

The thing that anyone who's actually met Donald Trump will tell you is that he's incredibly charming and fun to talk to, unless he thinks you're unattractive, in which case he'll ignore you, or he thinks you're very attractive, in which case he'll try to touch or kiss you (allegedly). He's basically like my German grandpa, where he's fun and endearing when he's in your living room, but if you gave him a microphone and had him speak at a rally for two hours straight, he'd probably say some weird stuff. (Again, like my grandpa, he shouldn't be president. Also why are we electing *any* grandpas president? No more grandpas!)

By the end of the week, I think most people at our show thought, *Huh. This guy isn't a monster after all.* There have certainly been other hosts who left with way worse reputations. (No, I will not tell you who they are. But their initials are R.C., and then after the R is an "ussell," and after the C is a "rowe.")

One of the strangest things about the week was how Trump was physically present for all of it. He was running for *president* and still put in the same number of hours hosting our show as Justin Timberlake. He flew to a rally one night after rehearsal but otherwise he was just . . . there.

Also, Trump was there *alone*. He brought no handlers, no campaign manager, no security. I would just walk into his dressing room—the door was wide open—and he would say, "Hey! Get in here! Did you see what Ben Carson said today? What a whack job!" It was incredible. (I never knew that "whack job" meant "future secretary of housing and urban development.")

By contrast, Hillary Clinton had appeared on SNL a month before Trump, and she had brought about fifteen people for a five-minute appearance. Secret Service guys, advisors, liaisons, friends . . . Trump brought no one, which really foreshadowed how he would run his campaign (and how he's currently running the country).

One thing I love about SNL is that we welcome hosts and musical guests from all over the country (and the world) with a wide range of social and political views. People forget that it's a variety show, and that means a variety of viewpoints, politically and culturally. (And comedically.)

People think of SNL as this bastion of liberal extremists from New York and California, but we have conservatives and libertarians, and more of our cast members are from Middle America than from New York or California. And like America in general, we have a lot of moderates and a lot of people who don't care about politics at all. After all, the majority of our show has zero to do with politics, and the sketches you loved most growing up were rarely the political ones. (Except for "Janet Reno's Dance Party.")

Once a host arrives—even one you're ambivalent about—you do your best to make them look good or at least minimize how bad they make you look. Or you write your own pieces that don't rely on the host at all, which is what I did that week.

Actually, I tried writing some sketches for Trump at first, but our senses of humor might have been slightly different . . .

I pitched him three ideas.

The first idea was an ad for "Rosetta Stone: Mexican," which would teach you low-level racist phrases you could say to someone who was Mexican. Like: "You're gonna pay for the wall." "Yes, *you* are." "Yes, *usted* will."

Weirdly, he didn't go for that one!

The next idea was that *if* he became president—which again, at the time, seemed *laughably impossible,* probably even to him—that would mean there would be an animatronic Donald Trump in the Hall of Presidents at Disney World.*) And my idea was that during the Hall of Presidents show, the animatronic Trump would just roast all the other presidents. Like: "George Washington! Look at his little wooden teeth. Did you

---

* And now there is. He's introduced by Abraham Lincoln!

chop down the cherry tree to get more teeth, you nerd?" Or "Want to see my impression of FDR?" (And then Trump would do his famous "cripple" impression.)

He actually liked that idea at first and he tried it at the table read. Then I think he realized that it wouldn't look good for him to go on TV and make fun of the father of our country and call FDR a cripple, and so we didn't do it. Dammit! Almost had him!

The third idea, which I thought was a real long shot, was that Cecily, Vanessa, and I wanted to write one of our recurring Porn Stars sketches, but make it a campaign ad for Donald Trump. And this is perhaps way less surprising in retrospect, but Trump was *very* into that idea!

So that week I ended up writing a sketch about two porn stars endorsing Donald Trump for president. (Trump at one point turns to Cecily and says, "Hey, didn't you used to be a brunette?") And I wrote a Drunk Uncle with Bobby Moynihan, where we found out that Drunk Uncle was basically the Platonic ideal of a Trump supporter.

Personally, I think I acquitted myself as well as I possibly could have that week. But there was still a larger question: Why was Trump hosting in the first place?

If you were to go back and examine all the hosts in SNL history—especially after the #MeToo movement—you're gonna find a lot of problems. There have been some hosts over the years who are real "Confederate statues" of entertainment. But they hosted because they were an important part of the cultural landscape at that moment—which certainly applied to Donald Trump in 2015 as much as it did to anyone else who hosted that year.

In Lorne's defense, at the time that he booked Donald Trump, no one thought he could possibly get the nomination, let alone get elected president. In fact, I remember that Lorne was worried about booking Trump because he might have already flamed out and disappeared from the race by the time the show happened. He was way more worried about Trump being irrelevant than he was about Trump being a legitimate candidate.

Also, anyone who had even a passing knowledge of Donald Trump knew that he was a Democrat! No one thought he would actually do any of the things he was saying. No one thought he would even keep *saying* the things he was saying.

Don't forget: Hillary Clinton went to Donald Trump's wedding! It seemed to a lot of people at the time, especially among New Yorkers, that he and Hillary weren't that dissimilar and that Trump's "conservative" agenda was all a façade. (This was, of course, very naive.)

I do remember wondering: *Will anyone in the audience boo Trump when he walks onstage?* But not a single person did. I think the audience (like a lot of America) still liked Trump as a person and didn't think he was an existential threat to democracy, like a lot of people think now. (Also, lots of people still like him and aren't worried that he's undermining democracy in the slightest, which I find hard to comprehend.)

As for the idea that SNL somehow "humanized" Trump by having him on the show, I think that's a tough argument since he was already the most humanized presidential candidate—and maybe the most humanized *human*—in history. He had been on every TV show, the cover of every newspaper and magazine, was essentially the third co-host on *Morning Joe,* and was the only actor to appear in both *Home Alone 2* and *Playboy Video Centerfold 2000.* He was very, very human.*

Oh, and Trump had already hosted our show ten years earlier.

Now, if by "humanize" you're instead implying that we were somehow "endorsing" Donald Trump by having him on, then by that logic, we had already endorsed Hillary Clinton, Bernie Sanders, Chris Christie, Jon Huntsman, Mike Huckabee, and Rudy Giuliani. And if viewers *were* influenced by seeing Trump host, then wouldn't they have noticed *how bad the show was*?!

I mean, it's a really, really bad episode. And it's not because of Donald Trump's *politics*—it's because of Donald Trump's acting and his comedic instincts.† No one watched that episode and thought, *I was on the fence about Trump, but now I see how good he is at sketch comedy!* They thought, *Huh. Maybe Jeb Bush and Ted Cruz should do a* Key & Peele–*type show together? That might be funnier.*

All this being said, I would *guess* that, in hindsight, Lorne would not have asked Trump to host if he had known how insane and divisive Trump would later get. But Lorne is also very contrarian, so maybe he would have!

In the end, I think Trump hosting was a wake-up call for our

---

* As Michael Che once said, "Donald Trump on a TV show makes total sense. It's Donald Trump as an elected official that's bonkers."

† Trump later bragged that he had "improvised" a lot of the show. I was like, "Oh my god, thank you for saying that! Please, take all the credit you want!"

show. It became clear that he *wasn't* like any other political guest. He was a uniquely divisive and dangerous candidate. And that episode of SNL has not aged well, politically or comedically. Just ask IMDb Trivia, which states:

> Due to the overwhelmingly negative reaction from critics and fans to this episode, some reviewers have subsequently referred to it as "The Episode That Shall Not Be Named."

Which I'm guessing is not what Lorne (or J. K. Rowling) ever intended.

The Chapter About Alcohol
and Drugs

"The point is not to be debilitated by your pleasures."
—Jay McInerney

"When I read about the evils of drinking, I gave up reading."
—Henny Youngman

My grandfather always told me a story about John F. Kennedy, the patron saint of Irish Catholics. He told me that when JFK was a teenager, his father, Joe Kennedy, made him a promise: "Don't drink until the age of twenty-one, and I'll give you a million dollars."

My grandfather made the same exact promise to me. Except for the million dollars. In fact, he offered me zero dollars. He didn't even offer to buy me a beer when I turned twenty-one. He just told me the story hoping I would think, *If JFK can do it, so can I!*

I made it to about fifteen.

Which in fairness might still be the world record for "Latest an Irish Kid Has Ever Started Drinking." (Also, I later found out that Joe Kennedy had only offered his son a *thousand* dollars. And that JFK gave back the check because he was already drinking.)

An alleyway in Middle Village, Queens, was no Camelot, but that's where I had my first drink, during sophomore year of high school. I'd imagine JFK had something elegant his first time—a fine scotch or an Old Fashioned. I had ten ounces of a 40 of Colt 45. And I was *flying*. I snuck into Scott Callahan's parents' garage, stole a five-iron from his dad's golf bag, and started running through the streets of Queens hitting rocks at trashcans.*

But except for a handful of dumb nights where I had a few screwdrivers or White Russians (both of which now make me sick just thinking about them), I didn't drink in high school. It just wasn't that interesting to me, and most of my friends didn't drink either, outside of a couple stray beers. I also felt (and still believe) that it's just better to wait until your brain is fully cooked before you start eating it away with poison.

That's the thing about alcohol. It's really fun, but at the end of the day, it's poison. We like to dress it up and pretend it's not. And order a "skinny poison," because we're worried about how many calories are in our poison. But it's poison. And I should know, I drink poison almost every single day.

Drinking worries me more than almost anything, because it sneaks up on you. I've had relatives drink themselves to death, and I've seen friends sabotage their careers or lose years of work because they couldn't stop drinking. Almost every single stand-up comedian is either a functional alcoholic or *was a*

---

* To this day, the five-iron is still unaccounted for, and Scott is now a lieutenant in the New York City Police Department.

functional alcoholic and is now sober. There's very little in between.

Part of it is the ritual: You get offstage and either your set went great and you want a drink to keep that feeling going, or your set went horribly and you want to make that feeling disappear.

It's the same at SNL. You either go straight home after a show and relax, or you go out with everyone you just performed with and have between three and fifteen drinks. Part of it is just social. There's always something happening after work—a network party, a screening of a new movie, Michael Che's birthday, a museum benefit, Michael Che's bris. And it's really hard to get through small talk with vague acquaintances without at least one drink. Then you finally escape the small talk and find your friends and you're like, "Oh man, that was awful. Let's get a drink!"

You really have to be vigilant, take days off, and limit how many drinks you have or it takes a rough toll on you over time. There are definitely some "Ghosts of Christmas Past" who come back to visit SNL and look like garbage and their brains don't work and that makes you realize, *Oh. Alcohol destroys your body.*

Then again, a Manhattan is a pretty amazing drink.

When I was growing up, my parents almost never drank. Not even a glass of wine at dinner. My dad might have a beer at a Giants game, or my mom would have a gin and tonic once a month at a party. But for them, not drinking was a reaction to the generation before them. My grandfather lost his brother to alcohol at a young age and my other grandfather showed up drunk one Christmas with presents that weren't for my grandmother. They were for my grandmother's *friend* who he was having an affair with. (My grandparents had been married *thirty-nine years* at that point.)

I'm always trying, and mostly failing, to drink less. I'll go a few days or even a week without drinking at all and I'll think, *AHHHHHHHHH, THIS IS BORING AND DRINKING IS FUN!!!*

My doctor calls this "a bad sign."

Part of the problem is that I'm a pretty fun drunk. (Maybe this is a classic introvert/extrovert dependency issue? But I'm no psychiatrist!*) Some people get angry or aggressive when they're drunk. I get *ambitious*. You'll find me at three in the morning at a bar, and we'll start *making plans*. Hundreds of times I've said things like, "Let's go on a trip tomorrow! Let's just get on a plane and go!" Or: "We need to start a company *tomorrow*. We could just, like, make movies! Why not???" Or: "Oh my god, we should go to *law school*! How awesome would that be! We'd be *lawyers*!!! Holy shit, we gotta do law school *tomorrow*!"

Needless to say, I'm not a lawyer. Nor do I have a company that makes movies. Nor have I ever just "gotten on a plane" and gone somewhere with a stranger. Because the next day I'm like, "What the hell happened last night? Did I suggest law school *again*?? I need to shut off my phone for forty-eight hours and avoid all human contact." You know, healthy stuff.

I'm also easily "dared" into doing dumb things when I'm drunk, like running along the tops of parked cars or diving headfirst into bushes like a maniac. I've also climbed trees in

---

* (yet)

the middle of Manhattan and attempted to "hide" from my friends. For example:

I've pretended to use pay phones to make phone calls while actually using them as urinals. (Weirdly, I've also pretended to use urinals to have peace and quiet to make phone calls.)

In short, I've been an idiot and a social menace. And I apologize to my fellow citizens, any visiting foreign dignitaries, and New York City mayors Dinkins through Bloomberg. (Mayor De Blasio, you killed our groundhog, Staten Island Chuck, so let's call it a draw.)

Drugs always scared me because I was worried that I would like them and they would derail my entire life. I never smoked weed until college and I never even *saw* cocaine until I was twenty-seven and a writer's assistant at SNL walked into my office and said, "Do you mind if I do coke in here?" I was truly honored.

Maybe my friends in high school and college were doing drugs all along and never offered them to me, but I honestly think I got lucky and hung out with people who were ambitious and didn't have time (or money) for drugs. And they were probably scared like I was.

I also have a terrible constitution for drug use. Any time I've smoked pot, I've had a classic "my heart is going to explode and I'll never be the same person ever again!" type of reaction. For example, I smoked the tiniest bit of weed with my friends and went to see the classic film *10,000 B.C.* The previews started and I thought, *Whoa. This movie screen is pretty big* . . . Then we saw a preview for *The Grinch* and I thought, *Oh no. His heart is growing. Maybe mine is, too* . . . Then *10,000 B.C.* started, and the opening shot is a thousand wooly mammoths charging at the screen. I got up, walked out of the theater, and paced up and down in the lobby until my friends came out and took me home. Not even to my own home. They took me to *their* apartment because I "refused to be alone," and gave me multiple blankets because I was shivering on their couch. Then I slept for twelve hours.

So that was my general reaction to pot. But around the age of twenty-eight, I went on a date with a girl and she offered me a pot cookie. I was worried I might feel paranoid, but I had such a deep, eternal faith in *cookies* that I was confident they would cancel out the effects of marijuana with their inherent deliciousness. I'm sad to report that for the first time in my life, cookies let me down.

We were at a Girl Talk concert in New York and having a great time. Then we went back to my apartment and the cookie suddenly hit me. I became so paranoid, I was convinced that she had *poisoned me*. So I did what any other twenty-eight-year-old man would do: I snuck into the bathroom and called my parents.

It was 2 A.M. and my parents had been asleep for at least four hours. My mom answered the phone and said, "Hello?" I said, in a heavy whisper: *"Mom. It's me. You gotta do something. This girl poisoned me. She gave me PCP."*

Why I took it to the level of PCP, I'll never know. I must have recently read an article about a guy taking PCP and eating his friend's face off. But I'd certainly never been offered PCP, and I'm pretty sure it's not available in cookie form.

As soon as my mother heard that I had been "poisoned," she said: "Don't move. We'll be right there."

Then, because I was also still super high, I went back in the other room and *forgot that I had called my parents.*

Cut to: an hour later. My date and I are on the couch, having a grand old time, when there's a knock at the door.

"Who could that be?" she asked.

"Oh shit. I know who that could be."

I open the door. My parents come barging in, like, *"Who the hell poisoned our son? Where's the PCP queen?!"* I start frantically apologizing to my date. She is so high, she thinks this is the funniest situation in the world. She's like, "Who are these awesome old people you hired to scare me?"

My heart feels like it's left my chest and is dancing an Irish jig on the radiator. My mom helps me lie down in bed and makes me a cup of hot tea to help me relax. I'm so paranoid at this point that I become convinced that *my own mother is trying to poison me.* So I fake-drink the tea, and pour it to the side of my bed like I'm in a spy movie.

And while I'm falling asleep, shivering, I hear my dad lecturing this poor girl about the dangers of drug use. "Do your parents know that you're doing this?"

"Uh, no, they don't. Because I don't *call them every time I do drugs!*"

Weirdly, there was no second date.

The next morning, I called my younger brother, who was still living at home at the time. And he said that at 2 A.M., my parents had come knocking on his door and said, "Hey, honey. Just wanted to let you know that we're going into the city for a bit."

"The city? But it's 2 A.M. And you're parents."

"Yeah, it's no big deal. We're just gonna drive into Manhattan for a bit. See what's going on. Nothing to worry about. Sleep tight, okay?!"

Then a couple minutes after they left, I called my brother too. "Casey, you gotta do something. This girl *poisoned me.* She gave me *PCP.*" And my brother said he just laughed and realized: "Oh, *that's* where my parents went."

Despite this, I tried a pot cookie one more time. (With the same friends who escorted me home from *10,000 B.C.,* so they bear some responsibility as well.) We were in the woods in Pennsylvania for New Year's Eve (which already sounds like a horror movie) and everyone decided to eat a pot cookie, so I naturally ignored the previous evidence that I should not eat one and ate one too.

My doctor calls this "another bad sign."

We went for a walk in the falling snow, which was delightful. Like walking through a Robert Frost poem, only high. Strongly recommend this part of the experience. Then we came back inside and someone decided to put on the film *Cloud Atlas*.

Now, in fairness, *Cloud Atlas* does sound like the perfect movie to watch when you're high. It was directed by the Wachowskis, so you know it's going to look amazing. It features the classic duo of Halle Berry and Tom Hanks, and takes place in both 1930s England and 2140s Korea. And the logline of the film is: "As souls are born and reborn, they renew their bonds to one another throughout time." This movie should *only* be watched high.

So the movie starts, and Tom Hanks is on an island in the Pacific Ocean in 1849. Okay, sure. It's like old-timey *Cast Away*. That's cool. And his name is Dr. Henry Goose. Hilarious. Love that. Then the pot cookie starts to really kick in right when the movie shifts to "Neo Seoul" and Tom Hanks (spoiler) becomes Asian.

And that put me over the edge. (Tom Hanks is white, goddammit!) I stood up, said I "had to go to the bathroom," then hid in a closet in the basement for two hours until the movie ended and my friends finally found me.

"How was *Cloud Atlas?*" I asked.

"I'm not really sure . . . ," my friend said. "I think I got too high, 'cause it almost looked like Tom Hanks was Asian?"

In conclusion: Don't drink and do drugs until you're older, when drinking and doing drugs are extra embarrassing. That way your brain will be in good enough shape to remember all the humiliating stuff you do when you drink and do drugs.

Or as my doctor put it: "That's bad advice, Colin."

My Visit to Google

"The human spirit must prevail over technology."

—ALBERT EINSTEIN

"Jesus, you should sue Google!"

—EVERY FRIEND I TELL THIS STORY TO

In the summer of 2016, I finally had a week off for the first time in two years. I was planning to sit on a beach and do nothing but surf and get slightly less pasty-white in the sun.

My agent called and said, "Hey, before you leave town, would you meet with some folks from Google? They want you to create some kind of content for their virtual reality platform. And they'd love to show you the latest in VR technology."

Like so many other foolish moments in my life, I thought, *Why not? What could go wrong?*

Until then, I had only heard wondrous tales of the Google headquarters. Every detail sounded like porn for office workers: Unlimited granola bars! You can skateboard around the office! There's a chair that's also a swing of some kind! Things that I'm sure no one at the office actually uses after their first week of work. But it all sounds so kooky and fun!

I had also invested a large part of my savings in Google stock, because I trusted the company (as much as one can trust any for-profit company) and I always thought: *They must hire the smartest people on Earth!*

I arrived at the Google building in Manhattan and met with three employees who worked in the VR department: Jennifer Kurtzman, Nick Fox-Gieg, and their ringleader Asa "Google Hired Me Ironically" Block. I only know these names because I had to write them down in an "incident report" an hour later.

They brought me to a weird, undecorated room with four metal desks pushed against the walls. "Sorry," they said. "Our normal VR space is under construction."

But that's the beauty of VR, right? You can be in an empty room with four metal desks and still get transported to a magical universe.

They put a VR headset on my head, plus noise-canceling headphones and VR gloves so I could see my hands in the virtual space. I was "fully immersed." For the very first demonstration of the afternoon, Asa Block said, "Let's show him the diving board."

I was suddenly in a futuristic landscape with an eerie glow on the horizon. The only thing I could see was a modern-looking pool with an enormous diving platform next to it. Then I heard him say, "Let's take him to the second level."

They clicked a button and suddenly I was on the second floor of the diving platform. I looked down at the pool from two stories up and it looked a little small for a diving platform of this size. Also, for context, I'm afraid of heights, but over the years I've forced myself to confront that fear as much as possible. I dove off a three-meter springboard when I was younger and it was terrifying. I had to convince myself to breathe and relax and visualize that everything would be okay. It was just water. And water couldn't hurt me. (That much.)

So being two stories above the pool was okay for me. Disorienting, but okay.

Then they said, "Let's take him to the *top* level."

Seconds later, I was magically at the top level of the diving platform, which was fifteen meters (or fifty feet) in the air. It felt extremely real. I slowly turned around and could see for miles in every direction.

"Walk to the edge," he said.

"Okay . . ."

I very slowly walked to the edge of the platform.

"Look down."

I looked down. The pool looked way too small to dive into. It seriously felt like I was four stories off the ground.

"Okay, now jump."

"What happens if I jump?" I asked.

"You'll see."

"Are you sure it's okay to jump?" I asked.

"Yes," he said.

I asked again, "Are you *sure* it's okay? There's nothing in front of me?"

He said, "Yup! It's all clear in front of you."

I stood at the edge of the platform, took a deep breath, and jumped.

.   .   .

I hit something HARD and thought, *Oh my god. I missed the pool and landed on the concrete deck. I'm dead. I just jumped fifty feet onto concrete and I died.*

I really thought that. Because that's how good the virtual reality was.

Meanwhile, in *real* reality, what happened was: This full idiot Asa Block had placed me *directly in front of a metal desk,* and when I jumped, I jumped right into the exposed metal edge of the desk. I hit my knee and my elbow, and sliced open the side of my stomach, like so:

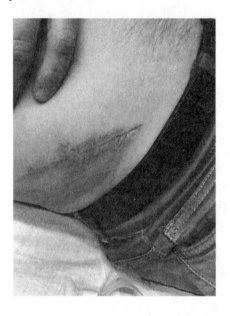

They pulled the VR equipment off me and said, "Oh my god! Are you okay?"

I said, "What the hell just happened? What did I hit?"

Asa said (moron voice), "Um, a desk."

I asked (I think fairly), "Why the fuck did you place me in front of a desk before you told me to jump?"

And Asa said, "Because no one's ever jumped before!"

Now, honestly, for a split second after I heard that, I switched from being furious to being oddly proud? Like, *Whoa . . . no one else has been brave enough to jump? I'm, like, a hero!*

That thought was also virtual reality. In *real* reality, I had just leapt into a desk like a doofus.

The three of them helped me into a chair, and no one had any idea what to do next. I was genuinely in shock, because the experience of suddenly leaving the VR world was jarring and I was trying to figure out how badly injured I was. My main concern was my knee, because it was bleeding and it hurt to put any weight on it. I thought, *Did you just fuck up my only week of vacation in two years, you fucking asshole?*

But because I'm afraid of conflict and I was fairly humiliated by the experience of jumping into a desk, I said, "I think I'm okay . . . my knee seems a little sore . . . but let me just sit for a second and see how it feels." In other words, I was in shock and I was *being a fucking trooper* to not make the situation more awkward, and here's what happened next: While I'm sitting there, trying to decide whether I needed to go to a hospital, Asa Block said, "While you're sitting there, would you like to try another VR game? It doesn't require any moving around. It's just my cellphone and a headset."

Because, again, I was in shock and trying to be cool about what had happened, I said, "Oh . . . uh . . . okay."

At this point, Jenn, Nick, and Asa all seemed sympathetic and remorseful about what had happened. Asa put the headset on my head and pressed a button to start the game. But he was somehow so bad at even pressing a button that instead of starting the game, *he projected his text messages in front of my eyes.*

The texts were between Asa and one of his coworkers elsewhere in the building.

ASA: OMG Colin Jost just jumped into a desk.

COLLEAGUE: Hahahaha what?? Is he okay?

ASA: Yeah he's fine but he's being a huge baby about his knee.

I was being a huge baby about my knee? The fucking dickface who put me in front of a desk and told me to jump into it said I was being a huge baby about my knee. At this point, by the way, I was also *bleeding through my shirt.* You know, *like a baby would.*

One of my great regrets in life is that I didn't punch Asa in the face.* I will be on my deathbed someday and my grandchild will say, "Grandpapa, is there anything we can bring you that might ease your suffering?" And I will say, "Yes. Bring me the face of Asa Block, so that I might punch it."

But in that moment, I talked myself out of it because I knew it wouldn't solve anything, even though, my god, it would have been satisfying. Instead I showed the text messages to Asa Block and said, "Really interesting messages."

He took his phone back and said, "Oh . . . uh . . . yeah . . ."

And I said, "Why don't you read them out loud for us?"

---

* Even though, as established earlier, I am really bad at punching.

And he said, "Oh . . . uh . . ." And then he awkwardly read out loud what he had just texted his friend.

I have to imagine that in that moment, even Asa's two colleagues thought, *Holy shit, how is Asa this dumb? And he's our boss?*

Asa made some half-hearted apology, not because he actually felt any human sympathy for someone he directly injured, but because he was embarrassed that he got caught. So I channeled what Michael Che would call my "inner white girl named Megan," and I said to him, "Why don't you go get your supervisor?"

Asa shuffled out and came back five minutes later with a man named Andy Berndt. Andy was extremely apologetic at first and offered a doctor or a ride to the hospital. Again, he seemed to be genuinely sympathetic. Then, at the end of his whole apology, he said, "Though in fairness to Asa, no one has ever jumped before."

Now I had two people I wanted to punch.

That *really* pissed me off. Here I was, being extremely reasonable about a situation that was entirely their fault, sitting there with blood soaking through my shirt, and this ass-for-brains was somehow implying it was *my fault* for jumping when Asa *told me to jump*.

Beyond the stupidity of that line of thinking, can you conceive of a worse way of "managing" a problem? Imagine you were shopping in a supermarket and you took a can of chili off the shelf and a hundred cans of chili fell on top of you. Now imagine that the manager of the store apologized but also said: "In fairness, maybe you shouldn't be eating all that chili, fatty."

Also, doesn't Google pride itself on "thinking outside the box" and not assuming that every outcome will be the same forever? How could someone not anticipate that at some point someone might jump? Clearly, the fact that I jumped should indicate that jumping was a possible outcome, you full morons.

Can you tell I'm still upset?

At this point, I couldn't even look at their dumb faces anymore. I thought, *Fuck you, assholes. I need to go to a hospital.*

I went to the emergency room, had an MRI on my knee, and had to walk on crutches for my entire vacation. I got stitches in my abdomen and couldn't go in the sun or the water. And I chipped a bone in my elbow, which is still visibly floating around in my skin. Weirdly, the doctor's diagnosis wasn't: "You're being a huge baby." It was: "Wow, this dude Asa sounds like a piece of shit." That was his *medical opinion.*

Google, a trillion-dollar company, did not even pay for my medical bills. Nor did they offer anything beyond an email to my agent saying, effectively, "Sorry, please don't sue us." I never heard from anyone higher up in the company about the complaint I filed. It ended with Andy Brendt and his "no one ever jumps" logic.

I didn't sue, because I have no interest in doing that—there are way bigger problems in the world (and, obviously, within Google). But if *Punch Court* existed (which in my mind is *People's Court* but the winner gets to punch the loser), I would tell Asa Block, "I'll see you in *Punch Court.*"

Ultimately, the real anger was directed at myself. Because only I could visit a virtual space and then have to go to a real-life hospital.

Notes from the Censor

"We all have different parts to play . . . and we must all be allowed to play them."

—EARL OF GRANTHAM, *Downton Abbey*

I f you've ever met someone who works in Hollywood in any capacity, that person has probably complained to you about "notes."

"The studio is giving us all these notes!"

"The pilot I wrote got noted to death!"

"I just found a note that says, 'We have your daughter.' Can someone deal with this while I finish my screenplay?!"

I've never understood why writers and directors are surprised by notes. Did they expect a studio to give them between 3 and 25 million dollars and then just disappear? "Here's our entire profit margin for the year—go nuts! No questions asked! We don't care if it sucks and we lose all our money, we just admire the creative process!"

Notice how few artists are using their own money to make movies and TV shows. *Because it's really hard to get that money back*. There's a reason Johnny Depp is an actor and not a portfolio manager at Merrill Lynch.

At SNL, we're fortunate to receive very few network notes, because we're on at 11:30 P.M. on Saturday and no one knows what "standards" are at that hour. Most people are either asleep or halfway to alcohol poisoning, so if someone says "dick" on NBC, no one's gonna freak.

We're also somewhat insulated from notes by Lorne, because he's built up a level of trust with the network over his four decades at SNL. The same way we trust Alex Trebek to sell us Colonial Penn Life Insurance because we've seen him host *Jeopardy!* since colonial times.

Occasionally we do get notes, though. Usually from advertisers who sponsor the show. For example, I had this joke on Weekend Update a few years ago:

McDonald's is reportedly unveiling a new slogan: "Lovin' Not Hatin'." Which narrowly beat out their other slogan: "Eat the Rats This Clown Killed."

The only trouble was, McDonald's was a prominent advertiser on that particular show. So we received the following note from NBC's advertising department:

In the McDonald's joke, could the clown not specifically kill *rats*? We're fine if the clown kills *something*, but we'd prefer if it wasn't specifically rats. McDonald's has never sold rat meat.

Seems a little defensive, but fair enough. I guess it's pretty aggressive for us to say, "McDonald's hamburgers are made of rats!" So instead the joke became:

McDonald's is reportedly unveiling a new slogan: "Lovin' Not Hatin'." Which narrowly beat out their other slogan: "Eat What This Clown Killed!"

Which might make the joke even better? I don't know. I just like the idea that Ronald McDonald is an equal opportunity murderer. (Except for rats.) And it made me like McDonald's more as a corporation, because they were relatively cool about the joke.

Unlike another sponsor of our show: Volkswagen.

Here's a joke I told at dress rehearsal:

Publishers announced that in less than a week, the new
edition of Adolf Hitler's book *Mein Kampf* has sold out of
the first 4,000 copies. *Mein Kampf* is of course German for
The Art of the Deal.

Now, I don't like comparing anyone to Adolf Hitler, but
that's just a well-structured joke. And technically, it doesn't
even reference Donald Trump. It could be about any author of
a book titled *The Art of the Deal*.

Regardless, we didn't get a network note about Trump. We
got a note from *Volkswagen*. They were advertising on the
show and they said, "Could you not refer to Adolf Hitler? Because if you mention Hitler, then people will think of Nazis
and then they'll think of Volkswagen."

WHAT?

It was the most self-incriminating logic I had ever heard.
Never in my life had I associated Volkswagen with Hitler. Then
Volkswagen brought it up and I thought, *Oh, I gotta look into
this!*

Turns out Hitler himself drew a design that ended up looking like the original Volkswagen Beetle. And he promoted
Volkswagen as "The Car of the People." (No creepy under-
tones there.)

My favorite detail is that Hitler received an early prototype of a Volkswagen convertible for his fiftieth birthday. Just in time for his midlife crisis!

So I get why Volkswagen would try to distance themselves from the Nazis, but no one hears "Hitler" and thinks, *The Volkswagen guy!* That's what was so confusing about the note. And it happened *again* in an even crazier way a few weeks later.

There was a Republican debate sketch where Ted Cruz was talking about the kinds of things New Yorkers do, and everything he listed was clearly just a plotline from *Seinfeld*. And Volkswagen asked our show to remove a reference to the "Soup Nazi" because they thought *that* would remind people of Volkswagen. Hmmmm. I wonder if they're hiding something? Because that level of paranoia is . . . well, Hitler-esque.

Turns out Volkswagen *was* hiding something! They had been lying for years about emissions figures on many of their cars. And they had designed software to trick inspectors into thinking their vehicles were compliant. The Car of the People!

They were such overly sensitive babies about the unrelated Nazi references on our show that when the emissions scandal broke, Rob Klein, Zach Kanin, and I wrote a Volkswagen commercial parody. The voiceover said: "Sure, Volkswagen has gotten in a bit of trouble recently with this whole emissions scandal, but let's not forget what our company was founded on: the vision and values of Adolf Hitler." Then music kicked in and we showed Hitler driving a VW Beetle thru the 1960s, '70s, '80s, etc., dressed in the style of the times and having a blast.

Hearing "Goin' Down to the Country" while Hitler cruises along the California coast in a '60s Volkswagen Beetle definitely made us laugh. The Volkswagen Corporation, on the other hand, found it less funny. And they were about to sign a huge advertising deal with NBC, so even though the ad was fully produced, we were never allowed to air it.

Perhaps someday it will appear on YouTube or on Volkswagen's website: www.oops.ger.

All that said, I've heard the 2020 Volkswagen Jetta is remarkably fuel-efficient. And it was just rated "Best in its Class" by J.D. White Power and Associates.

The other notes we get from the network are "standards notes," because unlike cable or Netflix, you can't curse or call someone a "filthy Irishman" on network TV.

Every week, we receive a list of words or phrases in various sketches that are "flagged" by the network censor as inappropriate or offensive. And I've made a point of collecting these notes over the past ten years because they might be the single most entertaining part of our job.

Here are some of my favorites, in no particular order, and with zero context. (All phrasing and emphasis is directly from the censor.)*

- Please revise "You piece of <u>shit</u>" and let's talk over the term "cuck."
- Let's have an alt line for "I'm <u>teabagging</u> your dead body."
- Please delete "Jesus comes from sperm."
- Lose the line: <u>"I'm gonna sit on your dick so hard that you die."</u>
- Lose the entire Ariel Castro beat and revise "gimp."
- During Drake's performance of *Hype,* lose "shit," 2 "fucks" and "n*gga." Please confirm "Oti" means "no" in Yoruba.
- Let's discuss the "wheelchair" riff.
- Delete "God lives for <u>Puss</u>" and let's discuss options that are not centered on female/male genitalia.
- I'm assuming Mike, Kyle, Sudeikis, and Russell Crowe will not be in "black-face"?
- Let's find another term for "dago."
- Let's lose the "balls" and make the "penis" a rocket.
- During Future's musical performance, please revise <u>8 "bitches," 10 "fucks" and 9 "n-words."</u> Also, in his song "March Madness," let's change the <u>19 "fucks"; 27</u>

---

* Also, so I don't get myself canceled, I should probably point out that these were not notes on *my* sketches. (Except for a couple, like the O.J./ *Grease* Mash-Up Musical.)

"n-words" and 5 "bitch" references. Looking forward to a clean version! [*What's left in the clean version?*]

- Lose all "tits," "titties" and the phrase "Jessica's titties." Also, have an alt for "Cowboys and Indians."
- In the "O.J./Grease Mash-Up Musical"—Revise the last beat of the song: "He killed Ron Goldman/like a stabby stabby slashy slashy stabbady-slashy-do/And then his ex-wife/like a jabby jabby knifey knifey jabbady-stabby-do."
- Obviously blur Vanessa's "exposed breast."
- Completely bleep: "Who shit in my room? Who the hell took a shit in my room."
- Let's soften the line "I got banged twice." Delete "his fingers."
- Lose the phrase "That escaped convict with the big dick."
- Caution on "double fisting" beat.
- In "New Medication Ad," what do you envision during the "offensive" Asian impression beat? Keep me posted.
- Please revise "1-800-Pubes for Kids" which does not fall within our pre-approved range of phone numbers.
- Caution on staging when Pete sucks the poison out of Dwayne Johnson's butt and when simulating the standing "69" position. I would avoid direct "head to crotch" contact. Flirt with the presentation of them "going to town" without it being accurately depicted. [*Flirt?*]
- Let's discuss "toilet babies."
- Revise the line "you'll feel like you're cock of the wops."
- Let's discuss the line: "From the Barrio to the boardroom, Puerto Ricans are on the move."
- Let's revise the Hillary Clinton line where we infer that she kills herself.

- This re-write is problematic. Let's lose the line "I put Marcus's <u>thing in my mouth. I rolled it around.</u> I did something else. And then I put it back." Please call me regarding the general tone of this sketch.
- Please delete "me licky ballsalotta."
- Caution on the presentation and staging of Jay Pharoah "violently making love" to a Japanese sex doll.
- In the Christmas scene, lose the phrase "I'm never gonna get to <u>suck any dick</u> at all!"
- In the "Treehouse Gang" sketch, let's see how the "molested" as well as "AIDS" references play out.
- Caution on "butt-crack" staging. Lose "#legally gatarded."
- Please ensure the "jizz" cream is not white.
- Substantially pixelate the "dog boner." Caution on presentation of the dog's "butt plug."
- Let's try to film a network-friendly "orgy" scene.
- If this ad is selected, please clear "Chevy" brand with our Sales Dept. given the "murder-rape" line.
- Let's soften the term "<u>jerk off</u> the mobsters' penises."
- Tiffany Haddish Monologue - Let's discuss the "<u>smell his balls</u>" line and provide translation of Japanese dialogue.
- Revise "<u>Titty</u> Parade" and the visual of a "<u>Titty</u> Parade."
- Let's discuss "<u>puss.</u>"
- Let's discuss the term "<u>cump.</u>"

And my personal favorite:

- Please ensure Madonna's areolas aren't visible.

Worst Emmys Ever

"Everyone's allowed a past they don't care to mention."

—BILL CALLAHAN

In Che's defense, he never wanted to host the Emmys. I said, jokingly, "Why not? What could possibly go wrong!" The same way Che often says, "Look on the bright side . . ." and then just trails off without describing a bright side.

The day after we hosted, the actual headline in *Variety* was: "Worst Emmys Ever."* Which was so extreme that I went past being upset and mortified and started finding it hilarious. First of all, do you realize how bad the Emmys normally are? An average Emmy Awards is borderline unwatchable. One time it started with an interpretive dance number. Another time it had five different reality show hosts, plus some kind of In Memoriam for the *set* of *Seinfeld*. It's just all over the place. So saying "Worst Emmys Ever" is the equivalent of saying "Worst Rattlesnake Bite." They're all pretty bad and we're just trying to survive them.

---

* The review in the *New York Post* was actually quite positive. I know because that's the only review my grandpa sent me.

The basic problem is: You have to give out roughly two thousand awards in three hours. So 1 percent of the show is determined by comedy or creativity, and 99 percent is determined by time and how we're running out of it. Our very first meeting, before we even pitched a single idea, the producers said: "We need to cut time."

"But . . . we have nothing."

"We know. And it's too much."

What I didn't understand, having never hosted an awards show before, is that you need to violently prioritize the one or two ideas you really care about or they will get pushed aside. Maybe that seems obvious, but there were so many moving parts that had nothing to do with me, that I felt like a dick saying, "We *have* to do this one thing."

Instead, everything we had been working on disappeared.

We had an In Memoriam–style compilation called "Things You'll Never See on TV Again," which had clips from shows that seem horrifying in retrospect. Like when Al Bundy says, "Hey, Peg? Shut up," and the audience goes wild. Or when Cosby offers a female guest a drink and does "funny eyebrows." Or when Maury Povich had a game called "Is This a Man or a Woman?" and the audience had to guess. Or that old ESPN segment called "Jacked Up!" where they celebrated the hardest hits to a football player's head. Or basically anything A. C. Slater said on *Saved by the Bell.**

Neal Brennan had an idea where we would go into the audi-

---

* For example:

JESSIE: "Haven't you ever heard of the women's movement?"

A. C. SLATER: "Sure! Put on something cute, and *move* into the kitchen."

ence and play a game with some of the nominees called "Real Show or Fake Show?" and we would say the name of a show, like *Yellowstone* or *Mary, Queen of Squats,* and they would have to tell us if it's real or fake. (Answers: *Yellowstone* is real; *Mary, Queen of Squats* I am now going to develop.)

We wanted to make fun of the fact that every awards show host now gives out "snacks" halfway through the show. So we were going to give out hot steaming crabs on giant trays, and put newspapers down in the aisle and give everyone bibs and little mallets for breaking the shells. (In fairness, after five minutes of hot crab smell I think half the audience would have puked.)

We had a bit with Larry David where he stood up in the audience and asked if he was gonna lose so he could leave early.

We had a sketch where the guys from *Queer Eye* would give makeovers to fictional characters, like Hodor from *Game of Thrones* and Eleven from *Stranger Things.*

We had Bill Hader as Stefon coming out as the head of programming for Hulu and listing all the new shows they have coming up.

We wanted to cut off people's acceptance speeches by having the microphone slowly lower into the stage, so they'd have to lean down or lie on the floor to keep speaking.

And we wanted to do a segment called "Things They Wouldn't Let Us Do at the Emmys," like our original character named "Steve Harvey Weinstein" who would yell things (*Family Feud*–style) like, "Show me . . . *ejaculating into a plant!*"

There were probably fifteen viable ideas (and 150 nonviable

ideas) that we would have loved to try. What we ended up with was: a five-minute monologue and Che's pretaped piece about Emmy reparations (and even that almost didn't make the show, until we begged the producers to move it into the first half so it didn't get thrown away at the end). And that's it.

We wound up with a show that ended right on time, at the expense of having almost zero comedy.

Still, afterward, we were mostly happy and relieved that it went as well as it did, because the days leading up to the ceremony were such a shit-show. (Plus, I got food poisoning and was on an IV the day before.) I was genuinely thrilled that the show came off without a gigantic fuckup . . . Which was another dumb trap I fell into: Worrying about the show going "smoothly" instead of taking big swings (even if they failed spectacularly).

Like Steve Harvey Weinstein always says, "Shoot your shot, playah. And aim for the houseplant!"

The other weird thing about hosting an awards show is that you have no idea who will actually win, and if people are unhappy with the results, they will be unhappy with 85 percent of the show. It was really strange to listen to all the stars on the red carpet celebrating the level of diversity on television, but then the first ten winners were all white. (One of them was so white that when he won, he thanked his *horse*.) You could tell the audience was thinking, *What the fuck*. Especially after *The Marvelous Mrs. Maisel* won for the fifth time. It's a great show, but when any one show dominates, that just multiplies the number of unhappy people in the audience. This is important, because audiences at awards shows are already among the worst audiences a performer will ever encounter. Here are several reasons why:

1. Everyone is hungry. No one has eaten a carbohydrate in a week so they can fit into their outfits (men and women alike) and they've just been stuck in a limousine in an hour of L.A. traffic and then have to walk a red carpet where photographers are screaming at them to smile and someone from an entertainment show like *Hollywood Buttholes!* is trying to trick them into a sound bite that will end their career.[*]

2. Everyone is nervous. They're nervous if they're nominated and could win. They're nervous if their loved one is nominated and could win (but mostly nervous that their loved one will forget to mention them). They're nervous if their *rival* is nominated and could win and therefore steal more jobs from them. They're nervous that they'll say something positive about the #MeToo movement and almost immediately get #MeToo'd by someone else in the room. They're nervous about getting caught laughing or smiling on camera at the wrong moment. (Like their agent makes a joke about someone's dress and they laugh and then realize that the host had just said that "slavery was an unspeakable evil" and it

---

[*] These are all celebrity problems, obviously. But we're talking about celebrities, so these are the problems!

looked like their reaction to that statement was joyous laughter.) They're nervous that one boob or most of their penis has been hanging out for almost forty-five minutes and everyone's been too polite to mention it. Basically, they're nervous about screwing up and never being invited back to Hollywood again. But, very quickly, everyone is not nervous anymore. Instead . . .

3. Everyone is sad. Steve Martin once said that when you're hosting an awards show, you really only have the first fifteen minutes to make people laugh, because after that, people start losing. And they very quickly stop laughing. When you think about it, almost everyone in that audience will be a loser by the end of the night (or the guest of a loser). And I'm allowed to say that, because I've been nominated for an Emmy thirteen times and lost thirteen times. The saying "It's an honor just to be nominated" would totally be true . . . if they didn't announce a winner. I'm not advocating for "participation awards" or anything. But just think how much happier everyone would be if the five nominees all won the award. It would be an actual fun party instead of a slow-motion journey into sadness. Then a bunch more adults would have trophies for their bookshelves or (power move) their bathrooms. And they'd have less anger and resentment toward their peers, and maybe that would make them less likely to scream in an intern's face because they ordered from the wrong Thai restaurant. Just an idea! And finally:

4. Everyone is tired. Because they've been hungry, nervous, and sad for almost three hours. Anytime a host tries to

tell a joke or do a bit at the end of the show, everyone in the audience openly hates them. After a three-hour ceremony, everyone is just desperate to leave and use the bathroom and finally eat some cocaine and they have zero patience for "a big finale." The host just needs to run out, thank God, bless America, then dash offstage and start drinking.

The highest grade a host of an awards show can possibly achieve is a B-plus. Half the audience is pissed off that the host said something offensive, and the other half is pissed off that they didn't go far enough. Nobody wins.

Even the announcement of who's hosting now upsets 75 percent of the population. Everyone seems to have some magical person in their heads who *should* host. Then a dozen articles pop up with the headline "Here's Who *Should* Host Instead." And the list is compiled by someone with absolutely no understanding of the entertainment industry, so the people on the "Should Host" list include: four comedians who have been asked to host a hundred times and have said no a hundred times, three actors who don't do comedy and have zero interest in doing comedy, two "up and coming" comedians who are barely known within their immediate families, one "legend" who may or may not be dead, and someone who makes the person writing the list look "subversive," like Beto O'Rourke or Amanda Knox. ("Or they *co-host?*")

Awards shows are the least efficient use of everyone's time— from the hosts, to the presenters, to the audience, to the people watching at home. So much energy is spent planning these events—not to mention the time people spend grooming and having outfits made—for a final product that has almost zero resonance two days after it's finished. It borders on madness.

That said, I would love to do it again and do it properly. Even though I'm sure no one will ever invite us back. But the fact that I'm even suggesting this will make Che furious. Which I consider a win.

Tomato, Potato

"We sometimes encounter people, even perfect strangers, who begin to interest us at first sight, somehow suddenly, all at once, before a word has been spoken."

—Fyodor Dostoyevsky

"Haha, he is potato salad boy!"

—Czech teens mocking me

Scarlett and I were wandering the streets of Paris after a romantic Senegalese dinner, followed by a nightcap of three piña coladas. It was the kind of evening that made you think, *I hope there's a toilet in the lobby!*

It was 2 a.m. on a dimly lit cobblestone street when a gang of vicious sixteen-year-old French thugs with flowing blond hair and designer sneakers pulled up on bicycles and started throwing rotten tomatoes at us. Now, as a comedian, I had always expected to get hit with rotten tomatoes at some point in my career, because that's what happened in the '80s cartoons I saw on TV. If you told a joke, and the joke bombed, then you should expect a tomato or at least a squash.

I asked the Internet where the practice of throwing rotten vegetables came from, and the first answer was: "Before restaurants were affordable, people carried food with themselves to eat while they were out from home each day. Meat was expensive, so vegetables and hunks of bread ['He's a *total* bread hunk'] were preferred. So armed, if one happened to be displeased by a performance or a public speech, one could conveniently hurl food objects at the speaker."

That's a classic Internet response that sounds completely reasonable and true, yet could also have zero basis in fact. Especially since the second most popular explanation was: "You cannot recast Thor. If you recast Thor, then we will come for you. First on Rotten Tomatoes. That is an initial soft warning to the system to correct its fault. If that is not paid attention, then hand bombs are used or the theatre is set on fire."

Wow! So, two great explanations . . . One of them requires me to notify the FBI, but otherwise I'm very impressed with both of their thoughtful answers. (Note to Marvel: Maybe don't recast Thor?)

I also learned that when President Howard Taft was campaigning for office, someone threw a cabbage at him and he quipped, "I see one of my adversaries has lost his head!" Bam! You just got Tafted! Take a seat, cabbagehead!

Anyway, enough history. Back to Paris.

So the teens on bicycles pelted us (actually just me) with rotten tomatoes, until I realized they weren't actually rotten. They were fresh, hard tomatoes, which kind of hurt. It felt like getting hit with a water balloon that doesn't break. Or with a baby's head.

I turned, saw the teenagers, and my mood suddenly shifted from romantic bliss to vengeful bloodlust. I was Keanu Reeves in *John Wick,* but instead of killing my puppy they had soiled my favorite windbreaker. *You don't do that to Jost Wick.*

I started running at them, which they did not anticipate. Two of them freaked out and fell on the ground. They all scattered and biked away, except one kid who couldn't get back on his bike fast enough. He ditched the bike and sprinted away into the night. And thank god he did because what the hell would I have done anyway? Punched a French teen? At best I would have assaulted a high school child. At worst (and most likely) I would have gotten the shit kicked out of me by high school children, in front of my girlfriend.*

So they fled the scene, and then I looked at the abandoned bicycle and realized it was the Parisian equivalent of a Citi Bike. That's right, this kid *rented a bike* to go around throwing tomatoes at foreigners.

I saw this, and naturally, after three piña coladas, I started thinking, *Street Justice.* I decided: *I should take his bike and ride it around for a while, so he has to keep paying for it.* Keep in mind: This is way more of a punishment for me than for him. It's 2 A.M. and I'm forcing myself to ride a bike for an hour so that a French kid has to pay an extra three euros.

Very quickly I got winded and realized the futility of my plan. But I was also still angry and refused to let this crime go unpunished. Because I'm French Batman.

I tell Scarlett, "We're bringing the bike to our hotel room." And she says, "No, we're not." And I say, "Okay, great counterpoint." Plan B it is.

I think, *Where can I put the bike where the teen can't retrieve it, but it will still keep charging him for the whole night?*

---

* I can see the headline now: "American Comedian Curb-Stomped by Wispy Teen Models."

I bike around until I find what looks like a construction site next to a big old building. I lift the bike over my head like a maniac and throw it over the fence into the construction area. Boom. Mission accomplished.

Scarlett then takes a video of me walking back to her with no bike and a sadistic grin on my face. She asks, "Where did the bike go?" And I say, "Oh, nowhere special."

Then she walks over to the "construction site" where I threw the bike and says, "Hey . . . you know that's the Musée d'Orsay, right?"

There's a beat. And then we both start running back to our hotel.

The next morning, police knocked at our door and we stayed absolutely still until they went away. We didn't leave the room for another five hours and missed almost an entire day of our vacation in Paris.

So take *that,* French teens!

The saddest part of this story is: It's not the only time I've been pelted with vegetables by European teenagers.

I'll repeat that: Euro teens have hit me with loose vegetables on *multiple occasions.*

Apparently, even in Europe, I have a very punchable face.

The first incident was in Prague in my mid-twenties. It was my first real trip to Europe, and after visiting Berlin and Rome with two friends from college, I thought, *How civilized!* Then we arrived in Prague. The first people we encountered were a stag party of drunk Scottish dudes who immediately started screaming the N-word for no reason at all. This was around

1 P.M., mind you, and they were about to have prostitutes for lunch.

My friends and I opted for a regular meal at a restaurant that I would describe as the Bubba Gump Radish Company. They served eight kinds of radishes, from "mashed" to "unseasoned" to "plain radish." As we walked out of the restaurant, there was a group of Czech teenagers across the street, huddled around a large wooden bowl filled with potato salad. Makes sense so far, right?

These teenagers were each about six-foot-five, 280 pounds— so the potato salad was definitely working. They were reaching into the bowl with their bare hands (size-wise, bear hands), scooping out handfuls of potato salad, and then smashing it into their enormous mouths. I thought, *Is this country okay?* I had always heard that Prague was "the jewel of Eastern Europe," not "the potato sack of the former Austro-Hungarian Empire."

As though hearing my criticism telepathically, one of the teenagers took one look at me, scooped up some potato salad, and threw it at me from across the street. Just a heaping handful of potatoes and mayonnaise (and maybe a sprig of dill) flying through the air and landing all over my shirt.

"Heh heh," one of them laughed, like Frankenstein. "He potato salad boy now!"

Now, I can get very angry very fast, but I also have a keen sense of self-preservation. I looked at them, then I looked at myself and my two friends. When *I* am the most threatening person in a group, that group is not going to win a street fight against Czech Shreks.

So I yelled, "Hey!" Then I paused for five seconds. ". . . why would you do that?!"

My response was so pathetic that I think they actually felt bad for me. It was like *Of Mice and Men,* but if Lenny felt bad for George. Instead of punching my head off my body and using it for a soccer ball, they all sort of hung their heads in disgrace and one of them muttered, "Soh-ree . . ."

Then *I* felt bad for *them*! These poor tree sloths wasted a handful of their precious potato salad on an American nerd, and they didn't even get to rip the nerd's eyes out!

My friends and I quickly walked away before they changed their minds. But we also felt a very small amount of pride for saying *something,* and not just accepting the potato salad shower as a way of life.

To celebrate, we met up with the Scottish stag party and started murdering hookers.

It's all in my new movie, *Hostel 5: Hot Potato.*

The Time I Fought in WrestleMania*

*and almost won

"Never back down. Never quit."

—John Cena

"I would really try to avoid a major head injury."

—The doctor at WWE

Anytime you're in a ring with twenty-five gigantic wrestlers in front of 82,000 screaming fans at Giants Stadium, you're probably wondering, *Have I made a huge mistake?* Especially when your name is announced and the entire stadium starts booing and yelling, *"Kill him!"*

In fairness, I was wearing an Odell Beckham, Jr., Cleveland Browns jersey about two weeks after he got traded from the Giants, when the wound was fresh and deep. Even the wrestlers I saw backstage were like, "Damn. You sure you want to wear that jersey, dude? These fans carry batteries."

It completed a triumvirate of trolling: First I had worn a Mets hat in Philadelphia, then a Yankees hat in Boston, then I came home to the Meadowlands in New Jersey, where so many of my fellow Staten Islanders were buried in shallow graves, and I taunted my favorite team, the New York Giants, because the bit was too good not to do.

It all started with Michael Che being a huge WWE fan. I was a big fan growing up. Che was a big fan *currently*. Like as a grown-up. By the end of our experience, I would be a fan again too, in a whole new way.

Che texted me one day, "Hey . . . you like wrestling?" It was like in the movie *Airplane!* when the pilot brings a young boy into the cockpit and says, "Joey, do you . . . like movies about gladiators?"

I texted back, ". . . where is this going?"

He said, "You might hate me, but I said we'd do something with the WWE."

Now, my generation of wrestling started with Hulk Hogan, André the Giant, Ric Flair, Macho Man Randy Savage, Ultimate Warrior, and of course, The Undertaker. And my passion ran deep. I was a Marty Jannetty fan. I was a Legion of Doom fan. I was a Papa Shango fan. I didn't just love The Undertaker, I loved his manager, Paul Bearer, way before I understood that his name was a play on "pallbearer." I had a Mr. Fuji trading card. I cheered for the Repo Man. I enjoyed the Quebecois villainy of Dino Bravo. I couldn't use a toothpick around my brother without saying, "My name . . . is Razor . . . *Ramon*."

I watched Virgil wrestle the Million Dollar Man for his "freedom" (this was in 1991). And I watched the Brain Busters destroy Tito Santana with a spike pile-driver, only to see El Matador team with his former archnemesis Demolition to defeat Rick Martel and the Fabulous Rougeaus.

I got *into it*. As Hawk and Animal would say, "Oooooooo, what a rush!"

So the idea of being anywhere *near* wrestling was both thrilling and weirdly intimidating. It was like being cast in a remake of *Caddyshack*—did I really want to go up against the memory of greatness?

From the beginning, Stephanie McMahon (who invited us to WWE) kept telling us, "This is all leading to an appearance at WrestleMania." Which we heard but never fully processed. It's like an NFL rookie being told, "Ideally, this ends with you playing in the Super Bowl." Sure . . . but let me catch a couple passes in preseason first.

As I quickly learned: There is no preseason in wrestling.

The WWE is the largest traveling show in the world. Our first stop was Monday Night Raw in Philly and there were eighteen 18-wheelers in the parking lot. It was a random Monday in March and they had sold out the entire Wells Fargo Center. They do this *every single Monday* in a different city. And *every single Tuesday* for SmackDown. Sometimes they'll fly to Japan for a weekend of shows, then fly back to, like, Indiana for a show that Monday.

These guys* *work*.

After seeing their schedule, I thought, *Wow. The Rock is the only person who could film a movie or a TV show every single day*

---

* I'm using "guys" to encompass both genders, because for some reason when you write "guys and . . ." the next word is always "gals." (Or "dolls," which is even worse?) I'll stop digging myself deeper!

and it would feel like a relief compared to the WWE schedule. So I guess Dwayne Johnson is almost lazy now? Let's get that rumor started.

I was so impressed by the whole operation and how much everybody cared about every last detail. They were performing in arenas, but if one element of a costume was off, or one line of dialogue seemed hacky, they were all over it. That requires serious dedication.

And it starts with Vince McMahon, who is clearly the Lorne Michaels of wrestling. (Not to say Lorne couldn't hold his own in the ring. Not many people know this, but he was a *luchador* in Tijuana from 1972 to 1974. That's why if a sketch is going particularly poorly, he'll stare into the distance and whisper, *"Que lastima . . ."*) Vince was literally directing WrestleMania from a booth next to the stage, all while putting out production fires and rewriting dialogue for a match in ten minutes' time. Yet if you went up to him and said, "Hi, Mr. McMahon!" he'd stop everything and look you in the eyes and say, "Colin, thanks for being here."

I thought, *Vince McMahon knows my name?* Also, *"Thanks for being here?"* I would be there even if I *wasn't* wrestling. At least twenty of my friends showed up at WrestleMania without knowing Che and I were on the card.*

Before we were allowed to wrestle, we had to pass a physical. This seemed like a smart precaution. Dr. Ronald Primas (to

---

* That was the best part, actually—having a random friend from sixth grade text me: "Wait . . . why are you in the ring?"

this day, not sure how he became our doctor) came to our offices at SNL and started drawing blood, which must have really freaked out the other cast members. "Holy shit! Is NBC doing drug tests now? We are *fucked*."

He called me up a few days later and said, "Well, the good news is, you don't have hep C."

"Oh . . . cool . . ."

"But you're not *immune* to hep C. So if you get in the ring and one of the wrestlers has hep C, you could get it."

"Oh . . . huh . . ."

"And I can't give you the *vaccine* for hep C because there's not enough time for it to take effect."

"Oh . . . okay . . ."

"So . . . I really hope you don't get hep C."

"Yeah . . . well . . . me too . . ."

"Oh, and your vitamin D is a little low, but that should be fine. Anyway, byeee! Don't die!"

We then had to pass a "flexibility" test on the morning of WrestleMania. So we met with the in-house WWE doctor, who, naturally, was ripped. (Every single employee at WWE—from the stagehands to the lawyer who presented my contract—was ripped. There was a wrestler back in the day named I.R.S., and I'm now convinced he was just their actual accountant.)

The flexibility test involved looking to the left, then looking to the right, then attempting to touch my toes. "Any pain?" the doctor asked.

"No . . ."

"Okay, then you're good to wrestle. Don't die."

"Don't die" became my mantra.

We were then sent over to a practice ring where a lot of the wrestlers were warming up. There, we were taught basic moves like "how to climb into the ring," "how to get thrown out of the ring," and "how to tuck your head to avoid a major spinal injury." Beyond that, we had very little idea about what might happen in the match. The WWE is remarkably similar to SNL in that everything is constantly changing up until the moment you're in front of a live audience.

It's also similar to SNL in that everyone you meet—from the wrestlers to the crew to the producers—is a total pro. Everyone was extremely knowledgeable and happy to give advice, which we desperately needed. They also encouraged us to enjoy it—as much as you can ever enjoy getting the crap beaten out of you on live TV.

And Braun Strowman, who pummeled us within an inch of our lives, was super cool afterward. My dad went up to him to say hi, and he broke my dad's arm in six places. My brother asked for an autograph and he ripped his ear off, signed it "I hear you, bro," and threw it in the trash. Then my mom yelled, "Why are you doing this?" and he said, "Because you needed to see a real man for once in your miserable life."

Such a fun, nice dude behind the scenes.

I had my entire family and all of my friends from high school come to WrestleMania. I'd been on SNL for thirteen years and this was the first time my friends were excited about anything I'd done. It felt like a bachelor party, except I wasn't engaged yet.

Every wrestler we talked to—from Triple H to Titus to surprise guest-star John Cena—told us there was no feeling in the world like walking out to a stadium full of fans who either *loved* you or *hated* you. (There was no in-between.) You could tell they were almost jealous that we were about to experience it for the first time.

Our entrance and our walk to the ring seemed to last for fifteen minutes.* Once we were in the ring, time suddenly disappeared. One minute we were hiding under the mat (which was *terrifying,* by the way—from underneath you realize it's just a bunch of wooden planks with 350-pound giants slamming into them at the speed of gravity), the next minute I saw Che getting tossed over the rope.

Then I saw a glimmer of hope: Braun Strowman's leg was stuck in the ropes. I ran at him in a daze, grabbed his leg, and tried to throw him over the top rope. For a very brief moment, I felt like a professional wrestler.

Then he kicked me fifteen feet across the mat, picked me up over his head, and threw me out of the ring and into the stands. I wobbled backstage, did a "postgame" interview that I have no memory of doing, and visited two "doctors" who turned out to be wrestlers Scott Hall and Kevin Nash. Let's just say their "medical treatments" were not covered by Obamacare.

After it was all over, Che asked me, "Do you hate me? Was it awful?" And I laughed and said, "It was honestly one of the best moments of my life."

The whole next week, random people on the streets of New

---

* We both walk pretty slow, so that might be accurate. Seth Meyers always said that during my first television appearance as a stand-up, it took me thirty seconds to walk to the mic.

York would shout, "Hey! Saw you on WrestleMania! That was awesome, bro!" A hot dog vendor near 30 Rock yelled, "Dude! You almost won!" It was the most I'd ever felt like I was back in high school and had no awareness of show business and just wanted to feel like a superhero for a day.

Che talked me into wrestling and I talked him into hosting the Emmys. It's pretty clear that Che has better taste.

Eggs in My Legs

"One must confront vague ideas with clear images."

—Jean-Luc Godard

"Whoa. What is happening with your leg???"

—Doctor #2

I had traveled to Central America about six different times and never had a problem before.

Except for the time my girlfriend Liz and I were shaken down at gunpoint by the police in Guatemala, and they threatened to throw us in jail unless we paid them two hundred dollars.

Or the time in Costa Rica when my friends and I bought "weed" from a bunch of teenagers on dirt bikes, who, after they sold it to us, openly laughed like Disney villains and then drove circles around us with their bikes. Maybe that was a subtle sign not to smoke the weed? But we did and it was clearly laced with something because we started hallucinating that our hotel pool was full of sharks and that the local teens were coming back to kill us in the night, so we moved all the furniture in our hotel room against the wall to barricade the door and windows.

Or the time I contracted a parasite in Honduras and had stomach pain for months until I finally pooped into a cup and sent it to a lab and they said, "Oh, this isn't good." And I said, "You mean it isn't good to have a job where you receive cups of poop in the mail?" And they said, "No, the job itself pays well and you get used to the poop cups. We meant what's inside *your* poop—it isn't good, parasite-wise." And I had to take several rounds of medicine and keep pooping into cups until the parasite went away. (I sent a couple extra cups after it went away, just for fun.)

Or the time my girlfriend Nasim and I were taking the "scenic route" (my idea) through the Nicoya Peninsula in Costa Rica, and after about six hours of driving the bumpiest, dustiest roads you could imagine in a 2006 Nissan Sentra (also my idea), night fell and we were driving in the middle of the jungle when we came upon a river that had overtaken the road, and, horrified at the prospect of driving three hours in the direction we had just come, I decided we could make it (a great slogan for the Nissan Sentra, by the way: "You *could* make it"), and we drove into the river and stalled exactly halfway across, and then we were sitting in a 2006 Nissan Sentra in the middle of a river in the middle of the night, wishing we had cellphone reception so we could call a tow truck or google "Can snakes get inside your river car?" when miraculously a giant truck came down the road out of nowhere and the driver offered to drag our car out of the river, at which point I turned to Nasim and said, "Could I offer you a stay at the Four Seasons?"

But *other than all of those incidents,* I had never had a problem in Central America before. So when I got bitten by something in Nicaragua last year, I figured it was a mosquito and ignored it. It just itched a little!

Then I noticed that it wasn't just one bite. There were six bites on my right leg and three more on my left leg. But again, I thought they were mosquito bites. Plus, the hotel we were staying at had this incredible homemade rum, so that really helped me ignore the bites for a couple days. It was vacation! We were having fun! So what if my legs were starting to swell up! That probably means they want to dance!

When I arrived back home, I took a moment to properly examine my legs. And what my eyes saw made my brain worried. Let me show you what I woke up to the next morning. **Viewer discretion is advised. (Even though it's probably too late.)**

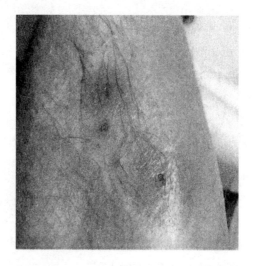

These were three of the nine bites. And when I pressed down into my skin, instead of the skin bouncing back to its regular position, it stayed indented. So I did what any other thirty-five-year-old man would do—I texted that photo to my mom and wrote, "This bad?"

Since my mom is a doctor, it kind of makes sense. But she's also a human being who doesn't love opening her phone to a raw photo of her son's infected leg. Especially since my last text was probably "Is today Christmas?"

My mom called me immediately.

"Do you have to keep going to Central America for vacation, Colin? What about Colorado?"

"Well, it's harder to go surfing in Colorado."

"Surfing, like how you got stitches on your face last year?"

"Mom."

"What about Disney World? They have surfing at Typhoon Lagoon. Plus, you can swim with sharks."

"Mom, I'm thirty-five."

"Your father and I are *sixty*-five, but we still go to Disney four times a year."

"That's because you're psychotic."

"They have a new *Avatar* ride at the Animal Kingdom."

"Mom, what do I do about my leg?"

"Well, it looks like MRSA so we should start you on antibiotics just in case."

"MRSA??"

For those not familiar, MRSA is a staph infection that's resistant to most antibiotics, because humans have used antibiotics so often that some parasites have adapted and built up a resistance. Like how we as a society have seen so much of Kim,

Khloe, and Kourtney Kardashian that by the time Kendall and Kylie came along, we were like, "Sure, this is normal."

MRSA is usually treatable by stronger types of antibiotics, like doxycycline, which my mother prescribed, but those don't always work. I was particularly freaked out because my best friend from high school almost died from MRSA, and one of our directors at SNL got MRSA and was in a coma for three months. (He also texted "Is today Christmas?" but it was March.)

I took doxycycline and waited a few days, but my legs only got worse. You know things are bad when you're "marking the circumference of the wound" with a ballpoint pen and you realize the wound keeps expanding. It was like the reverse of the polar ice caps.

Enter Doctor #2. My mom referred me to her colleague at the fire department who said, "Wow. What happened to your leg? That looks nasty." Adding, "Did you ever consider going to Disney World instead?"

My leg was described as "nasty," "angry," "vicious," and "wicked." Basically, any adjective Donald Trump used to describe Hillary Clinton, doctors used to describe my leg.

Doctor #2 agreed with my mom's diagnosis but sent me to Weill Cornell Medical Center for a second opinion because my legs still weren't improving. I should also mention that this was a show week at SNL. So I would stay up till 5 A.M. writing sketches, fall asleep for a couple hours at work, then run over to the hospital for what became a daily 8 A.M. leg exam. (Not to be confused with my daily leg workout at Curves.)

Lorne's office referred me to Lorne's doctor (Doctor #3),

the delightfully named Dr. Pecker. And I was slightly worried because normally when Lorne's office refers you to one of Lorne's doctors/dentists/lawyers/plumbers, that person is "the best" at his job, but "the best" means "he doesn't take insurance and charges two thousand dollars an hour."

But it was all worth it to tell the elderly woman next to me in the waiting room: "I'm here to see Pecker." And then watch her inch away and pretend to read *Highlights* magazine.

Dr. Pecker examined my leg and said, "Hmm. That looks pretty angry." To which I said, "You should see it after the Knicks lose!" To which he said, "Please stop."

Dr. Pecker then did something I never thought I'd see a doctor do—he turned on his computer and went to WebMD. My first thought was: *Whoa! I could totally be a doctor!* My second thought was: *Am I being pranked?* I kept waiting for Michael Che to text me: "You thought 'Dr. Pecker' was real???"

"This isn't my area of expertise," Dr. P admitted.* "But I want to see something . . ." He typed in my symptoms and looked concerned. Then he switched over to Google Images and started looking back and forth between my leg and the horrifying photos on his computer. It was a real "Scared Straight" moment for my legs.

He turned to face me, leaving photos of Nicaraguan farmers with eggs and worms exploding out of their skin in the

---

* Dr. P is a great doctor. I feel like I should point that out because I mentioned him using WebMD. But that's only because this kind of illness isn't his specialty! Even Wolfgang Puck has to look up a recipe online if he's making something exotic like Icelandic Horse Casserole. (Which I've eaten in Iceland and I'm sad to say, it's delicious.)

background. "This *could be* MRSA," he said. "But it could also be something called *cutaneous leishmaniasis.*"

Cutaneous leishmaniasis falls into a category called "neglected tropical diseases" (which are tropical diseases whose parents were working all the time and never made it to any of their baseball games). It occurs primarily on the beaches of Central America and Africa, where female sandflies bite your skin and infect it with parasites that can lead to fever, low red blood cell count, and an enlarged spleen (which I've heard ladies love). Around 25,000 people a year also die from it, and it was described in the sixteenth century as "white leprosy."*

"I want you to see another doctor," said Dr. P. "Someone who specializes in infectious diseases." (Always reassuring.)

"When are you available this week?" he asked. And I thought, *Uhhh, at 1 A.M. on Saturday?* But instead I said, "I'll make it work whenever!"

I went back to SNL until 2 A.M. and then, at 7 A.M. the next morning, I met with the director of infectious diseases for Weill Cornell, Dr. Ole Vielemeyer, who—you'll never believe this—is German.

Now, I'm the opposite of most people: I always trust a German. To quote one of my favorite episodes of *The Simpsons:* "No one who's German could ever be evil!"† I also trusted Dr. Vielemeyer because he had a good sense of humor. I realize that when one is choosing an infectious disease specialist,

---

* Even among sixteenth-century lepers, they still had to make it about race.

† I know this was a joke, but I'm just going to quote it unironically.

"strong sense of humor" is not the first quality you look for. But I always trust a doctor with a sense of humor, because if they ever get super serious, you know things are really bad.

I showed Dr. Vielemeyer my leg, and his face lit up with what I can only describe as schadenfreude.

"Oooo, that is quite nasty!" he said. "Let's take a piece out!"

He took out a scalpel and removed the central black spot from one of the bites. "Interesting . . . ," he said, as he placed the little chunk into a plastic tube. "We'll send this to the CDC for testing."

"Cool, cool, cool. Love when the CDC is involved."

He asked me questions about my travel and the timeline of the bites and how they grew. Then he peered at the wounds for a while longer, with the excitement of a ten-year-old examining an ant he's just incinerated with a magnifying glass. Finally, Dr. Vielemeyer sat up, clapped his hands on his knees, and looked almost giddy to share his diagnosis.

"Okay! So, best-case scenario—something laid eggs inside your legs."

I'll pause there for a moment.

You might understand how I found that statement confusing.

"I'm sorry . . . that's the *best-case scenario*?"

"Well, yes. Because if something laid eggs inside you, all we have to do is wait for them to hatch, and then you're golden!"

Now, if you've watched YouTube videos of "spider eggs hatching inside humans" as many times as I have, then the word "golden" would not be the first adjective that comes to mind. In general, the idea of "Let's see where these eggs are heading!" didn't appeal to me all that much, considering that my legs were the nest.

"So . . . what kind of animal would have laid eggs inside me?" I asked.

Secretly I was hoping he'd say "turtle."

"Most likely a botfly," he explained. "They sometimes use human flesh as a host for their larvae."

He could not have been more casual about that statement. He said, "They sometimes use human flesh as a host for their larvae" the same way I would say, "They sometimes put cheese on my hamburger."

This, of course, led me immediately to google "botfly eggs in humans," which led to me wishing I could remove my eyeballs and all of my memories. It was one of many instances where I have cursed the efficiency of Google. I started typing "botfly" and Google Images was like, "DID YOU MEAN YOU WANT TO SEE A HIGH-RES IMAGE OF BOTFLY LARVAE EXPLODING OUT OF SOMEONE'S NECK?"

The great news for botflies is that they made CBS's list of "10 Most Terrifying Parasites Ever!" (Exclamation point very much theirs.) And botfly larvae were also featured on the Animal Planet show *Monsters Inside Me*, which has outstanding episode titles such as: "Something's Eating My Son Inside Out," "They Hijacked My Eyeball," "My Child Will Only Eat Cat Food" [what?], "Something's Eating My Dreams," and my favorite: "You Left a WHAT in My WHAT?" (The second WHAT is def a butt.)

I was curious to know what the "typical approach" was for larvae growing under your skin, so I asked Dr. Vielemeyer, "Should I just wait for the eggs to hatch?"

"Well, if you want, you could also try to suffocate the larvae for a few days and then remove them with tweezers."

If I *want*?

All I could think of was a thousand tiny baby botflies crying, "Help me, Colin! I can't breathe!" and I would lean down and whisper, "It's okay. It'll all be over soon." Then I'd put on Lenny Kravitz's "Fly Away" and clear out a matchbox to use as a mass grave.

Again, this was the best-case scenario.

"And what's the *worst*-case scenario?" I asked, still struggling to imagine how baby insects crawling down my legs was a hopeful outcome.

"Well, you could have MRSA and that's usually treatable, but not always. Or, if it turns out to be *leishmaniasis,* then the options can get a little dicey." (Lil' Dicey, by the way, should either be a combo rapper/chef or the mascot for a casino.) "Sometimes you can freeze the wound and kill the infection and sometimes you have to just wait it out and hope it heals itself, but that can also leave scarring."

"And what's the most likely scenario?"

"Well, it's possible that the botfly laid its eggs inside you, then the site got infected with MRSA. So let's treat you for MRSA while we wait to see the test results. And then we'll know whether you have bites from flies, or flies growing inside you."

Boy, I couldn't wait to find out! It was like opening a present on Christmas morning. "Mommy, is it fly *bites* or fly *babies*?!"

"You'll have to wait and seeeee, Colin!"

. . .

I went back to work, started a new round of antibiotics, and began "suffocating the larvae" with tape and bandages. By the time our show happened on Saturday night, the swelling had gone down and I had removed the remaining eight "sites" from my legs with tweezers. (Otherwise, per union rules, NBC would have had to pay the larvae as extras.)

And since I work in comedy, my colleagues were super supportive all week, with comments like: "Did your leg bugs hatch yet?" "What are you gonna name your kids? Will it be a George Foreman thing where all the bugs are named Colin or Colleen?" And of course, "Leggo my eggos."

I went back the next week for a checkup with Dr. Vielemeyer, who was pleased with my progress.

"Better!" he said. (We still hadn't heard back from the CDC because of the government shutdown at the time.) "This should continue healing on its own."

I was almost sad that our journey together—me, Dr. V, and our thousands of unborn insects—was coming to a close.

"Do you have any other questions for me?" he asked.

I thought for a moment, then asked what in retrospect was the worst question to ask an infectious disease specialist: "So what's the worst thing you've ever seen?"

Which . . . why? Why would I ever ask that? It's like going on WebMD and searching for "disgusting."

Dr. Vielemeyer sat back, crossed his arms in happy reflection, and told me in that alarmingly casual German way, "Oh, I don't know. I suppose it was the time that my colleague was pregnant and started getting morning sickness halfway through her pregnancy, which was strange . . . And then one day she threw up, and a two-foot bloody worm jumped out of her mouth and landed on the floor of her bathroom, and she was like, 'Uh-oh!' "

He paused.

"But the good news was, she was able to save the worm and she wrote her thesis about it!"

And they say German fairy tales don't have happy endings.

Epilogue

Leaving Home

"We need illusions in order to dream. And then we need to discard illusions in order to grow."

—Lindsey Buckingham

"Soooo . . . when are you leaving SNL?"

—My agents

I have a recurring, almost constant fear of being mediocre. I grew up average in so many ways—sports, height, the size of my breasts—and I worry that I'll end up average, which will feel like a complete failure.

Average, of course, is so much better than *below average.**
But when you meet people who are extraordinary, average feels humiliating. I wish it didn't, but it does.

I've worked at a variety show for the past fifteen years, and variety is exactly what I've craved throughout my life—in my career, in the friends I've made, in the women I've dated, and in the polymaths I've admired, like David Lynch, David Byrne,

---

* Except in terms of "acquiring STDs."

and David from the Bible, who slayed Goliath *and* played a little guitar.

Despite having a demanding, not-in-any-way-routine job at SNL, I've still felt desperate to do a dozen other projects on the side, like writing screenplays and pilots, performing stand-up every off week, submitting pieces for *The New Yorker,* acting in movies and commercials, rewriting movies and commercials, and now writing a book.* But I've realized that part of my reason for doing a hundred things at once is a deep fear of doing one thing as well as I possibly could—and failing. I've always been reluctant to throw myself fully into one project because if it doesn't work out or people don't like it, then I would have to face the reality that my best effort wasn't good enough.

It's the same reason I was afraid of opening up completely in a relationship—because what if the person I was dating didn't like me after that? Then I'd have nothing left in reserve to win them back. I'd be like David Blaine after he was frozen in a block of ice in Times Square: cold, disoriented, and not sure what exactly just happened.

So I've basically built an emotional escape hatch in my work and my relationships. I've had one foot out the door in case things go haywire and I need to put on a fake mustache and stow away on a Viking River Cruise to Finland.†

And my greatest fear—besides my trypophobia, or fear of holes—is leaving SNL and never finding anything I like doing more than SNL.

---

* Which has turned out to be the most creatively satisfying and least financially rewarding of all these pursuits.
† "Viking River Cruise: Travel like a Viking, minus the rapes!"

.   .   .

When I was young, my dad worked at the Procter & Gamble plant on Staten Island, in an area that's still called "Port Ivory" after the Ivory soap they manufactured there. When the factory closed down, my dad took a job at another factory where they made Lancôme cosmetics, and he still says that was the best job he ever had. He loved the people he worked with. He loved learning about the chemical process behind all the products (nerd!). And Lancôme even offered a program to teach their employees French, which seems odd for a group of factory workers, but as they say in France, c'est la lee!

Then he got offered a job as the vice president of a local moving company and it seemed like a huge opportunity to "make it big" in a whole other way. More money, more decision-making, and a piece of the company if it expanded to other cities. He took it and left Lancôme, and less than a year later the new job had fallen apart. His boss was a nightmare, the company was a mess, and my dad was miserable. He got fired and couldn't get his old job back at Lancôme. My dad was unemployed for a while after that, and all I remember is that he was really depressed. After all, no one feels sadder than an unproductive German.

So whenever I thought about leaving SNL and attempting something new on my own, I thought about my dad. What if I left this incredibly rewarding job working with people I love in hopes of achieving something greater—and what if it sucked? Or the project fell apart? Or I was suddenly working with people I hated? I was worried that I would look back and regret losing something good in pursuit of something better.

.   .   .

Recently I asked my dad, "Do you regret leaving your job at Lancôme? Do you wish you had stayed there for your whole career?"

And he said, "You know, I loved that job, but leaving was the best decision I ever made. Because eventually I started teaching, which meant I was home with you and your brother more after school. And I got to impact the lives of thousands of kids who came through my classroom, which is something I never knew was important to me until I went and did it."

He taught at Staten Island Technical High School for twenty-five years, and except for how much he hated the New York City Board of Education, he truly loved his job. Anytime I went to visit, it seemed like his students really loved him, too. When I started doing Weekend Update, so many people on Staten Island would say, "You're Mr. Jost's son?? He's the *best!*"

Except for one kid who said, "He gave me a shitty grade, but whatever, he's still pretty nice." (If that's your *worst* review in twenty-five years, you're doing something right.)

The other part about leaving SNL is that it means growing up. Because no one who works at SNL is really an adult.[*]

It's certainly not a good place to work while you're raising a family or nurturing a healthy relationship. In terms of "family-friendly jobs," SNL ranks somewhere between long-haul truck driver and Somali pirate. That's why, when I started at the

---

[*] Even Lorne is basically a seventy-five-year-old teen.

show, out of the roughly thirty writers and cast members, only two of them were married and only one had kids.* It's a job for young, single people, because when SNL is at its best, the cast and writers are essentially living at work. They might go home for a few hours, but they're still thinking about the show. That's an amazing and fulfilling life—to a point. And I think that after fifteen years, I've finally reached that point.

I feel like I'm only now having my quarter-life crisis, at the age of thirty-seven—partly because I've been emotionally frozen in the same job since 2005, and partly because advancements in nanotechnology will extend the human lifespan by decades, making thirty-seven a very realistic quarter-mark.

I've started to notice subtle changes in my life, like wanting to spend time with people who don't work at SNL. Or wanting to attend human activities like birthdays, weddings, and dinners that start before 10 P.M. I've even woken up on a Sunday after a show and thought, *I would love to be raising a baby right now!*† Which is a far cry from when I used to wake up on a Sunday and think, *Can I make it to the bathroom, or should I just puke on this plant?*

These changes are what most therapists would call "healthy." I've met someone I love and who I feel more comfortable with than I ever have before. I feel more confident committing to what I'm working on and standing by whatever I create, regardless of whether people like it or not. And I'm drawn to larger ideas, and creating worlds that are far more complex

---

* And the two who were married are no longer married.

† As soon as I have a baby I will realize how foolish this sentence was.

than the ones I can explore in a five-minute sketch that I only have twenty-four hours to write, cast, and produce.

I've worked very *broadly* for the past fifteen years. And now I'm ready to work more *deeply*. Neither is better or worse, by the way. While comedy sketches may seem fleeting—and many are—there are some that strike a weird nerve and linger in American culture for decades, like Will Ferrell's "Cowbell," or the phrase "Debbie Downer," which people now say all the time like it's an expression from the 1920s when it's actually from a Rachel Dratch/Paula Pell sketch where people couldn't stop laughing at a sad trombone noise.

Being forced to generate *something* every week means at some point you'll be tired enough to let down your guard and write the dumbest idea that pops into your head because your brain can't think of anything better. And sometimes that turns out to be the best sketch you wrote all year.*

But now I'm ready to sleep semi-regular hours and write without the constant swirling pressure of a live show every Saturday night. Because working at SNL is a drug—it's highly addictive, and if I don't stop soon I think my mind will be warped in an irrevocable way. And while whatever I do next will almost certainly be less *fun* than SNL, it could also be better in some way I never expected.†

---

* Other times it's the worst sketch. Example: "Trampoline Cowboy," a sketch I wrote for Taylor Lautner where he was dressed as a cowboy and bounced on a trampoline for five minutes while making odd observations about modern life. My coworkers at the table read probably thought: *Wow. We can't get that five minutes of our life back.*

† Like I become best friends with the Pope!

. . .

I'm preparing mentally to leave SNL in the near future. Which is a very scary sentence to write, even though it's intentionally vague.* As Lorne says, "Careers are made by choices." And this is a choice I need to make. (Lorne also says, "Don't leave the show," but I can't listen to *everything* Lorne says.)

I will miss SNL in a deeply spiritual way, because it's the thing I've cared most about for the past fifteen years. It's been my entire identity and the vast majority of my career. It's how I met most of my friends, all of my enemies, and my future wife.

Plus, my office has become a storage locker for everything Scarlett refuses to keep in our apartment. So when I leave, NBC will have to burn the robotic koala I rescued from a dumpster on Forty-eighth Street. And the black dreadlocked puppet that Che makes me hold so he can post "racist" photos of me on Instagram. And the upsettingly sharp butterfly knife I bought in a sewing machine repair store next to the Port Authority because I heard David Letterman used to shop there. Not to mention the bocce ball set we use in the hallway at 5 A.M. on writing night when we can't think of any funny ideas. Or the "Certificate of Recognition" I received from a congressman on Staten Island, days before he was charged with twenty counts of fraud, federal tax evasion, and perjury. Or the various other disturbing trinkets from the past decade and a half: an autographed candle from Taylor Swift, a photo of Kurt Co-

---

* I'd at least love to do Weekend Update through the 2020 election. Maybe Donald Trump and I will leave our jobs at the same time!

bain leaving SNL less than a year before he died, a folding chair from our match at WrestleMania, a large axe I bought in Kentucky because I was afraid of sleeping alone in my car, a VHS tape celebrating the 1986 World Champion New York Mets, a bottle of rum from Lil' Wayne, a pair of sneakers from Usain Bolt, a framed photo of Leslie Jones with the engraving TO MY DELECTABLE CAUCASIAN, and an old black-and-white photo of Bill Murray putting Richard Pryor in a headlock, which I stole from Bill Murray's house while I was drunk at his Christmas party. (I'm really sorry, Mr. Murray.)

I've been very lucky to have a job this great for this long. When I look back someday, I think my time at SNL will seem like the best years of my life. But I also think my best life is still to come.

If not, I can always beg Lorne for my job back.

Acknowledgments

Thank you to Erin Doyle, Mike Shoemaker, Seth Meyers, Bryan Lourd, Chris Reisig, Gena Ciccone, John Solomon, Mike Calcagni, Rob Madison, and Jack Howard for reading early drafts of this book and telling me which parts to cut so I don't get fired.

Thank you to my editor, Tricia Boczkowski, for a lot of hard (and very timely) work, to Lindsey Arenberg for all her help putting this book together, to Matt Frost for organizing the book tour, and to Richard Abate, David Miner, and Tim Duggan for believing I could write this book in the first place.

Thank you to Lorne for giving me a career, and to all my friends at SNL, past and present, for making me laugh to the point of crying almost every single day for fifteen years. That is a very special and rare thing. (Or maybe I have emotional problems?)

Thank you to my family, especially my grandparents Helen and Bill Kelly, who helped raise my brother and me after already raising four kids of their own.

To the Fire Department of New York for employing 75 percent of my family.

To Mr. DiMichele, Dr. Tricamo, and Mr. Connelly for your incredible efforts at educating me. I'm sorry they didn't work.

And to my friends from Staten Island, Regis, and the Lampoon, who are the reason I got into comedy in the first place. Any terrible jokes in this book are kind of your fault.

And finally, thank you to Scarlett for being my first reader and for always protecting me from my worst instincts. Remember that Mexican tribal mask I tried to put in our living room? Thanks for stopping me from doing that.

Photo Credits

Page 158: Courtesy of the author

Page 165: Barry Brecheisen / Getty Images

Page 168: Dana Edelson / NBC

Page 170: NBC

Page 171: NBC

Page 172: Will Heath / NBC

Page 173: Will Heath / NBC

Page 174: Dana Edelson / NBC

Page 176: Dana Edelson / NBC

Page 177: Will Heath / NBC

Page 178: Dana Edelson / NBC

Page 180: Dana Edelson / NBC

Page 181: Dana Edelson / NBC

Page 182: Will Heath / NBC

Page 183: NBC

Page 184: NBC

Page 185: Dana Edelson / NBC

Page 186: Will Heath / NBC

Page 188: Will Heath / NBC

Page 189: NBC

Page 190: NBC

Page 191: NBC

Page 206: Courtesy of the author

Page 232: NBC

Page 245: Denise Doyle Chambers

Page 254: Courtesy of the author

Page 260–61: NBC

Page 262: Apic

Page 263: Sueddeutsche Zeitung Photo / Alamy Stock Photo

Page 292: Courtesy of the author

Courtesy of the author
e left: Courtesy of the author
e right: Courtesy of the author
m: Courtesy of the author
Courtesy of the author
e: Courtesy of the author
m: Courtesy of the author
Courtesy of the author
e left: Courtesy of the author
e right: Courtesy of the author
m: Courtesy of the author
Mike Shoemaker
e: Courtesy of the author
m: Dana Edelson/NBC
Courtesy of the author
le left: Mary Ellen Matthews/NBC
le right: Mindy Tucker
m: Michael Fragosos
Courtesy of the author
le: Dana Edelson/NBC
m: Art Streiber
Will Heath/NBC
le: Phil Provencio
m: Will Heath/NBC
Mathieu Bitton
le: Brian Ach/Stringer
om: Courtesy of the author

TYPE

; set in Dante, a typeface designed by
dersteig (1892–1977). Conceived as a
for the Officina Bodoni in Verona,
as originally cut only for hand com-
Charles Malin, the famous Parisian
between 1946 and 1952. Its first use
tion of Boccaccio's *Trattatello in laude*
ippeared in 1954. The Monotype Cor-
rsion of Dante followed in 1957.
eled on the Aldine type used for Pi-
Bembo's treatise *De Aetna* in 1495,
noroughly modern interpretation of
e face.